Documentary

Documentary

A HISTORY OF THE NON-FICTION FILM

Revised Edition

Erik Barnouw

OXFORD UNIVERSITY PRESS
Oxford   New York   Toronto   Melbourne
1983

OXFORD UNIVERSITY PRESS

Oxford London Glasgow

New York Toronto Melbourne Auckland
Delhi Bombay Calcutta Madras Karachi
Kuala Lumpur Singapore Hong Kong Tokyo
Nairobi Dar es Salaam Cape Town

and associate companies in
Beirut Berlin Ibadan Mexico City Nicosia

Library of Congress Cataloging in Publication Data

Barnouw, Erik, 1908–
    Documentary: a history of the non-fiction film.

    Bibliography: p.
    Includes index.
    1. Moving-pictures, Documentary—History.
I. Title.
PN1995.9.D6B37   1983   791.43'53   82-19053
ISBN 0-19-503301-9 (pbk.)

Printing (last digit):   9 8 7 6 5 4 3 2

Printed in the United States of America

ACKNOWLEDGMENTS

Ideas for a history of documentary film have nudged at me through years of film writing, producing, research, and teaching. But I could hardly have carried through with it except for the opportunity that came in 1971–72 to travel with my wife to some twenty countries, visiting film archives and studios and interviewing documentarists. This unique odyssey was made possible by a commitment from Oxford University Press, a leave from Columbia University, and a grant from the JDR 3rd Fund; to all, a great debt of gratitude is hereby acknowledged. The names of many of the artists interviewed will be found in the source notes. There is hardly any adequate way to thank the countless archivists, projectionists, interpreters, and others with whose help we viewed over 700 documentaries of diverse periods and places, and scanned stills, scripts, and other materials. In thanking the organizations they represented, we want especially to thank the individuals involved. We hope the result will seem, to some extent, to have justified their patient help to two wanderers with an excessive documentary appetite.

The organizations—(Canada) Allan King Associates, Canadian Broadcasting Corporation, Canadian Film Archive, National Film Board of Canada, Potterton Productions; (Japan) Iwanami Productions, Japan Association of Cultural Film Producers, Japan Film Library Council, NHK, Nippon AV Productions, Toho Company, Towa Company; (South Korea) Motion Picture Promotion Union, National Film Production Center; (Hong Kong) Broadcasting House, Farkas

Studio, Filmo Depot, Zodiac Films; (India) Films Division of the
Ministry of Information and Broadcasting, Krishnaswamy Associates,
National Education and Information Films Ltd., National Film Archive, Naya Sansar Productions; (Egypt) General Cinema Organiza-
tion, Higher Institute of Cinema, Visual Images Technical Centre;
(Yugoslavia) Dunav Film, Film and Television Academy, Jugoslo-
venska Kinoteka, Neoplanta Films, Zagreb Films; (U.S.S.R.) Asso-
ciation of Film Makers of the U.S.S.R., Central Documentary Studio,
Gosfilmofond, Institute of Fine Arts; (Poland) Association of Polish
Film Makers, Krakow Festival, Film Polski, Filmoteka Polska, Wy-
twórnia, Filmów Dokumentalnych; (East Germany) Hochschule für
Film und Fernsehen, Staatliches Filmarchiv, Zentrale Filmbibliothek;
(West Germany) Institut für Film und Bild, Riefenstahl-Film; (Swe-
den) Film Centrum, Svensk Filmindustri, Svenska Filminstitutet,
Sveriges Radio-TV Arkivet; (Denmark) Danske Filmmuseum; (Neth-
erlands) Centrale Filmotheek, Nederlands Filmmuseum; (Belgium)
Cinémathèque Royale; (France) Cinémathèque de la Coopération,
Cinémathèque Française, Musée de l'Homme, Slon; (Italy) RAI;
(Switzerland) Locarno Festival, Praesens Film; (Great Britain)
BBC-TV, British Film Institute, British Transport Film Unit, Film
Centre International, Granada TV, Imperial War Museum; (United
States) Contemporary Films, George Eastman House, International
Film Seminars, Library of Congress, Museum of Modern Art, Na-
tional Archives, Time-Life Films, Tricontinental, U. S. Information
Agency. To all, our warmest thanks.

Since publication of the original edition of this book, much has
happened in film and television. A wave of new technologies has
brought upheaval. Documentarists have found many new opportunities in the new technologies, and the field has burgeoned as never
before. These developments have led to this revised, updated edition
of *Documentary: A History of the Non-Fiction Film.*

New York City   ERIK BARNOUW
January 1983

CONTENTS

1

GLIMPSE OF WONDERS

attacca subito

Workers Leaving the Lumière Factory, 1895. Filmed by Louis Lumière.

Museum of Modern Art

Prophet

The inventors of cinema, who were legion, included diverse showmen, and others with interests far from showmanship. Some of these were scientists who felt a compelling need to *document* some phenomenon or action, and contrived a way to do it. In their work the documentary film had prenatal stirrings.

Thus the French astronomer Pierre Jules César Janssen wanted a record of Venus passing across the sun, an event of 1874. He developed what he called a *revolver photographique*—a cylinder-shaped camera in which a photographic plate revolved. The camera automatically took pictures at short intervals, each on a different segment of the plate. The result—photographed by Janssen in Japan—was not yet a motion picture, but it was a step in that direction, and it gave ideas to others. For Janssen the important thing was: it documented the event.[1]

About the same time the English-born Eadweard Muybridge was doing experiments sponsored by Leland Stanford, former Governor of California. Stanford, a horse-breeder, sensed that the devices used by his trainers to improve gait and speed were based on imprecise knowledge of how a horse runs. Muybridge, already a celebrated photographer, undertook to provide data. He placed a series of cameras—at first twelve, later several times that many—side by side along a track. From these cameras, parallel threads ran across the track. A horse galloping through them clicked the cameras in swift succession. The photos gave information on each stage of the gallop.

The study of animal motion became an obsession for Muybridge. By 1880 he had learned to project sequences of his photos with an adaptation of the magic lantern, and thus to present a galloping horse on a screen—at various possible speeds. The results were eye-opening to many who saw them. Muybridge had foreshadowed a crucial aspect of the documentary film: its ability to open our eyes to worlds available to us but, for one reason or another, not perceived. Muybridge applied the technique to numerous animals and later to men and women—athletes, dancers, and others, sometimes photographed in lovely nude sequences. These often evoked the poetry of ordinary, familiar actions: a woman stooping to pick up a jug. Such painters as

Muybridge sequences—from *Animal Locomotion,* published 1888.

Thomas Eakins and Jean Louis Ernest Meissonier began to use Muybridge's work as a guide in depicting figures in motion.[2]

The celebrated French physiologist Étienne Jules Marey followed the work of Janssen and Muybridge with intense interest. Having seen a Muybridge galloping-horse projection, Marey wanted to do similar work with bird-flight, but birds could hardly be made to trip a series of threads on a pre-selected route. So Marey followed Janssen's lead, devising a *fusil photographique,* a photographic gun, with which he could follow a bird in flight while "shooting" at split-second intervals. At first, as in Janssen's camera, the photos were successive images on the same glass plate; but in 1887 he switched to strips of photographic paper and the following year to celluloid strips, putting forty images on one strip. Besides birds in flight, he "shot" such phenomena as a cat falling backwards from a height and landing on its feet. He too learned to project the results on a screen. He was approaching motion picture technology, but his embryo documentaries were scarcely three or four seconds long.

Georges Demeny, who began as assistant to Marey, was especially interested in problems of the deaf. He felt deaf people could be taught to lip-read, perhaps to speak, if they could see over and over the characteristic mouth movements connected with sounds. So in 1892, with his own adaptation of Marey's equipment, he began to shoot and project close-ups of mouths articulating short phrases—"Vive la France" or "Je vous aime." Again an experimenter with special interests provided intimations of things a documentary film might be and do.[3]

The achievements of these and other experimenters were widely

heralded. It remained for protean professional inventors like Thomas Alva Edison and Louis Lumière—racing against scores of other inventors throughout the world—to develop the experiments into a commercial reality and an industry. Edison began the process; Lumière and others carried it forward.

To some extent, Edison shared the documentary ardor of the early experimenters. Before he created his peep-show *kinetoscope*—launched with explosive but short-lived success in 1894—he had met Muybridge and Marey and discussed their work with them. He himself often spoke of the archival and instructional value of motion pictures and sound recordings—in education and business. But in practice his film work quickly took a "show business" direction. In the end it was Louis Lumière who made the *documentary* film a reality—on a worldwide basis, and with sensational suddenness.

The reason why Lumière and not Edison played this key role is rooted in sharp contrasts between their technical inventions. The camera with which Edison began film production was an unwieldy monster; several men were needed to move it. Also, Edison was intent on integrating the invention with another Edison specialty, electricity, to ensure an even speed of operation. For both these reasons, the Edison camera was at first anchored in the tarpaper-covered studio called "the Black Maria," built at West Orange, N.J. This camera did not go out to examine the world; instead, items of the world were brought before it—to perform. Thus Edison began with a vaudeville parade: dancers, jugglers, contortionists, magicians, strong men, boxers, cowboy rope-twirlers. They appeared at a fixed distance from the camera, usually against a black background, deprived of any context or environment.

Serpentine Dance—performed by Annabelle. Filmed in the Black Maria for Edison's peepshow kinetoscope, 1894.
Library of Congress

The Louis Lumière camera, on the other hand—the *cinématographe,* launched in 1895—was totally different. It weighed only five kilograms; according to film historian Georges Sadoul, this was about a hundredth of the weight of the Edison camera. The *cinématographe* could be carried as easily as a small suitcase. Handcranked, it was not dependent on electricity. The world outdoors—which offered no lighting problems, at least during the day—became its habitat. It was an ideal instrument for catching life on the run—"sur le vif," as Lumière put it.

A remarkable fact about this small box—a trim hardwood item of much elegance—was that it could with easy adjustments be changed into a projector, and also into a printing machine. This meant that an *opérateur* with this equipment was a complete working unit: he could be sent to a foreign capital, give showings, shoot new films by day, develop them in a hotel room, and show them the same night. In a sudden global eruption, Lumière operators were soon doing precisely that throughout the world.[4]

Louis Lumière, first magnate and major prophet of documentary film, was the son of Antoine Lumière, a painter who had turned to portrait photography, photographing well-to-do clients against backdrops he had painted. Louis and his brother Auguste received a technical education, but Louis left school at an early age because of severe headaches, and took up laboratory work for his father. While still a teenager he invented a new procedure for preparing photographic plates, which gave such startlingly fine results that the Lumières began to manufacture plates for others, using the new formula. Soon the family sold the photo studio and on the outskirts of Lyon organized a factory to manufacture plates. Louis designed the equipment and supervised every detail of the installation. By 1895 the factory had 300 workers, sold fifteen million dry plates a year, and was the leading European manufacturer of photographic products—surpassed internationally only by the Eastman plant in Rochester, N.Y. The elder Lumière now lived in semi-retirement, painting landscapes. Louis and Auguste produced further inventions, always patented in both their names, although in the case of the *cinématographe* Louis was the sole inventor, having worked out all the problems during one night of insomnia near the end of 1894.

In March 1895, at a meeting in Paris to promote French industries, Louis Lumière demonstrated his invention with the short film *Workers Leaving the Lumière Factory (La Sortie des Usines).** In June he gave a demonstration at a photographic meeting in Lyon. This time he photographed convention members—they included the astronomer Janssen—as they arrived by river steamer; next day, at the meeting, he let them see themselves disembarking. The familiar, seen anew in this way, brought astonishment. Other closed showings were held for scientists in Paris and a photography assemblage in Brussels.

A public unveiling was planned, but Louis Lumière held this off until late in December 1895. Early in the year he had placed an order with the engineer Jules Carpentier for twenty-five *cinématographes*. Throughout the year Carpentier was at work, in constant consultation with Louis Lumière. Every secret of the apparatus was meanwhile guarded: the only existing *cinématographe* was the one used at the demonstrations. All films shown and shot during 1895 were made with this equipment by the Lumière brothers themselves—almost all by Louis.

The films made during this year numbered several dozen, all about a minute long—at the moment, this was the maximum length of a reel. They included several films that were soon to be world famous. One of the most successful was Louis Lumière's *Arrival of a Train*

---

* In this volume titles will be translated into English where advisable for clarity, with the original title supplied in parentheses when the film is first mentioned. Many Lumière films were shown under a number of different titles; the French titles here used are as they appeared in Lumière catalogues.

Lumière's *Arrival of the Conventioners,* 1895. Leading the way, astronomer Janssen.

Cinémathèque Française

(*L'Arrivée d'un Train en Gare*), filmed at La Ciotat in southern France—the first of many such "arrival" films. In this we see a train approach, from long-shot to close-up. The camera is placed on the platform near the edge of the track. The arrival of the train—virtually "on camera"—made spectators scream and dodge. As we see passengers leave the train, some pass close to the camera, seemingly unaware of it. The use of movement from a distance toward the viewer, and the surprising depth of field in the sequence, offered audiences an experience quite foreign to the theater, and different from anything in the Black Maria performances.

While a few of these early films involved deliberate performances for the camera, such as *Feeding the Baby* (*Le Repas de Bébé*) and *Watering the Gardener* (*L'Arroseur Arrosée*),* most were "actuality" items. None used actors; Louis Lumière rejected the theater as a model for motion pictures. He presented instead a panorama of

---

* In this renowned little film, a boy steps on a garden hose being used by a gardener. When the gardener examines the nozzle to see what is wrong, the boy withdraws his foot and the gardener is drenched. Some regard it as the first fiction film.

French life that grows more fascinating as the years recede: fishermen and their nets; a boatride; swimmers; firemen at work; men sawing and selling firewood in a city street; a bicycle lesson; the demolition of a wall; children at the seaside; a blacksmith at work; a potato-sack race at a Lumière employees' picnic. The events are small but vivid.

In mid-December of 1895 Carpentier began delivering to Lumière the *cinématographes* ordered early in the year. Manufacturing methods had been developed, and Lumière now ordered 200 more. A world-wide offensive was in the making.

The training of *opérateurs* was meanwhile beginning. In the film *Workers Leaving the Lumière Factory* a youth with a cap is seen leaving on a bicycle. He was Francis Doublier, and he was chosen to be one of the first of the Lumière world travelers; soon he would film the Tsar of Russia. Another was Alexandre Promio, to be sent to Spain, Italy, and elsewhere. Another was Félix Mesguich, an Algerian youth just completing military service with the Zouaves. He visited the Lumière factory looking for a job, was interviewed by Louis Lumière himself, and was hired. He knew nothing of photography, but this did not seem to trouble Lumière, who apparently felt Mesguich had the proper personality and precision of mind. His training, and that of several dozen others, began promptly at Lyon.

With equipment and personnel for world exploitation assured, Louis Lumière was finally ready for the première run in Paris. It began on December 28, 1895, in the Salon Indien—a room in the basement of the Grand Café on the Boulevard des Capucines, with its own entrance from the street. Louis and Auguste did not attend. They had delegated arrangements for this première to their father, Antoine, who was glad to emerge from semi-retirement for the ceremonial occasion. The brothers were busy with preparations for larger events.

The run began quietly, with little advance notice, but soon queues waited at every performance. The Salon Indien, which seated 120 people, was soon giving twenty shows a day, at half-hour intervals. At one franc a ticket, receipts ran to 2500 francs a day. To meet the overflowing demand the Lumières began showings at additional locations. By the end of April, four concurrent Lumière programs were running in Paris. One developed into a permanent cinema.

Fishermen . . .

Embarkation . . .

Swimmers . . .   Photos from Library of Congress

Among those at the first performance was the magician Georges Méliès. He at once expressed ardent interest in buying a *cinématographe* but was put off with various excuses by the elder Lumière. Within two months the Lumières had more than 100 purchase offers, including many from abroad. They were answered with a form letter, stating that a date for the sale of equipment had not been set. For the immediate future other plans were afoot.

Starting in February in London, an avalanche of foreign *cinématographe* premières began. Within six months after the Paris opening the *cinématographe* was launched by the Lumière organization in England, Belgium, Holland, Germany, Austria, Hungary, Switzerland, Spain, Italy, Serbia, Russia, Sweden, the United States—and soon thereafter in Algeria, Tunisia, Egypt, Turkey, India, Australia, Indochina, Japan, Mexico. Within two years Lumière operators were roaming on every continent except Antarctica.[5]

A triumphant opening in a foreign metropolis followed by a run of weeks or months became a normal sequence. Foreign concessionaires shared in the revenue, but only Lumière operators handled the equipment. Their instructions warned them to reveal its secrets to no one, not even kings and beautiful women. Invited to a banquet, a Lumière operator took his *cinématographe* with him and kept it between his feet. Showings generally began at a small theater or a hotel, earning quick revenue. In a number of cities, success prompted a move to a larger location or additional screenings elsewhere.

Meanwhile—a spectacular feature—operators filmed new items and soon announced a "change of program" with local events. The filming of these was done as publicly as possible; the idea was to lure people to the shows in hope of seeing themselves—which they sometimes did. In any event, the local items were often the high spot of the run: in Spain, *Arrival of the Toreadors* (*Arrivée des Toréadors*); in Russia, *Coronation of Nicholas II* (*Couronnement du Tzar*); in Australia, *Melbourne Races* (*Les Courses*)—all 1896 products. To local audiences they seemed ultimate proof that the *cinématographe* was no "trick."

At Lumière headquarters in Lyon the arrival of such material from abroad rapidly enriched the catalogue, so that operators went forth with increasingly international assortments. The Lumière program

Lumière poster, Krakow, 1896.

shown by operator Félix Mesguich at Proctor's Pleasure Palace in New York in March 1897 included:[6]

The Baby's First Lesson in Walking

The Electrical Carriage Race from Paris to Bordeaux

A Gondola Scene in Venice

The Charge of the Austrian Lancers

Fifty-ninth Street, Opposite Central Park

A Scene near South Kensington, London

The Fish Market at Marseilles, France

German Dragoons Leaping the Hurdles
  (also a reverse view of this picture)

A Snow Battle at Lyon, France

Negro Minstrels Dancing in the London Streets

A Sack Race Between Employees of Lumière & Sons' Factory, Lyon

The Bath of Minerva, at Milan, Italy
  (also a droll effect obtained by reversing the film)

In 1897 the *cinématographe* was already giving its audiences an unprecedented sense of seeing the world.

By the end of that year some hundred Lumière operators at work throughout the world had swelled the Lumière collection to more than 750 films. In advertisements and press releases "Lumière" and *"cinématographe"* were always featured; the name of the operator seldom appeared in print. Thus the creators of many Lumière films are not known. A fire destroyed pertinent company records. Louis Lumière in later years recalled the names of some of the operators; others are mentioned in memoirs—their own or those of others. Thus we know that Maurice Sestier went to India, then on to Australia. Félix Mesguich handled screenings in various French cities, then was sent to the United States, and later did service in Russia. Alexandre Promio ranged widely, with early activity in Spain, Italy, Switzerland, Turkey. Latin America was opened by operators Porta and Tax. Francis Doublier, accompanied by Charles Moisson, launched the program in Russia, and later traveled widely in Asia, ultimately settling in the United States.

The Russian tour of duty involved extraordinary and tragic events.

Lumière advertisement, *Times of India,* July 7, 1896.

Two days after filming the coronation of Nicholas II, Doublier prepared to shoot another occasion: presentation of the new Tsar to his people, who would receive souvenirs. Hundreds of thousands gathered for this purpose. A murderous crush developed as they pressed forward in impatience, and were thrust back by battalions of police. Then the boards over two huge cisterns gave way, and large numbers of people fell to their deaths. In the resulting panic, countless others were trampled to death. From a near-by roof Doublier watched in horror. He later described the experience.

When we came to our senses we began to film the horrible scene. We had brought only five or six of the 60-foot rolls, and we used up three of these on the shrieking, milling, dying mass around the Tsar's canopy where we had expected to film a very different scene. I saw the police charging the crowd in an effort to stop the tidal wave of human beings. We were completely surrounded and it was only two hours later that we were able to think about leaving the place strewn with mangled bodies. Before we could get away the police spotted us, and added us to the bands of arrested correspondents and witnesses. All our equipment was confiscated and we never saw our precious camera again.[7]

Presumably, the film was destroyed. Some observers estimated the death toll at 5000. No word of the disaster appeared in the Russian press.

For the wandering operators, improvisation became a habit. Because they handcranked, in shooting and projection, they quickly learned the uses—comic, dramatic, symbolic—of slowed or speeded motion. During projection a sequence could also be reversed, for amusing or meaningful effect. This device was used early in the Salon Indien: a wall was razed, then put itself together again. This became a standard feature in *cinématographe* showings. Promio, in Venice, photographed famous edifices from a moving gondola, creating highly acclaimed traveling shots. These became a model for scores of shots by Lumière operators from moving trains, carriages, trams, and other vehicles. In the Lumière catalogue they were called "panoramas." There was even a sequence from a rising elevator.

A Lumière operator could expect triumphs and tribulations. At the Taj Mahal Hotel in Bombay, in mid-1896, an Australian portrait photographer, Walter Barnett, came upon the disconsolate Maurice Sestier, the Lumière representative. Sestier had launched the *cinématographe* with enormous success in Bombay at Watson's Hotel and the Novelty Theater—featuring "Reserved Boxes for Purdah Ladies and Their Families"—but he had a blistering letter from the home office in Lyon: the items Sestier had shot in Bombay were regarded as incompetent and unusable. None were placed in the Lumière catalogue. Later in Australia—where Barnett became associated with him —Sestier was notably more successful with his *Melbourne Races*.[8]

The moments of triumph could be sweet. Mesguich, finishing his first American projection in June 1896 at the B. F. Keith Music Hall in New York, was at first terrified to find crowds hammering on his improvised booth. Opening the door, he found himself seized bodily and carried to the stage amid deafening shouts and applause as the orchestra played "The Marseillaise." Mesguich recounted in his memoirs: *"Ovation grandiose! Inoubliable! Inoubliable!"*[9]

At the end of 1897, with the same suddenness with which the world-wide exploitation had begun, the Lumière company announced

Francis Doublier. Photographed in 1945, with an 1896 *cinématographe*.

Félix Mesguich.

a change in policy. The company would discontinue its world demonstration tours, and would proceed to sell its equipment to any one who wished to buy. The Lumières would thenceforth concentrate on manufacture and sale—of *cinématographes,* raw film, and films in the Lumière catalogue. Thus a strange and dizzying chapter ended.

It meant the early withdrawal of the Lumières from film production. Within a few years their catalogue was taken over by others.

All this may have been as Louis Lumière had planned it: he was most at home in research and manufacture. The monopolistic opening drive could not in any case have been maintained. Lumière had been in a neck-and-neck race with other men working on cameras and projectors. At the time of the Lumière whirlwind, a number of these had achieved some success: Max and Emil Skladanowsky in Germany; Birt Acres and Robert William Paul in England; Thomas Armat and C. Francis Jenkins in the United States—and others. Some had even begun demonstration tours. But Lumière's swift campaign and the standard set by his equipment and films caught them all short. Now there was a frenzied scramble to catch up—to pirate, adapt, imitate, surpass.

In the United States Thomas Edison, when he sensed that the *cinématographe* had doomed his peep-show *kinetoscope,* had hastily arranged to take over the projector developed by Armat and Jenkins—which thus became the "Edison Vitascope"—and to launch it in New York at Koster & Bial's Music Hall—on the site later occupied by Macy's department store—two months before the *cinématographe* reached the United States. The Vitascope was also, almost instantly, dispatched on foreign promotion tours, vying with the *cinématographe* and with others. World struggles now became fierce and often violent. Lumière had made clear the possibilities of profit.

Throughout the world new enterprises sprang up. In the United States, Edison was confronted by Biograph, Vitagraph, Essanay, Selig, Lubin, Kalem; in France it was Méliès, Pathé, Gaumont; in England, Urban, Hepworth, Williamson; in Italy, Ambrosio, Cines, Itala; in Germany, Messter; in Denmark, Nordisk; in Russia, Drankov; in India, Madan; Japan had its own M. Pathé—inspired by, but unrelated to, the French Pathé brothers.

Some of these companies were founded by former peep-show operators; others, by alumni of traveling shows. Most entrepreneurs, including Edison, sought or built portable equipment for field work.

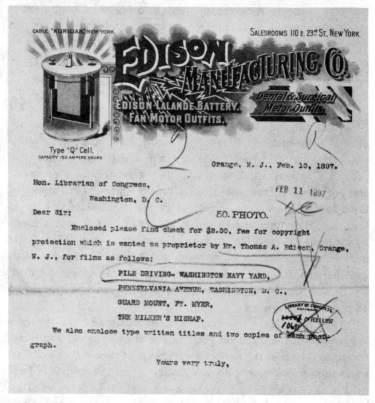

Copyright application, 1897. The Edison company began the practice of submitting a *paper* print of an entire film—as a "photograph"—for copyright protection. The paper strips survived the nitrate films; much of our knowledge of
early films is based on new negatives made in recent years from these paper
strips. This copyright procedure lasted until 1912, when an amendment to the
copyright law made special provisions for films. See Niver, *Motion Pictures
from the Library of Congress Paper Print Collection 1894–1912.*

Pile Driving—Washington Navy Yard, 1897.
From the Edison paper strip submitted with the
above application.

Library of Congress

Alexanderplatz in Berlin, by Skladanowsky, 1896.

Staatliches Filmarchiv der DDR

Many started with nonfiction items—calling them *documentaires, actualités, topicals, interest films, educationals, expedition films, travel films*—or, after 1907, *travelogues.*

The Lumière company, withdrawing from this chaotic arena, had in three years achieved extraordinary things. It had reaped, financially speaking, the main harvest from the novelty value of film. It had set a new industry in motion on five continents. It had enshrined the word *cinema,* an early shortening of *cinématographe,* in innumerable languages—rivaled only by derivatives of the Skladanowsky term *bioskop.* It had put France in the lead as film producer and exporter, a position it would hold for more than a decade. It had also set an entertainment pattern—a program of short filmed items, predominantly of a documentary sort—that would likewise persist for many years.

In scores of countries, the visit of a Lumière operator marked the beginning of film history. New entrepreneurs took up where the Lumière emissaries had left off. Many did so with Lumière equipment or imitations of it; some with the help of former Lumière operators. The Lumière pattern thus continued under other auspices.

In Sweden, where the Lumière opening run had lasted more than a year, Alexandre Promio taught cinematography in 1897 to Ernest

Peter Elfelt, court cinematographer, Copenhagen.

Danske Filmmuseum

Florman, son of the court photographer, who thus became Sweden's first cameraman. The Danish royal photographer Peter Elfelt had visited Paris in 1896 and had tried to buy Lumière equipment, but had been refused. However, he managed to have similar equipment built by a Copenhagen master mechanic, and began film production and public showings; early projects dealt with Greenland dogs, street scenes, and royal ceremonies. In England, former Lumière operator Félix Mesguich went to work for Charles Urban, who had come to London as Edison representative; his company soon became one of England's most vigorous enterprises, specializing in documentary films. In Spain, Fructuoso Gelabert of Barcelona, crediting Lumière as his inspiration, began in 1897 to manufacture film equipment; the next year he filmed the visit of Queen Maria Cristina and her son Don Alfonso XIII to Barcelona, marking the start of Spanish film production. Another Spaniard, Antonio Ramos, on finishing military service in the Philippines, became one of the first to buy a Lumière *cinématographe;* also buying twenty Lumière films, he inaugurated the motion picture era in the Philippines. Later, after Spain lost the Philippines to the United States, he moved to Shanghai and in 1903 became its first film entrepreneur. His Ramos Amusement Corporation long dominated the Shanghai scene. In India the portrait photographer Harischandra Sakharam Bhatvadekar had been an enthralled spectator at one of the first Lumière showings and then became an early—probably the first—Indian purchaser of a *cinématographe*. In 1897 he photographed a wrestling match at Bombay's Hanging Gardens, marking the start of Indian film activity.

Although the establishment of permanent cinemas accelerated, Lumière-style tours continued, shifting from cities to towns and villages. With programs in the Lumière pattern, they carried the film to rural fairgrounds throughout Europe, and also to distant colonial areas. From 1901 to 1907 the tent showman Abdullaly Esoofally moved throughout southeast Asia with showings in Singapore, Sumatra, Java, Burma, Ceylon. He then traveled in India, eventually settling there. His tent, 100 feet long and propped by four posts, could hold 1000 people. He later recalled:

When I started my bioscope shows in Singapore in 1901, little documentary films I got from London helped me a lot in attracting people. A short documentary about Queen Victoria's funeral and another about the Boer War showing the British Commander-in-Chief Lord Roberts' triumphant entry into Pretoria against the forces of Paul Kruger, the President of the Transvaal republic, proved wonderful draws. People who had merely heard or read some vague reports about the war were thrilled beyond description when they saw the famous figures of the Boer War in action.[10]

Throughout the world, such showings had common characteristics, but there were also variations. Speakers who stood beside the screen, explaining things, were especially popular in Asian countries. In Japan, where they were known as *benshi,* they acquired great prestige.

For many years the one-reel film remained the staple, but there were changes. Improvement in equipment brought longer reels. At the turn of the century a one-reel film was one to two minutes long; five years later it was five to ten minutes long. And while documentary items in most countries outnumbered fiction films as late as 1907, the mix was changing. Fiction films were increasing in number and beginning to dominate audience interest. The documentary was declining—in quantity and in vigor.

Several factors were involved. The documentary was to some extent a victim of its quick successes. Many producers continued to follow the formulas that had won such instant acclaim. Meanwhile the fiction film was in a period of innovation—by Méliès, Porter, and soon many others. It was in fiction, not documentary, that the art of editing was beginning to evolve—and to change the whole nature of film communication.

Still other factors stifled the growth of documentary. The films of Louis Lumière himself, shot in 1895–96, had often been fascinating reflections of French middle-class life. But in the *cinématographe* tours his emissaries, as a matter of promotional practice, had sought royal sponsorship—with triumphant success. King, Tsar, Kaiser, Emperor, Maharajah had readily played their part in launching the wonder of the century—and had meanwhile tended to become infatuated with it, not only permitting but expecting film coverage. All this facilitated access to official functions and clinched other permissions, but the film men paid a price. They became purveyors of royal performances, agents of imperial public relations.

In the Swedish film archives—typical, in this respect, of most such collections—one finds the following 1907 items:

Oscar II and Sofia's Golden Wedding Anniversary
The Kaiser at Swinemünde
Wilhelm II and Nicholas II Coming Aboard the Deutschland
Kaiser Wilhelm Visit to London
Kaiser Visit to Portsmouth
Pictures From the Life of Oscar II
Funeral of Oscar II

The 1908 items include:

British King Inaugurates Olympics
King Carl I of Portugal and Crown Prince Ludwig Philip Assassinated
English Royal Couple Visits Stockholm
Gustaf V and Queen Victoria in Berlin
Crown Princess Margaret Visits Lund
King Gustaf Visits Ystad
Prince Wilhelm and Princess Maria Arrive in Stockholm

In the United States the situation was no different. Theodore Roosevelt, even before he became President, was an especially eager performer. In 1898 during the Spanish-American War he showed—according to Albert E. Smith, Vitagraph co-founder and cameraman—"a willingness to halt his march up San Juan Hill and strike a pose."[11] During speeches he noted any cameraman and gave him the full benefit of vigorous grins and gestures, sometimes walking to the side of the platform to do so. He inevitably became a favorite subject; Library of Congress film files include innumerable Theodore Roosevelt items, many collected by Roosevelt himself.

Along with world-wide ties to rulers there came, perhaps inevitably, growing involvement with military leaders. Spanish-American war coverage was such a bonanza for Vitagraph that Biograph the following year sent its co-founder and chief cameraman, W. K. L. Dickson—Edison's aide during *kinetoscope* days—to photograph the Boer War. During his work there he acquired a primitive telephoto lens. Albert E. Smith, for Vitagraph, also headed for Africa, with assurance of a lucrative contract with Koster & Bial's Music Hall. Film men were on hand for the Boxer Rebellion, and provided footage of the Russo-Japanese War from both sides. The military, after initial suspicions and hostility, became as cooperative as royalty. In the Boer War, when Smith felt he needed close shots of Boers in action, British soldiers were put in Boer uniforms to provide a few skirmishes. When Dickson, for Biograph, wanted to film Lord Roberts, British Commander in Chief, at work with his staff, Lord Roberts had his table taken out in the sun "for the convenience of Mr. Dickson." He was, according to Dickson, delighted to be "biographed."[12]

The leading film-producing countries of this period were nations with colonial empires. Not surprisingly, their work reflected the attitudes that made up the colonial rationale. Coverage of "natives" generally showed them to be charming, quaint, sometimes mysterious; generally loyal, grateful for the protection and guidance of Europeans. Europeans were benevolently interested in colorful native rituals, costumes, dances, processions. The native was encouraged to exhibit these quaint matters for the camera.

Most "native" shots probably gave western audiences a reassuring feeling about the colonial system, but there were exceptions. The 1903 film *Native Women Coaling a Ship and Scrambling for Money*, made in the West Indies by an Edison cameraman, must have left some disturbing feelings. It presented a picture of degradation such as seldom reached the screen.

Advertisement for telephoto lens, 1901.
From the end pages of *The Biograph in
Battle,* by Dickson.

Along with colonialist tendencies, documentary film was infected
with increasing fakery. This started early. When Albert E. Smith returned to New York from Cuba with his San Juan Hill footage, he
was worried: in spite of the Roosevelt posturing, it looked like a dull
uphill walk, in no way fitting the "charge up San Juan Hill" trumpeted
by newspapers. Meanwhile theaters clamored for the Cuban material,
already publicized. So Vitagraph held off its distribution until Smith
and his partner J. Stuart Blackton had shot a table-top "battle of Santiago Bay" complete with profuse cigarette and cigar smoke, explosions, and cardboard ships going down in inch-deep water. Combined
with the shots brought from Cuba, it became the hit of the war coverage. The public apparently did not suspect its true nature.

In the feverish competition of the time, such activity was not so
much "deceit" as "enterprise." Deceit was sometimes avoided by special promotional phrases. A 1902 film shot by Méliès in Paris, de-

picting the coronation of Edward VII in Westminster Abbey, was announced as an authentic "reconstitution." This material, as in the case of the Cuban film, was intercut with genuine footage—shot outside Westminster Abbey.

In a period when news weeklies had long been illustrated with wood engravings "from photographs taken in the field," there was not likely to be concern about the precise meaning of a "reconstitution." The public was accustomed to news pictures having an uncertain and remote link to events. The relationship was scarcely thought about.

Reconstitutions and fakes had an impressive record of "success." Memorable genuine footage came back from the 1906 San Francisco earthquake, but other footage of the event, contrived in table-top miniature, was equally applauded. Several volcanic eruptions were triumphantly faked, as in Biograph's 1905 *Eruption of Mount Vesuvius*. Film companies did not want to ignore catastrophes or other headline events merely because their cameramen could not get there; enterprise filled the gap. In this spirit the British producer James Williamson shot his 1898 *Attack on a Chinese Mission Station* in his back yard, and some of his Boer War scenes on a golf course. The snows of Long Island and New Jersey provided settings for such action as Biograph's 1904 *Battle of the Yalu* and a competing Edison film, *Skirmish Between Russian and Japanese Advance Guards*. In the latter we see soldiers surge back and forth before the unmoving camera, while many fall in their tracks. To help audiences identify the players, Russians were dressed in white, the Japanese in dark colors. The acceptance of such items probably discouraged more genuine enterprise—at least among some competitors.

A different kind of fakery was exemplified by a project of Doublier, who in 1898–99 continued his travels in Russia—no longer for Lumière, but under the auspices of producer Ivan Grunwald. Visiting predominantly Jewish districts in the south of Russia, Doublier found an intense curiosity about the Dreyfus affair. The court-martial of Dreyfus had taken place in 1894, before the debut of the *cinématographe,* but agitation by Émile Zola, along with confessions of forgery by a colonel in the French War Office and the colonel's subsequent suicide, brought interest in the scandal to a new pitch in 1898. Doublier proceeded to satisfy it with footage that originally had no connection with Dreyfus. A few words to the audience, and their own imagination supplied connections. Footage of a young French captain at the head of an army parade was promptly accepted as "Dreyfus." A large Parisian building became "scene of the court-martial." A tug going out to meet a barge became "Dreyfus taken to a battleship." A long shot of the Nile Delta became "Devil's Island," scene of the imprisonment.

Audience imagination was often relied on for such services. A curious instance involved a much-publicized 1907 African hunting trip by Theodore Roosevelt. William Selig, working in Chicago, found a Roosevelt look-alike and photographed him stalking through a studio jungle, followed by black "native" porters, also from the Chicago area. He encountered an aged lion, who was then shot on camera. The film was a great financial success. The name "Roosevelt" was never mentioned. The item was merely titled *Hunting Big Game in Africa.*[13]

In Denmark that same year Ole Olsen, founder of Nordisk—and previously a peep-show operator—had a similar smashing success. He bought two aged lions from the Copenhagen zoo and put them on a small wooded island; there a group went "on safari" and the lion was shot on camera. The "jungle" footage was intercut with close shots of a hippopotamus, a zebra, and other animals photographed in the Copenhagen zoo—downward from above to avoid backgrounds and fences. The film ended with a group posing with a lion skin; a black man was included for authenticity.

Amid such projects, the documentary tended to become a dubious and perfunctory part of film programs. The rise of multi-reel fiction films—and then of film stars—downgraded it further. In 1910 the newsreel, with weekly or semiweekly issues, made its debut. The Pathé and Gaumont newsreels were followed by numerous others throughout the world. They tended to turn the customary documentary items into a ritual composite: a royal visit, a military maneuver, a sports event, a funny item, a disaster, and a native festival in costume. The newsreel institutionalized the decline of the documentary. Little now remained of its first vitality; the Lumière period was over.

It had been an era of beginnings, and an astonishingly prophetic one.

As early as 1898 a *cinématographe* operator in Warsaw, Bolesław Matuszewski, had written *A New Source of History (Une Nouvelle*

Title page of Matuszewski manifesto.

Source de l'Histoire), a short book published in Paris.* Asserting
that the work of the camera deserved a place beside stamps, medals,
ornamental pottery, sculpture, etc., he proposed a "cinematographic
museum or depository" for material "of a documentary interest . . .
slices of public and national life." Its contents would be far more
meaningful for the young, he suggested, than the words in books.
Once established, material would flow in abundance into such an institution. He offered footage of his own. The depository should contain, he argued, not only meetings of rulers and departures of troops
and squadrons, but "the changing face of the cities."

He recognized that history does not always happen where one

---

* Polish title: *Nowe Źródło Historii.* It was reprinted in Warsaw in 1955 for a
meeting of FIAF–Fédération Internationale des Archives du Film. Another
Matuszewski volume, *La Photographie Animée,* was also published in 1898.

Louis Lumière.

Museum of Modern Art

waits for it, and that effects are easier to find and photograph than causes. He also realized that the film camera would often want to penetrate where not wanted. Yet in so doing, he felt, it might shed a valuable ray of light.

Film evidence, he suggested, would be able to shut the mouth of the liar.

The high cost of film would fall, he predicted, and come within reach of the many.

He urged the use of film in the arts, industry, medicine, military affairs, science, education.

He himself, in 1898 in Warsaw, showed to a group of doctors a film of an operation, exemplifying the versatility he foresaw for the medium.

The aura of prophecy surrounds much of the work of this first documentary period. It foreshadowed the many potential roles of a documentary film maker. Louis Lumière, in his first film, *Workers Leaving the Lumière Factory,* was making what would later be called an industrial film, and was acting as a promoter. In *The Arrival of the Conventioners* (*Arrivée des Congressistes,* 1895) he was a reporter. The maker of *Wood Cutters in the Street in Paris* (*Scieurs de Bois,* 1897) was more a genre painter. In the works of many Lumière operators, such as the "panoramas" of Venice and other cities and the later *Coolies at Saigon* (*Coolies à Saïgon,* 1897) and *Elephant Processions at Phnom Penh* (*Promenades des Éléphants à Phnom-Penh,* 1901), we see the documentarist as travel lecturer. The Pueblo *Eagle Dance* and *Wand Dance* filmed by an Edison cameraman in 1898 are considered early examples of ethnographic film. That same year zoologist Alfred Cord Haddon took a Lumière camera with him on a Cambridge Expedition to the South Pacific Torres Straits, to record and report research findings. In films of the Charles Urban Bioscope Expeditions, a series launched in 1903 to depict remote areas such as Borneo, we see the documentarist as popular educator. Urban assumed a similar function in science with his "micro-bioscope" series *Unseen World,* launched in 1903 and including such items as *Circulation of the Blood in the Frog's Foot.* He also made advertising films for Dewar's Whiskey and Swan's Soap. W. K. L. Dickson, in his Biograph coverage of the Boer War, performed as war reporter. But in Biograph's *Changing the Flag at Puerto Rico,* which brought United States audiences to their feet with the sight of a Spanish flag being ripped down and replaced by an American flag, the film maker was serving more as war propagandist. Edison's *Rout of the Filipinos* had a similar bugle-call purpose, fanning the imperialistic emotions of the hour.

None of these functions can be neatly separated. They never occur separately. The documentarist is always more than one of these. Yet different occasions, different moments in history, tend to bring different functions to the fore. This was true in the first decade of documentary history, and it remained true in later decades.

As the documentary entered a period of decline and seemed headed for oblivion, the documentarist-as-explorer showed the clearest signs of continuing vitality. Interest in distant places was effectively stimulated by the Urban Bioscope Expeditions. It was fanned for several years, starting in 1904, by the ingenious *Hale's Tours,* in which a small auditorium, shaped like a train, was entered from the back by paying a "conductor." Once seated, audiences found the car vibrating and shaking as wondrous scenes rushed by. *Hale's Tours* units were operated in many cities of America and Europe. More substantial were films shot on a 1909 Carnegie Museum Expedition to Alaska and Siberia, and the extraordinary footage filmed in 1911 by Herbert G. Ponting during the disastrous expedition of Captain R. F. Scott to the Antarctic. Sponsored by Gaumont, the material began to reach· theater screens with enormous success in 1912.[14]

It is perhaps not surprising that in the exploration field, the documentary had its first rebirth.

2

IMAGES AT WORK

allegro con brio

Nyla, the smiling one—*Nanook of the North.*

Explorer

Robert J. Flaherty, in his early years, had no thought but to follow in the footsteps of his father, a mining engineer. The boy grew up around mining camps of northern Michigan and Canada, with miners and Indians as companions. Later the father became a prospector searching the Canadian wilderness for mineral resources—for United States Steel and other corporations. Sometimes he took young Bob with him on these explorations, traveling many weeks by canoe in summer and on snowshoes in winter, meeting Eskimos, mapping the country, learning arts of frontier survival.

In 1910, at the age of twenty-six, young Robert Flaherty embarked on his own career as explorer and prospector. He was hired by Sir William Mackenzie, builder of Canadian railroads. Canada had decided on a railroad to carry wheat from its western lands to Hudson Bay, for shipment to Europe. Wheat-carrying trains and ships could also carry iron and other ores. What deposits were there in the Hudson Bay area? Young Flaherty was sent to prospect. Within a few short years, in four expeditions for Sir William Mackenzie, he won fame as an explorer, showed astounding resourcefulness and stamina, mapped unknown country, and brought back reports on mineral and pulpwood resources, as well as deposits of gypsum and lignite.

In 1913 as he prepared for his third expedition, Sir William Mackenzie said to him: "You're going into interesting country—strange people—animals and all that—why don't you include in your outfit a camera for making film?"[1]

Flaherty liked the idea. He bought a Bell & Howell camera, a portable developing and printing machine, and some lighting equipment. Since he knew nothing about film, he also took a three-week cinematography course in Rochester, N.Y. During his next two Mackenzie expeditions, in 1914 and 1915, he shot many hours of film on Eskimo life. The film activity, begun casually, soon became an obsession that almost obliterated the search for minerals.

Between the third and fourth expeditions he was married. Shortly afterwards in Toronto the young bride, Frances Hubbard Flaherty, recorded in her diary—February 1, 1915:

Robert Flaherty—prospector.

Museum of Modern Art

Moving pictures still the undercurrent of life. Printing almost finished and editing begun. R. refuses to let me see them until the first edition is in shape. . . . R. is full of the idea of the use of moving pictures in education, in the teaching of geography and history. Someone might well make it a life work. Why not we?[2]

A few weeks later Flaherty began test showings. Reactions gave cause for jubilation. The director of the Ontario Museum of Archaeology, C. T. Currelly, wrote him:

I cannot too strongly congratulate you on the moving pictures you exhibited in Convocation Hall. They are much the best I have ever seen. . . . I have never known anything received with greater enthusiasm.

Another spectator wrote to a New York acquaintance:

This will introduce Mr. Robert J. Flaherty of Toronto, who has a most interesting series of ethnological moving pictures of Esquimo life, which show the primitive existence of a people in the way they lived before being brought into contact with explorers. He is looking to bring them out in the best way. I know you are thoroughly in touch with the moving picture game from the inside and can at least give him some pointers. Do what you can. . . .[3]

Flaherty was not ready to launch his film. Heading north for his fourth Mackenzie expedition, he obtained more footage, came back to Toronto, and continued editing. In 1916, while he was preparing to ship the film to New York, his cigarette fell from the table onto scraps of film on the floor. Within moments his entire negative— 30,000 feet of film—was exploding into flames before his eyes. In trying to beat out the flames he was badly burned, and landed in a hospital. He was lucky to escape with his life.

What remained was his work print. It was not considered feasible, at that time, to make a new negative from it.

Flaherty persuaded himself the disaster had been for the best. In spite of enthusiasm he had aroused, he was not satisfied with the film. It was, he felt, too much a travelogue—"a scene of this and that, no relation, no thread." Talking it over long hours with Frances, he decided he must return to the north and make a different kind of film. It would center on one Eskimo and his family, and reveal characteristic events of their lives.

He began showing the surviving print to raise funds. It soon seemed an impossible task. The World War of 1914–18 occupied the attention of the world and brought other priorities. Prospecting trips to Hudson Bay were, for the duration, out of the question. And film people seemed indifferent. Flaherty himself, when he showed his film, found it more and more inept. He became all the more determined to make it as he knew he must. From 1916 to 1920—while three daughters were born to the Flahertys—he kept at the fundraising efforts. He earned modest funds with articles and talks about northern exploration. His in-laws talked about getting him a Ford agency; in his mid-thirties, he seemed to them at dead end. Then, as the war ended, the fur company Revillon Frères began to take interest in his proposals, and in 1920 Robert Flaherty finally headed north again. He was to get $500 a month for an unstipulated period, $13,000 for equipment and technical costs, and a $3000 credit at Port Harrison for "remuneration of natives." It took him two months to reach this subarctic post on the northeast coast of Hudson Bay. He stayed sixteen months.

He knew now how he must proceed. The full collaboration of Eskimos had already become the key to his method. This seemed a philosophical necessity but also, in working alone, a practical necessity. Some of the Eskimos soon knew his camera better than he did: they could take it apart and put it together—and did so, when the camera fell into the sea and had to be cleaned piece by piece. They scoured the coast for driftwood to help him build a drying reel for his film.

As his main character Flaherty chose a celebrated hunter of the Itivimuit tribe of Eskimos—Nanook. Nanook became chief fountainhead of film sequences. His zeal for the "aggie"—the film—came to know no bounds. One of his first suggestions was a walrus hunt, done as in former days, before the explorers came.

"Suppose we go," Flaherty said to him, "do you know that you and your men may have to give up making a kill, if it interferes with my film? Will you remember that it is the picture of you hunting the ivuik that I want, and not their meat?"

"Yes, yes," Nanook assured him. "The aggie will come first."[4]

In a diary scrawled in pencil with frequent abbreviations, Flaherty recorded his activities. On September 26, 1920, six weeks after arrival, he wrote:

It has been the day of days. Morning came clear and warm. Some twenty walrus lay sleeping on the rocks. Approached to within 100 ft & filmed

Eskimo drawing of walrus hunt—from *Flaherty Papers.*

with telephoto lens. Nan stalking quarry with harpoon—within 20 ft they rose in alarm and tumbled toward the sea. Nan's harpoon landed but the quarry succeeded in reaching the water. Then commenced a battle royal— & Esk straining for their lives on the harpoon line at water's edge—this quarry like a huge fish floundering—churning in the sea—The remainder of the herd hovered around—their "Ok ok!" resounding—one great bull even came in to quarry & locked horns in attempt to rescue—I filmed and filmed and filmed—The men—calling me to end the struggle by rifle—so fearful were they about being pulled into the sea.

Flaherty later wrote that he pretended not to understand their appeal and just kept cranking. The sequence became one of the most famous in *Nanook of the North.* The scene gives no hint of the presence of a rifle. Flaherty's focus was on traditional ways.

The work went on at relentless pace. Diary jottings noted ideas for sequences:

Pos scenes
unloading
the port
winter

tracking
the gramophone
Xmas
sledging
medicine—castor oil

The gramophone and castor oil were the only civilized intrusions permitted in the final film—perhaps because of the Eskimo warmth and humor they elicited.

Notes on Eskimo words and their meanings punctuate the diaries. An early entry was: "Again—*poonuk.*" Flaherty must have said "*poonuk!*" many times to his co-workers. He showed them every sequence immediately. If it seemed unsatisfactory, or if he wanted an additional shot from another angle or distance, the action was repeated.

Problems mounted. Sometimes it was so cold that film shivered into bits like "so much thin wafer glass." Some sequences involved long journeys with overnight stops in igloos built en route. A trip of many weeks to film a "polar bear aggie"—a dangerous project urged by Nanook—almost ended in disaster. They found no bear and, for weeks, no food for men or dogs. Halted many days by blizzards, they huddled in an igloo as its dome grew black with smoke and dripped black drops. They barely survived the trip. On the way back they used film to kindle a fire.

The building of an igloo became one of the most celebrated sequences in the film. But interior photography presented a problem: the igloo was too small. So Nanook and others undertook to build an outsized "aggie igloo." During the first attempts the domes collapsed —as the builders roared with laughter. Finally they succeeded, but the interior was found too dark for photography. So half the igloo was sheared away. For the camera Nanook and his family went to sleep and awoke "with all the cold of out-of-doors pouring in."[5] Daylight lit the scene. Flaherty was intent on authenticity of result. That this might call for ingenious means did not disturb him. Film itself, and all its technology, were products of ingenuity.

Printing his footage called for considerable ingenuity. Flaherty found that the light from his portable generator fluctuated too much. In his hut he therefore cut an aperture the size of one 35mm frame— and blocked out all windows. With the printing machine screwed to the wall, he used the sun for light, regulating the intensity with bits of muslin.

Quantities of negative shot during midwinter were developed in a rush in March and April of 1921. All available hands were recruited. The vast amounts of water needed were hauled up through a hole chiseled in six feet of ice and were then pulled by a ten-dog team and a fourteen-foot sledge to Flaherty's quarters, to be poured into wash tanks and later hauled away again. On some days tons of water were hauled. Keeping it free of fur hairs was a problem.

Late that summer Flaherty headed back to civilization. Pointing to the countless pebbles on the beach, he told Nanook that people in such numbers, far southward, would see the Inuit—"we the people," as they called themselves—in actions they had filmed together.

That winter *Nanook of the North* reached final form at the editing table. Flaherty had help from an assistant editor, Charles Gelb, but he himself dominated every moment. The editing process was undoubtedly helped by Flaherty's experience and dissatisfactions with the earlier film. This time he had been able to anticipate editing problems, providing crucial close-ups, reverse angles, and a few panoramic movements and tilts to yield moments of revelation. Flaherty had apparently mastered—unlike previous documentarists—the "grammar" of film as it had evolved in the fiction film. This evolution had not merely changed techniques; it had transformed the sensibilities of audiences. The ability to witness an episode from many angles and distances, seen in quick succession—a totally surrealistic privilege, unmatched in human experience—had become so much a part of film-viewing that it was unconsciously accepted as "natural." Flaherty had by now absorbed this machinery of the fiction film, but he was applying it to material not invented by a writer or director, nor performed by actors. Thus drama, with its potential for emotional impact, was wedded to something more real—people being themselves.

A few moments in the film reflected earlier documentary styles. Characters occasionally glanced at the camera as though at a film maker. Nanook, grinning over the gramophone, testing a gramophone disc with his teeth, looks at the camera as though for agreement and approval; his child, tasting castor oil, shares his pleasure with a smile to the camera. These seem holdovers from travelogue—characters posing for the camera, demonstrating their quaintness. Such shots soon vanished from Flaherty's documentary language.

Nanook the hunter. *Nanook of the North,* 1922.

In his subtitles Flaherty was especially felicitous. They showed a
rare gift for word-choice—"the rasp and hiss of driving snow"—and
for conciseness. They never overexplained. "Now only one thing
more is needed," a subtitle tells us as Nanook, having apparently
completed an igloo, starts to cut a block of ice. Audiences do not
know, for the moment, the purpose of the "one thing more." They
soon discover: a square of snow is cut from the igloo, and the ice becomes a window. It is even equipped with a snow reflector, to catch
the low sun. The sequence has often brought applause. Part of the
satisfaction lies in the fact that the audience has been permitted to
be, like Flaherty himself, explorer and discoverer.

Similarly, when Nanook has harpooned an unseen creature through
a hole in the ice, and we see him in a grotesquely acrobatic rope-tug,
sometimes winning but sometimes skidding head over heels toward
the hole as the antagonist gains momentum, Flaherty does not immediately identify the unseen creature as a seal. Again he allows us
the joy of discovery.

Especially valuable to the film are glimpses of children and their

Nanook and son—from *Nanook of the North,* 1922.

relations with others. During the igloo-building we see a child deter-
minedly shooting arrows at a small snow-animal. A subtitle says: "To
be a great hunter like his father." Finishing the igloo, Nanook turns
to give him a brief bow-and-arrow lesson, then warms the child's
hands in a moment of affection and intimacy, remote from travelogue.

Early in 1922 *Nanook of the North,* a product of two decades of
exploring and almost a decade of film activity, was ready for distributors. First to see it was a group from Paramount.

Paramount was then emerging as a leading force in an American
film industry that had seized world leadership. The 1914–18 World
War had choked off production in France—the prewar leader—and
had almost halted it in England and Italy. The American industry,
expanding fantastically while establishing itself in Hollywood, had
filled the vacuum. By the end of the war huge American production-
distribution-exhibition combinations were supplying the screens of
the world. Each felt it understood what audiences wanted: its world-
wide distribution records held the answers.

At the Paramount screening of *Nanook of the North,* as Flaherty later described it, the projection room was blue with smoke before the film was over. Then most of the men simply left the room.

The manager came up and very kindly put his arm around my shoulders and told me he was terribly sorry, but it was a film that just couldn't be shown to the public. He said that he had tried to do such things before and they had always ended in failure. He was very sorry indeed that I had gone through all that hardship in the North, only to come to such an end, but he felt he had to tell me and that was that.[6]

Four other major distribution companies reacted similarly. One executive explained that the public was not interested in Eskimos; it preferred people in dress suits. But finally the Pathé organization—like Revillon, of French origin—accepted the film for distribution and was able to open it at the important Capitol theater in New York on June 11, 1922—with immediate success. Most critics found it a revelation. "Beside this film," said the New York *Times,* "the usual photoplay, the so-called 'dramatic' work of the screen, becomes as thin and blank as the celluloid on which it is printed." The critic found it "far more interesting, far more compelling purely as entertainment, than any except the rare exceptions among photoplays."[7] Reviewing the films of the entire year, Robert E. Sherwood said of *Nanook· of the North:*

It stands alone, literally in a class by itself. Indeed, no list of all the best pictures of the year or of all the years in the brief history of the movies, could be considered complete without it.[8]

Hailed by almost all critics, the film was also a box-office success in the United States and a very substantial one abroad. Its fame spread rapidly throughout the world. European critics vied with each other in superlatives. A French critic compared the film to Greek classic drama.

Flaherty had spent on *Nanook of the North* approximately twice the amount .anticipated in the original arrangements. The total production cost came to $53,000. Such excess expenditures became a Flaherty habit. Revillon loaned the additional funds, to be repaid from distribution income; it recouped this investment and made a substantial profit, as did Flaherty. Documentary suddenly acquired a financial legitimacy it had not had for years. Paramount, first company to reject *Nanook of the North,* also became first to reconsider

its stance. Jesse Lasky of Paramount proposed sending Flaherty anywhere he wanted to go to bring back "another *Nanook.*" Contract
talks began, soon centering on the South Seas.

The ultimate in commercial accolade came from the Broadway
music world with the appearance of the song *Nanook:*

> Polar bears are prowling,
> Wintry winds are howling,
> Where the snow is falling,
> There my heart is calling:
> Nanook! Nanook!

The chorus went:

> Ever-loving Nanook,
> Though you don't read a book,
> But, oh, how you can love,
> And thrill me like the twinkling northern lights
>   above. . . .*

Much later the Flahertys, in Berlin, found the smiling face of Nanook
on the wrapper of an ice-cream sandwich—a "Nanuk." When Nanook
died on a hunting trip two years after the appearance of *Nanook of
the North,* the event was noted by newspapers throughout the world.
When documentary film makers from many lands were asked thirty
years later, on the occasion of the 1964 Mannheim film festival, to
select the greatest documentaries of all time, *Nanook of the North*
led the list.

While establishing a new genre, which has become firmly fixed in
documentary tradition, *Nanook* and its creator have been criticized
on various grounds. In this film as in later films, Flaherty exposed his
characters to extreme dangers. To be sure, they welcomed and even
sought these dangers, and this suggests the kind of dedication they
came to share with Flaherty. Nanook, who urged the most perilous
sequences, may well have sensed in the aggie a kind of immortality
for the Inuit and himself. In spite of his prowess in the film, he was
apparently already ill. A Flaherty diary entry notes that one night he
coughed splotches of blood on the wall of their igloo.

---

* *Nanook.* Words by John Milton Hagen and Herb Crooker, music by Victor
Nurnberg, copyright 1922 Cameo Music Publishing Company. Quoted by
courtesy of Harmony House (ASCAP), Mill Valley, California.

". . . small figures in a vast expanse . . ." Eskimo drawing, from *Flaherty Papers.*

Columbia University

Flaherty was a man of immense charm; his blue eyes riveted attention. Of imposing physique, he was a prodigious worker, ebullient companion, yarn-spinner, hard drinker, chain-smoker, and spared neither himself nor others. He loved music, and took his violin and phonograph records with him to the subarctic to entertain the Eskimos. He was an admirer and collector of Eskimo carvings and drawings; his photographic compositions in *Nanook* often suggest Eskimo drawings: small figures in a vast expanse of white.

But his total absorption in the Eskimo, and the nature of *Nanook of the North* and subsequent Flaherty films, seem also linked to his own conflicts. His first contacts with primitive people came early, and were dismaying. Indian hangers-on at the mining camps, who sometimes came to his mother's kitchen for food and warmth, were a pitiful lot, bearing the marks of civilized diseases, including alcoholism. Many had hacking coughs. He later described his mother as in tears over them. "It is too awful," she would say, "what the white man has done to them." When Flaherty first met Eskimos, he saw the same deterioration at work. But as he went further north, where contacts with explorers, prospectors, and entrepreneurs had been less extensive, he had glimpses of what seemed an earlier nobility. On this he riveted his attention.

He had reasons for doing so. One was a growing sense that he himself represented the cultural destruction that troubled him. He had originally plunged with all his heart into the role of explorer and prospector; before Nanook, his own father was his hero. Yet as he entered the Eskimo world, he knew he did so as the advance guard of industrial civilization, the world of United States Steel and Sir William Mackenzie and railroad and mining empires. The mixed feeling this gave him left its mark on all his films.

Flaherty did not come to grips with this inner conflict; he relentlessly avoided it, in *Nanook* as in most other films, by banishing the intruder from the world he portrayed. Flaherty wrote:

I am not going to make films about what the white man has made of primitive peoples. . . .

What I want to show is the former majesty and character of these people, while it is still possible—before the white man has destroyed not only their character, but the people as well.

The urge that I had to make *Nanook* came from the way I felt about these people, my admiration for them; I wanted to tell others about them.[9]

The urge to capture on film the nature of rapidly vanishing cultures has been pursued also by anthropologists, who have given it the name "salvage ethnography."[10] Flaherty was doing such work for deeply personal rather than scholarly reasons, but the outcome was similar. It has been called "romantic" in that Flaherty was not recording a current way of life but one filtered through memories of Nanook and his people. Unquestionably the film reflected *their image* of their traditional life. Yet a people's self-image may be a crucial ingredient in its culture, and worth recording. Anthropologists, while aware of the distorting lens, study it with care. In effect, so did Flaherty.

John Grierson, a Flaherty apostle, was also a frequent critic of the "romanticism" of Flaherty. "Consider," Grierson wrote later, "the problem of the Eskimo. . . . His clothes and blankets most often come from Manchester, supplied by a department store in Winnepeg. . . . They listen to fur prices over the radio, and are subjected to fast operations of commercial opportunists flying in from New York. . . ."

Moana, 1926.

Museum of Modern Art

But Flaherty knew all this; he was aware of the "fast operations." In a sense he had been part of them. His concern now was not to produce an exposé, but to celebrate what he valued. To this, generations have responded.

During the following half-century the fiction films of the early 1920's became museum curios—dress suits and all—but *Nanook of the North* retained astonishing validity, an aliveness scarcely affected by time.

By 1923 Robert Flaherty, with a Paramount contract and a roomy budget—"Write your own ticket," Jesse Lasky had said—was organizing an expedition to Samoa in the Pacific, this time with Frances Flaherty, their three daughters, an Irish nursemaid, and his brother David Flaherty. Robert Flaherty was world-famous, creator of a new kind of film, and from the South Seas he was to bring back "another *Nanook.*"

The genre, the tradition he had launched, was now in deep trouble. Behind *Nanook of the North* had been twenty years of exploring and living with Eskimos. The same process was now to be compressed into a year or two—which to Hollywood seemed a long time.

The Flaherty group headed for the village of Safune on the island of Savai'i. There they had been told they might find—before it was too late—the old Polynesian culture as it had been before the traders and missionaries came. This gave the new project a thrust similar to that of *Nanook of the North.*

The start was encouraging. When the people of Safune realized that Flaherty did not want to film them in the clothes the missionaries and traders had brought them, they were surprised and then deeply moved. "It seemed a new idea to them," wrote Flaherty later, "that neither Christ nor we, the papalangi, really wished to see them in white man's clothes. Through the influence of the missionary it had come about that the Samoan who had only a siapo was looked down upon." Urged by Flaherty, the chief asked all to wear siapos. It seemed to precipitate a reliving of old days, a remembering of things almost forgotten.

But all this could not make "another *Nanook.*" The struggle for survival that had been a central element in *Nanook* hardly existed in Samoa. Flaherty had read about sea monsters but there were none. Nature was benign. Food fell from the trees. To find a climax for his film, Flaherty finally revived the painful ordeal of tattooing, a Poly-

nesian manhood-initiation rite that had almost become extinct through
missionary influence.

Moana, released in 1926, was hailed by some as a worthy successor to *Nanook of the North.* A film of great pictorial beauty, it
was called an "idyll" by some critics—the sort of praise-word that has
often kept audiences away. Paramount tried to promote the film as
"the love life of a South Sea siren," but audiences lured by this were
bound to be disappointed. *Moana* failed at the box office. The failure
virtually ended Flaherty's association with big-studio Hollywood. An
American Indian film project was started under William Fox auspices, but was soon afterward halted.

Flaherty was still a world figure. Proposals and invitations poured
in. Would he like to make a film in Iceland? Australia expressed interest in a Flaherty visit. Such proposals generally came without
budgets. The German director Fred Murnau, sick of Hollywood,
wanted Flaherty to work with him on a film on Bali; after long negotiations, the project was abandoned.[11] Flaherty worked briefly with
Murnau on *Tabu*—a fiction film more Murnau than Flaherty.

Flaherty wanted to make a film in the Soviet Union about one or
another primitive tribe in Siberia, but he received no encouragement
from Soviet officials. Stress on the virtues of primitive cultures was
not likely to have high priority among the Soviets. After *Moana,* eight
years passed before another Flaherty-style documentary appeared.

But primitive-people films by others meanwhile followed the *Nanook* success. The 1925 feature-length documentary *Grass,* by Merian
C. Cooper and Ernest B. Schoedsack—the latter had been a combat
photographer in the 1914–18 World War—was distributed by Paramount with much success. It portrayed a staggering migration of
50,000 people over the Zardeh Kuh mountains in Turkey and Persia
in search of grass for their herds. The crossing of the torrential Karun
river with loss of life among men, women, children, goats, sheep,
donkeys, horses, provided one of the most spectacular sequences ever
put on film. The photography, sometimes from near positions and
sometimes from mountain tops, was often breathtaking. But the mi-
grants remain a mass of strangers to the audience; no individual portrait emerges from them. And the final emphasis was not on what
they had endured but—in a brash display of egotism—on the heroic
accomplishment of the film makers. The same team followed in 1927
with *Chang,* commissioned by Paramount and filmed in Siam, and

Ernest B. Schoedsack, at work on *Chang*—released 1927.

Museum of Modern Art

ostensibly following a *Nanook* pattern: a family struggling for survival, in this case against jungle animals. But the impressive animal sequences were set in a story framework that must have been part of Hollywood pre-planning, along with pretentious subtitled dialogue. Kru, a Lao tribesman, tells his child:

"The very last grain of rice is husked, O very small daughter!"

At a moment of crisis, a Lao call to battle:

"Out, swords! Out spears! Out, O Brave Men! Help us, O Lord Buddha!"

From their documentary beginnings the Cooper-Schoedsack team was clearly veering in other directions, more in line with studio ideas. They had their ultimate success a few years later with *King Kong*.

A more authentic project was the French film *The Black Cruise* (*La Croisière Noire*, 1926) by Léon Poirier—like Murnau, a temporary fugitive from fiction. Sponsored by Citroën, it recorded an unprecedented automobile journey from the northern to the southern reaches of Africa, and on to the French island colony of Madagascar. The feature-length project provided occasion for countless vignettes of tribal and village life. Again, no individual portraits emerge, and the expedition's interest remains superficial, with stress on the bizarre. Yet the record of such a journey inevitably offered documentary values, and preparations for a similar Citroën-sponsored Asian journey, from Lebanon to Indochina, were begun in 1929. Titled *The Yellow Cruise* (*La Croisière Jaune*) the film did not reach completion until many years later.

The explorer-as-documentarist tradition received some of its most tawdry contributions in the work of Mr. and Mrs. Martin Johnson, who had completed their first travelogue in 1912 and were still successfully at it two decades later. Self-glorification was the keynote. Unabashed condescension and amusement marked their attitude toward natives. They started *Congorilla*—about "big apes and little people"—in 1929 as the transition to sound was under way, so they included brief sound sequences and a narration to make it "the first sound film from darkest Africa." Both Johnsons were constantly on camera in sequences demonstrating their courage or wit, or both. In a forest clearing we see them recruiting forty "black boys" as carriers. When one gives his name, it sounds like "coffee pot" to Mrs. Osa

Martin Johnson, at work on *Congorilla,* 1929.

Morro Pictures

Johnson, so his name is written down as Coffee Pot. Johnson's narration speaks of "funny little savages," "happiest little savages on earth." His idea of humor was to give a pygmy a cigar and wait for him to get sick; to give another a balloon to blow up and watch his reaction when it bursts; to give a monkey beer and watch the result. During a shot of a crocodile opening its mouth, Johnson's narration comments: "Gee, what a place to throw old razor-blades." To catch two baby gorillas, seven huge trees are chopped down, isolating the gorillas in a tree in the middle; then it is chopped down.

A decade after *Nanook of the North* the explorer-as-documentarist was clearly in decline. The creator of the genre and of its greatest triumph seemed himself to be edging into obscurity. But meanwhile other documentary genres were moving to the fore—one of these, under the impact of huge social change.

Reporter

Denis Arkadievich Kaufman (1896–1954), known in film history as Dziga Vertov, was one of three sons of a librarian in Bialystok, in the

Polish part of the Russian empire. Early in the 1914–18 World War the family moved from war dangers to what seemed the comparative safety of Russia itself. In Petrograd—which had recently been renamed to shed the Germanic "St. Petersburg"—young Denis studied medicine and psychology and wrote poetry, falling under the spell of Russia's "futurist" poets, among whom Vladimir Mayakovsky was the leader.[1]

Futurism, a movement sweeping through Europe from its 1909 beginnings in Italy and France and invading all the arts, gloried in the clamor and rhythm of machines, and the dynamism of a world in change. Its poets tended to reject syntax in favor of word-montages; they were intoxicated with long catalogues of words in the manner of Walt Whitman, to whom they owed much. Its composers called for inclusion of sounds, as symbols of modern life, in orchestral instrumentation. The futurists were given to rhetorical manifestos, which often used unconventional typographical arrangements as means of expression and emphasis.

In 1916–17 Denis Kaufman, medical student and young futurist poet, organized an "audio-laboratory" of his own in which he built montages of sounds—sound poems on discs. They provided a foundation for things to come. He adopted the pseudonym Dziga Vertov—both names connoting *turning, revolving*. The names suggested a spinning top and perhaps perpetual motion—the keynote of the following years and of his role in them.

The bolshevik seizure of power in October 1917 found Vertov eagerly volunteering to the Cinema Committee in Moscow; he became editor of its newsreel *Film Weekly* (*Kino-Nedelia*), which began appearing in June 1918. This put him at the age of twenty-two at the heart of a swirling operation. To his modest editing table came footage from all fronts. In addition to German armies, invading forces of allied troops—American, British, French, Japanese, and others—landed north, east, and south, trying to suppress the revolution and, at first, keep Russia in the war against Germany. For the three years 1917–20 the combination of civil war and foreign intervention continued; blockade, hunger, chaos tore the land. Vertov's task was to assemble incoming bits of film—fragments of struggle, crisis, disaster, victory—and send them forth again, subtitled and in meaningful organization. The newsreel issues went in all directions—by "agit-train" back to the various fronts to be seen by revolutionary fighters themselves, and by similar trains and steamboats to villages and towns. The agit-trains distributed newspapers and books; some had printing presses operating en route. When a train was not in motion, film shows were held—at night in near-by streets or fields. One "agit-steamboat" plied large rivers towing a barge-cinema that seated 800 people —while carrying its own cameraman, who sent back footage to Vertov. The mission was to get out the news—unite people by keeping them informed of the ups and downs of agonizing struggle.[2]

In the midst of the newsreel work Vertov compiled longer releases including *Anniversary of the Revolution* (*Godovshtchina Revolutsii*, 1919), reusing footage in broader context. But in 1919 the blockade became so tight, and the black market so rampant, that stocks of raw film gave out and the newsreel schedules faltered. Old film was sometimes scraped and recoated by homemade methods to maintain schedules—at the cost of archive material. Astonishingly, in the midst of such crises the new government went ahead with its plans for a state film school—at first operating without film. It was a measure of the importance attached to film activity.

Late in 1920 the last intervention troops were finally ousted, and a kind of peace arrived. But the land faced other and more unprecedented struggles. Not surprisingly young Vertov, now a seasoned film man who had processed hundreds of thousands of feet of film, saw newsreels playing a role in these struggles. In the building of a new kind of society there would be other crises and victories which, like earlier battle news, must surely be made known at once throughout the Soviet Union.

With the end of fighting Vertov compiled a feature-length *History of the Civil War* (*Istoriya Grazhdanskoi Voini*, 1921) from footage he knew so well, and awaited new tasks.

But the following months brought famine and epidemics. A prostrate economy forced Lenin—barely recovered from an assassination attempt—to retreat from socialist theory and proclaim a New Economic Policy—"NEP," a temporary return to forms of private enterprise.

In the war-scarred film theaters fiction films began reappearing. There were not yet new Russian features—countless projects waited, begging for raw stock. Out of hiding, or newly imported by NEP entrepreneurs, came mostly foreign films—American, German, French, Italian—items such as *Drama on the Equator, The City's Temptation, The Devil's Admirers, A Night of Horror in the Menagerie, Daughter of Tarzan, Evil Shadows, The Adventuress,* and *Secret of the Egyptian Night.*[3]

Until this time Vertov had functioned as editor—of footage supplied by others. The events of 1920–22 propelled him into a wider range of roles: writer of polemic manifestos, theorist, producer. A typical Vertov manifesto addressed film artists in the name of a mysterious Council of Three:

Five years crowded with world-shaking events have entered your lives and left—leaving no trace. "Art" works of pre-revolutionary days surround you like icons and still command your prayerful emotions. Foreign lands abet you in your confusion, sending into new Russia the living corpses of movie dramas garbed in splendid technological dressing.

Spring is coming. At the studios new activity is awaited. The Council of Three notes with frank horror how producers leaf through works of literature looking for scenario material. Names of theater dramas and epics selected for studio enactment float through the air. In the Ukraine, and here in Moscow, several photoplays have already been made displaying every symptom of impotence.

The body of cinema is numbed by the terrible poison of habit. We demand an opportunity to experiment with this dying organism, to find an antidote. . . .

Vertov was sure what the antidote must be. He saw the traditional fiction film, descendant of theater artifice, as something in the same class as religion—"opium for the people." The task of Soviet films, as Vertov saw it, was to document socialist reality.

To build cinema on theatrical tradition seemed to him outrageous foolishness. Theater offered a "scabby substitute" for life; the same was true of theatrical film with its synthetic struggles and heroics—a dangerous weapon controlled by capitalists and NEPmen. He scorned producers and distributors who "snapped up the scraps from the German table . . . the American table." "Come to life," he urged film makers. He asked them to stop running from "the prose of life." They must become "craftsmen of seeing—organizers of visible life," armed with a "maturing eye."

His attacks—on almost everything being done—inevitably won for Vertov many enemies in the film world. But his views also had support—some of it in high places. Early in 1922 Lenin held a discussion about film with the Commissar of Education, Anatoli Lunacharsky. "Of all the arts," Lenin told him, "for us film is the most important," and he spoke especially of films "reflecting Soviet actuality." Such films, thought Lenin, "must begin with newsreels." Later he called for what came to be known as the "Leninist film-proportion," a doctrine that every film program must have a balance between fiction and actuality material.

In this context Vertov and his Council of Three were able to plunge into a new kind of film journalism—while continuing to pour out manifestos. In May 1922 *Film-Truth* (*Kino-Pravda*) began to appear, usually at monthly intervals, under the banner of Kultkino. It continued until 1925 and, like the civil war newsreel, had feature-length documentaries as by-products.

The mysterious *troika* or "Council of Three" behind this venture consisted simply of Dziga Vertov himself; his wife Yelizaveta Svilova, who became film editor; and Dziga's brother Mikhail Kaufman, one year his junior, a photography enthusiast since childhood who joined Dziga after being demobilized. He became chief cameraman, soon backed by scores of other cameramen throughout the Soviet Union. Occasionally he made films independently.

The title *Kino-Pravda* was itself a kind of manifesto. The newspaper *Pravda,* founded by Lenin in 1912, had become the official government organ. The film project, in calling itself *Kino-Pravda,* seemed to assert a central role for itself. And the title epitomized Vertov doctrine—that proletarian cinema must be based on truth—"fragments of actuality"—assembled for meaningful impact.

The ambitious project began in a squalid setting. Vertov described its first quarters:

We had a basement in the center of the city. It was dark and damp, with an earthen floor and holes that you stumbled into at every turn. Large hungry rats scuttled over our feet. Somewhere above was a single window below the surface of the street; underfoot, a stream of water from dripping pipes. You had to take care that your film never touched anything but the table, or it would get wet. This dampness prevented our reels of lovingly edited film from sticking together properly, rusted our scissors and our splicers. Don't lean back on that chair, film is hanging there—as

Mikhail Kaufman and camera.

Mikhail Kaufman collection

Dziga Vertov (at right), and assistant.

Staatliches Filmarchiv der DDR

it was all over the room. Before dawn—damp—cold—teeth chattering. I wrap comrade Svilova in a *third* jacket. The last night of work so that the next two issues of *Kino-Pravda* will be ready on time.[4]

Mikhail Kaufman, later recalling these days, said they never really thought of it as hard work. It was all done as a life-necessity, "like breathing or eating." On big stories Dziga mapped strategy, assigning topics but leaving wide latitude to the cameramen. Much of the time Mikhail followed his own interests, moving about from morning till night, shooting whatever seemed important. The epoch provided the themes. His camera was constantly with him; he felt lost without it. Once he went south for a rest—without his camera. "But when I could not see it with the help of my camera, it was not beauty for me."[5]

The emphasis—harking back to Lumière—was on action caught on the run, from any revealing vantage. Permissions were never asked. Staged action was abhorred. Concealed camera positions were used to catch moments in marketplaces, factories, schools, taverns, streets.

An issue of *Film-Truth* generally took up several topics. Subject matter was seldom spectacular. This was part of its essential quality: drama was revealed in "the prose of life." It caught the moment when a Moscow trolley line, long out of operation in torn-up streets, was finally put in repair and began running again. Army tanks, used as tractors, were leveling an area for an airport. A children's hospital was trying to salvage war-starved children; a flashback to scenes of the famine period emphasized the magnitude of the task. A traveling film team was shown arriving in a town, unpacking its gear, and preparing an open-air showing; a subtitle gave information on how to arrange a visit by such a film show—write to *Kino-Pravda*. Audiences clearly valued all this. It was often the one program item touching the historical moment. But the Vertov stress on unusual, revealing camera vistas and on meaningful juxtapositions must also have contributed to the impact. The subject matter might be "prose" but the treatment was lively, vigorous, sometimes witty.

In his continuing manifestos—no longer emanating from a Council of Three but from a wider group calling itself the Cinema-Eyes, or *Kinoki*—Vertov emphasized two points. One was the superhuman versatility of the film camera. He described this with the typographical zest of futurist poetry:

Basic and essential:

FILM-PERCEPTION
OF THE WORLD

The most fundamental point: *use of the camera*

> MAKE WAY
> FOR THE
> MACHINE!

as a cinema-eye more perfect than the human eye for exploring the chaos of visual phenomena filling the universe.

The cinema-eye works and moves in time and in space, seeing and recording impressions in a way quite different from the human eye. Limitations imposed by the position of the body, or by how much we can see of any phenomenon in a second of seeing—such restrictions do not exist for the cinema-eye, which has much wider capabilities.

> DOWN WITH
> 16 FRAMES
> PER SECOND

We cannot improve our eyes, but we can always improve the camera.

Elsewhere he wrote:

. . . I am cinema-eye—I am a mechanical eye. I, a machine, show you a world such as only I can see.

From now on and for always I cast off human immobility, I move constantly, I approach and pull away from objects, I creep under them, I leap onto them, I move alongside the mouth of a galloping horse, I cut into a crowd, I run before charging troops, I turn on my back, I take off with an airplane, I fall and rise with falling and rising bodies.

Freed from the tyranny of 16–17 images per second, freed from the framework of space and time, I coordinate any and all points of the universe, wherever I may record them.

My mission is the creation of a new perception of the world. Thus I decipher in a new way a world unknown to you.

Along with the surreal capabilities of the camera, Vertov stressed the editor's role:

But it is not enough to show bits of truth on the screen, separate frames of truth. These frames must be thematically organized so that the whole is also a truth.[6]

Kinoki team. At extreme right, Mikhail Kaufman. At left, Svilova. Beside her, Ilya Kopalin, later prominent as a director.

Staatliches Filmarchiv der DDR

In synthesizing his bits, Vertov was ingenious, resourceful, even tricky. His love of technical tricks brought frequent criticism; he often appeared to use them for their own sake. But they also yielded telling symbolic moments. In *Film-Truth* issue No. 24 (1925), on the first anniversary of the death of Lenin, we see streams of people filing past the dead leader in his coffin. In the midst of this, the living Lenin appears in the corner of the screen as though still speaking to them. It was a highly emotional moment for its audiences.

The ideas and methods of the *Film-Truth* series were carried forward in several long documentaries, including *Cinema-Eye* (*Kino-Glaz,* 1924), *Forward, Soviet!* (*Shagai, Soviet!,* 1926), *One Sixth of the World* (*Shestaya Chast Mira,* 1926), and *The Eleventh Year* (*Odinnadtsati,* 1928). Among these, *One Sixth of the World* was by far the most successful in the Soviet Union, and it also had considerable vogue abroad.[7] It was marked by a use of subtitles that seemed to anticipate spoken commentary. In most earlier documentaries, each subtitle explained the following shot, or a limited group of shots. In *One Sixth of the World* a long series of short, intermittent subtitles form a continuing apostrophe, in a style reminiscent of Walt

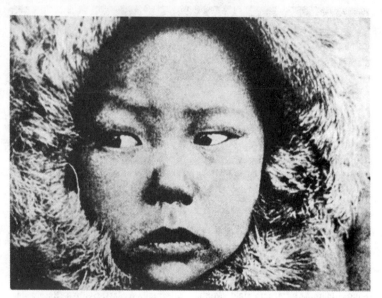

One Sixth of the World, 1926.

Staatliches Filmarchiv der DDR

Whitman, a poet much admired by Vertov. The film presents an astonishing diversity of vivid footage from all parts of the Soviet Union, fused by the intermittent commentary addressed to all its people. "You in the small villages" . . . "You in the tundra" . . . "You on the ocean. . . ." Having established a vast geographical dispersion, the catalogue turns to nationalities: "You Uzbeks" . . . "You Kalmiks." . . . Then it addresses occupations—scores of them. Each catalogue item brings one or more shots, never long enough to halt the momentum of the invocation. The invocation and footage include young, old; men, women, children; those at work, those at play. One enormously long sentence, presented in these short bursts, appears to continue for several minutes and finally concludes with ". . . you are the owners of one sixth of the globe."

The incantation-style of commentary continues, fusing other long sequences. One of these hails elements of change, each shown in a revealing vignette or two, again involving wide geographical range and diversity: a Muslim woman emerging from her hidden status; a worker at night school, learning to read; a clinic in action.

The enthusiastic reception won by this film is not surprising. To

men and women with only a dim awareness of the scope and resources of their land, and with a deep desire to believe in its destiny,
One Sixth of the World was a prideful pageant.

"The history of Cinema-Eye," said Vertov in a 1929 lecture during
a visit to Paris, "has been a relentless struggle to modify the course
of world cinema, to achieve in cinema a new emphasis on the un-
played film over the played film, to substitute the document for the
mis en scène, to break out of the proscenium of the theater and to
enter the arena of life itself."[8]

But when he spoke these words, it was already clear that he had
failed in this mission. In the chaos of the first post-revolution years,
the reporter-documentarist had briefly won dominance. But much of
what Vertov had reported was now being transmuted into legend.
The means of transmutation was not documentary, but fiction. Vertov had been part of a sequence of brilliant explosions that had made
Soviet cinema, in the mid-1920's, a sudden world wonder. But the
focus of interest had rapidly shifted from documentary to the works
of Eisenstein, Pudovkin, Dovzhenko, and others. Some of their works
had a documentary look; Eisenstein himself said of *The Battleship
Potemkin* (*Bronenosets Potyomkin,* 1925) that while it functioned
as drama, it "looks like a newsreel of an event." This quality led some
to associate it with documentary. But what Eisenstein assembled with
his montage was not "fragments of actuality" but fragments of his
own intense vision.

While Vertov's *One Sixth of the World* was winning acclaim, his
position in the Soviet film world was slipping. His views, so fanatically argued, made him troublesome. Besides, they represented an ultimate challenge to authority. Stalin was as interested as Lenin in
cinema, but was more intent on control. During the first Five Year
Plan, begun in 1928, determined efforts were made to coordinate film
content with political goals. Project approvals and budgets were based
on detailed scenarios. Vertov's documentary ideas collided with this
procedure: how could a documentarist predict—or guarantee—what
truths he would find and record in the arena of life? He at first said he
could not write scenarios. That attitude marked him as a man with
dangerous "anti-planning" views. To continue his work, he eventually compromised, submitting documents which he preferred to call
analyses—analyzing his intentions without specifying shots and sequences.

Thus he eventually won the chance to make a film he had long considered—on the documentary cameraman and his role in society. In this he set out to dramatize all the theories he had poured into manifestos and polemics. It would be his testament.

It was a reckless notion. At a time when technical experimentation was increasingly damned as "formalism," and the Stalinist view of "Soviet realism" increasingly favored explicit social doctrine, the new Vertov film with its intellectual pyrotechnics must have seemed a defiant gesture. Yet it became the film by which he was to be known throughout much of the world and even in the Soviet Union—in spite of mixed initial reactions.

The Man With the Movie Camera (Chelovek s Kinoapparatom,

The Man with the Movie Camera, 1929.

Mikhail Kaufman collection

1929) presents, on one level, a kaleidoscope of daily life in the Soviet Union: sleeping, waking, going to work, playing. At the same time it presents constant glimpses of a film cameraman—Mikhail Kaufman—in action, recording Soviet life for all to see. We see him climbing bridge spans, smokestacks, towers, roofs; riding on cars, trains, motorcycles; lying on the ground for underneath views of trains, traffic, marching men. We see the making of a film and at the same time the film that is being made. The interweaving of the two is constant and, in its playfulness, disarming, stimulating, often baffling. We get a through-the-camera view of a passerby; see him reacting to the camera; then we see the camera as seen by him, with his own reflection in the lens. The film incessantly reminds us that it is a film. The shadow of the camera is allowed to invade the shot.

In a startling sequence, action suddenly ends in a frozen frame. The frozen frame becomes a series of stills. We then see these as frames on a strip of 35mm film being examined, image by image, by a film editor—presumably Svilova. For a while, we cut back and forth between images as seen individually at the editing table, and related motion sequences in the finished film. Occasionally we also see an audience seeing the finished film. The film digresses to note parallels. A woman washing at her washbowl is linked with a window-washing shot; paper rolling through a printing press is associated with water flowing over a dam. Shots of a wedding, a death, a childbirth, a divorce, are joltingly intercut. Superimposures and trick shots become frequent as the film progresses. At one point we see a camera putting itself together, and the tripod walking off with it. Is Vertov telling us again about the superhuman abilities of the camera—or is this just playfulness? In a superimposure we see a camera on its tripod, seemingly the size of an Eiffel Tower, standing with the cameraman in the midst of a vast crowd of tiny people: a highly expressive image. Elsewhere we see a cameraman, with camera and tripod, climbing out of a glass of beer: what is Vertov telling us here? At the end of the film, camera and tripod take a bow by themselves.

Since much of the film shows Mikhail Kaufman in action, as photographed by assistants, *The Man With the Movie Camera* involves staging and contrivance to an extent previously rejected by Vertov. But the artificiality is deliberate: an avant-garde determination to suppress illusion in favor of a heightened awareness. The film is an essay on film truth, crammed with tantalizing ironies. But what did it fi-

Enthusiasm: Symphony of the Donbas, 1931.

Staatliches Filmarchiv der DDR

Three Songs of Lenin, 1934.

Staatliches Filmarchiv der DDR

nally mean for audiences? Had Vertov demonstrated the importance of the reporter as documentarist? Or had his barrage of film tricks suggested—intentionally? unintentionally?—that no documentary could be trusted? Of the brilliance of *The Man With the Movie Camera* there was never a doubt. It was dazzling in its ambiguity. Eisenstein, usually a Vertov supporter, felt he was slipping into "unmotivated camera mischief" and even "formalism."[9]

During the years following *The Man With the Movie Camera,* Vertov visited various western European countries and found audiences of *cinéastes* wildly enthusiastic. But his position continued to slip at home. The coming of sound found Vertov and Kaufman working in the studios of the Ukraine—a reflection of disfavor in Moscow. But in the Ukraine Vertov created one of the most inventive of early sound films, *Enthusiasm: Symphony of the Donbas (Entuziazm: Simphonya Donbassa,* 1931). Its effective use of non-synchronous sound undoubtedly reflected his early "audio-laboratory" experiments. Subsequently he completed a film he had long planned, built to some extent on cherished Lenin footage—*Three Songs of Lenin (Tri Pesni o Leninye,* 1934). Each of its three segments uses music as its cohesive force: the first is a celebration of achievement; the second, a dirge;

the third, a marching song. Unassuming, deeply felt, it has gradually won the status of a Vertov classic.

Vertov continued to work and produce, but he finally settled into the anonymity of a newsreel editing desk. He ended where he had begun, but no longer writing manifestos or polemics.

He had given the reporter-as-documentarist a moment at the center of cinema, and had influenced others. The importance he had given the newsreel set the stage for several careers. Notable was that of Esfir Shub (1894–1959), who during the NEP period had worked in Moscow as subtitler and editor of foreign films—preparing such items as Pearl White serials and Fritz Lang's *Doctor Mabuse* for Russian audiences. But she had a documentary fervor and repeatedly asked for permission to study old newsreels as feature-film material. After many refusals, this permission was finally granted, and in 1926 she went into action. Among the footage she studied, analyzed, and painstakingly catalogued was material accumulated by the Museum of the Revolution—much of it unmarked, disintegrating, and stored in rusty cans in Leningrad cellars. Here her months of work were rewarded by a historic find—one she had hoped for but almost despaired to achieve. A collection of "counterrevolutionary film" turned out to be the home movies of Tsar Nicholas II. They became a key element in her immensely absorbing feature-length documentary, *The Fall of the Romanov Dynasty* (*Padeniye Dinasti Romanovikh*, 1927).[10]

The long-time newsreel obsession with royalty, and the Tsar's own devotion to film—as in various other royal households, a court cinematographer had immortalized birthday celebrations, tennis matches, croquet games, boating parties, and innumerable rituals—now boomeranged in overwhelming fashion. Placed meticulously in proper time context along with footage of war, strikes, munitions assembly lines, arrests of troublemakers, breadlines, the "counterrevolutionary film" proved to have powerful pro-revolutionary impact. Brief subtitles were used to document or explain individual shots: we are told that the legislative body, the Duma, included 241 landowners, seven workers. We see endless parades of religious dignitaries, in opulent garb. Officers in dress uniform dance the mazurka at a battleship deck party. A subtitle occasionally makes a sharp propaganda stab. A close shot of a munitions assembly line is explained in these words: "The hands of workers preparing the death of their brothers."

The Fall of the Romanov Dynasty used documents of the years

1912–17. Its success led to two similar Esfir Shub projects: *The Great Road* (*Veliky Put,* 1927), covering the period 1917–27; and *The Russia of Nicholas II and Leo Tolstoy* (*Rossiya Nikolaya II i Lev Tolstoy,* 1928), dealing with 1896–1912. The three form an epic trilogy of Russian history from the birth of cinema to 1927.

Esfir Shub's scholarly achievement played an important role in encouraging the development of film archives. Her later editing work concentrated on other kinds of cinema, but she returned occasionally to the genre of newsreel compilation which she had so notably advanced.

The repertorial documentary pioneered by Vertov attracted other Russian film makers of the 1920's and resulted in some masterworks. The most celebrated was probably *Turksib* (1929), by Victor Turin, a feature-length film on the building of the Turkestan-Siberia railway. Turin's organization of his huge project, and his success in giving it cumulative dramatic impact, won wide admiration and influenced documentary film makers throughout the world. The Whitmanesque style of the subtitles, linking long sequences, was reminiscent of *One Sixth of the World* and, like Vertov's film, seemed to anticipate spoken commentary. Turin's tracing of small mountain rivulets into a raging, swollen river has been widely imitated. A memorable sequence—introduced with the simple title "Strangers . . ."—shows people in a remote Turkestan desert village watching the arrival of surveyors. This sets the stage for a later climactic sequence in which an engine for the first time arrives on the new track. Men—some on horseback —come cautiously to look it over as it stands at rest, puffing quietly. As the engine starts up, the terror of the horses and men and their temporary retreat provide fascinatingly authentic moments. Later we see them joyfully racing the engine across vast plains.

Another remarkable achievement in journalistic documentary, of special interest because it represented early Soviet observation abroad, was Yakov Blyokh's *Shanghai Document* (*Shanghaisky Dokument,* 1928). Blyokh generally worked in fiction and had assisted Eisenstein in the production of *The Battleship Potemkin.* In *Shanghai Document* he portrayed, in revealing actuality material, a city of divided societies: the suppressed, swarming Chinese, and the heavily armed concessions of the International Settlement. The final portion of the film reflects the rise of revolutionary resistance and the strife between various Chinese factions. It touches briefly on the bloody

Turksib, 1929.

Shanghai Document, 1928.

Salt for Svanetia, 1930.

slaughter in Shanghai by forces of Chiang Kai-shek as he sought to consolidate his anti-communist regime. *Shanghai Document* emerged as a film of great historic interest.

Another impressive reportorial project was *Salt for Svanetia* (*Sol Svanetii,* 1930) by Mikhail Kalatozov. It pictures a starkly isolated mountain community between the Black and Caspian seas. Culturally bizarre in its fierce isolation, it is also seen to suffer in strange ways from a total lack of salt. As we see a farmer lie in a field to rest from his labor, a cow comes to lick the sweat from his brow. When he urinates, cattle lick his urine. As a baby is born, a dog is at hand to lick the placental fluid from its body. The climax of the film is the coming of a Soviet-built road, which will bring salt to Svanetia.

The Stalin regime apparently felt that Kalatozov had been far too fascinated by the backwardness and superstition of Svanetia, and too perfunctorily interested in the socialist solution. The film was considered unbalanced and unfair to Svanetia. Kalatozov was for a time in disfavor—an increasingly frequent occurrence during this period.*

Another memorable documentary was *Moscow* (*Moskva,* 1927), made by Vertov's brother Mikhail Kaufman in collaboration with Ilya Kopalin, also a Vertov co-worker. It presented an absorbing kaleidoscope of life in the Soviet capital. Still another was Mikhail Kaufman's *In Spring* (*Vesnoy,* 1930), much admired by contemporaries but seldom seen abroad in original form. Portraying the springtime devastation of rain and flood—preliminaries to rebirth—Kaufman makes spring a metaphor for revolution. Portions dealing with this theme, in which religion is seen as a distortion of the symbolism of spring, were generally excised abroad.

Vertov's influence went beyond documentary. Many observers felt that he influenced fiction films of the 1920's, in that his work and polemics helped to turn them away from earlier artificialities. Thus he may have strengthened the Soviet fiction film, though he scarcely intended to do so. There may also be a Vertov influence in the use of climactic actuality sequences in a number of fiction films—as in Kuleshov's celebrated satire *The Extraordinary Adventures of Mr. West in the Land of the Bolsheviks* (*Neobychainiye Priklucheniya Mistera Vesta v Stranye Bolshevikov,* 1924) and in Ermler's *Fragment of an*

---

* Decades later, Kalatozov scored a world-wide success with *The Cranes Are Flying.*

In Spring, 1930.

Mikhail Kaufman collection

In Spring, 1930.

Empire (*Oblomok Imperii,* 1929). Both end with tours of restored and rebuilt Moscow: in the first, serving to disabuse the American Mr. West of his preconceptions of Soviet life; in the second, opening the eyes of a long-time victim of amnesia who had lost his memory during a battle of the revolutionary war, and regains it a decade later. The film has a *Rip Van Winkle* pattern: the hero is suddenly confronted with the vast changes that have taken place.

The work of Dziga Vertov and of those he influenced had unquestionable propaganda values for the Soviet government in the early and middle 1920's. Yet Vertov thought of himself not as a propagandist, but as a reporter: his mission was to get out the news. Conflict—or potential conflict—between the obligations of a journalist and the demands of doctrine was not yet sensed as a problem in the early Vertov days. This happy moment passed quickly.

During the Stalin period increasing international tension, increasing fear of encirclement, increasing armament production and secrecy, along with pressures on film makers to support policy and tactics, all this laid a heavy hand on fiction and documentary alike. A golden film moment—brief, like many a renascence in the arts—was over, and the spotlight shifted elsewhere.

Painter

All the arts were shaken by the rise of film. Practitioners of other arts re-examined their own roles, assailed cinema, staked out new positions for themselves, developed isms to fortify them, appropriated elements from cinema, wrote manifestos. Some transferred their main interest to film.

In the 1920's painters infiltrated in numbers into the film world. Along with sculptors, musicians, writers, architects, still photographers, and others they joined cine-clubs—the first was formed in Paris in 1924—to look at films, talk about films, and present their own experiments. The cine-club was in part a protest against the commercialism of cinema; even more, a recognition of its power over men.

Painters inevitably brought with them ideas and ways different from those of other film makers. Plot and climax were not among their habitual concerns. They tended to think of film as a pictorial art in which light was the medium, and which involved fascinating composition problems in that the interrelationship of forms was always evolving, developing unexpected and mysterious dynamics. They were also interested in texture and its interplay with light.

In 1921 two painters who had been members of a Zurich avant-garde movement—the Swedish Viking Eggeling and the German Hans Richter—began joint experiments in abstract film. Richter admired the "perfect order" of Eggeling's abstract paintings—"as clear as Bach." Together they hoped to generate a Bach-like feeling from movements counterpointed on the screen in fugue-like patterns. At first their experiments seemed remote from documentary, but they acquired a documentary link. The artists often photographed familiar objects—"fragments of actuality" in Vertov parlance—and used them as the basis for their interplaying movements. Thus they carried the ideas of Vertov to an ultimate conclusion. The artist was beginning with actuality, then creating his own expressive synthesis.[1]

Any sort of actuality could be used as a basis for such abstractions. Richter made his *Racing Symphony* (*Rennsymphonie,* 1928) from horse-race footage, which he organized into complex overlapping patterns. It was Muybridge fused with abstractionism.

A striking example of this abstract-documentary trend was *Ballet Mécanique* (1925) by the French artist Fernand Léger and the American artist Dudley Murphy. It won such vogue that Léger considered abandoning painting for film. Much of it is a composition built out of moving gears, levers, pendulums, eggbeaters, and other items. Its most celebrated sequence shows a cleaning woman climbing a flight of stairs. It was so edited that just as the woman appears to reach the top, she is seen to be at the bottom again. The effect is repeated many times, and audiences acquire an agonizing desire to see the upward journey completed. In this sequence, suggesting the degradation of repetitious labor, the film had strong philosophic overtones.

The work of Jean Painlevé gave the avant-garde film makers a link with science. Trained as a biologist, he experimented with photography of underwater life—sometimes in speeded, sometimes in slowed motion, often hugely magnified, and always artfully lighted—producing astonishing studies in the surrealism of natural phenomena, with their bizarre shapes and movements. Starting in 1928 with *Devilfish* (*Le Pieuvre*), *Stickleback Eggs* (*Oeufs d'Épinoche*), and *Sea Urchins* (*Les Oursins*), he later won wide celebrity with his *Sea Horse* (*L'Hip-*

pocampe, 1934) for which Darius Milhaud composed an accompaniment.

Most such experiments circulated largely in cine-clubs. But in 1927 one painter-documentarist, Walther Ruttman, released a work of such impact that it created a genre, which established itself in theatrical cinema.

Walther Ruttman (1887–1941) was born in Frankfurt, Germany. Along with painting, he studied architecture and music. He became a successful designer of posters. Admiring Viking Eggeling, he also became an early film experimenter, and in 1924 created a nightmarish dream sequence about black hawks for Fritz Lang's films on the *Nibelungen* saga. He also admired Dziga Vertov and Sergei Eisenstein. All these influences seemed to come together in *Berlin: Symphony of the City (Berlin: die Sinfonie der Grosstadt,* 1927), directed and edited by Ruttman and photographed by Karl Freund. It was by no means the first film about a great city; predecessors included Kaufman and Kopalin's *Moscow* and numerous short films including *Mannahatta* (1921) by the Americans Paul Strand and Charles Sheeler, and an earlier venture by a Swedish visitor to New York, Julius Jaenzon—*New York 1911.* But none of these had so strikingly suggested a painting heritage, and none spurred so many imitations. *Berlin* started a wave of "city symphonies," to which Ruttman himself later contributed films on Düsseldorf, Stuttgart, and Hamburg.

In *Berlin: Symphony of the City* the word "symphony" is significant. Ruttman was interested in rhythms and patterns. People form part of the patterns, but Ruttman is not especially interested in the people themselves. The film depicts a day in the life of the city: this dawn-to-dusk progression is the only "plot." An early morning entrance into the city, by railroad, opens the film. It is an extraordinarily dynamic opening, and characteristically devoid of human content. It is compounded of telephone lines bobbing up and down along the track, stroboscopic patterns of railroad bridge beams, tracks dividing and coming together as seen from the front of the train, jiggling movements of couplings—all these intercut with glimpses of landscape, changing from rural to metropolitan to industrial. In the city we first see a quiet sequence of empty streets, restfully interlaced; then the city awakes via a catalogue of opening shutters, blinds, curtains, windows, doors. All manner of machinery gradually goes into action. Machines are a major interest throughout and are often seen without human operators. An office sequence gives us frenzy compounded of typewriter and telephone activity. Eisenstein "shock" editing techniques are here injected: in the midst of phone calls we see monkeys chattering, dogs lunging at each other. Such animal-human intercutting is done at several points. A symphonic score by Edmund Meisel was composed to accompany the film, and was featured in big-city showings.[2]

In France the Brazilian artist Alberto Cavalcanti was at the same time making a strikingly similar film, *Only the Hours (Rien Que Les Heures*, 1926), about dawn-to-dusk life in Paris. Cavalcanti had been trained in Brazil for a career in architecture, but in Paris he moved into scene design, and from there into film experimentation. His Parisian film, begun after Ruttman's *Berlin* but completed and released earlier, is less severely compartmentalized. It had moments of humor, rare in Ruttman. Its opening suggests a Vertov trick: elegant ladies are seen descending a stairway, as though we are beginning a Hollywood high-life movie. But the action freezes: a pair of hands picks up the frozen frame, which has become a still photograph, and tears it into bits; the bits become garbage on a street. This is no Hollywood dream-movie, Cavalcanti is telling us; actuality will be the theme.

Rich-poor contrasts are suggested throughout the film, but no meanings are developed from them: rich and poor are mere threads in the fabric of city life. As in Ruttman's work, pattern and design are dominant interests. Over a girl selling newspapers Cavalcati superimposes a swirling ballet of newspaper titles and headlines. Paris as seen by various painters forms another such montage composition; another is developed from movie posters. Cavalcanti loves tricks. We see a gentleman eating a steak for lunch; over the center of his plate —replacing the steak—Cavalcanti superimposes a slaughterhouse scene. The fancy design of the luncheon plate remains visible, framing bloody mayhem. Cavalcanti wanders from topic to topic. He uses a few staged scenes, sometimes embarrassingly amateurish. He lacks Ruttman's sense of organization, but seems far more genial.[3]

Another city symphony also involved a foreigner drawn to Paris. He was Boris Kaufman, brother of Dziga Vertov and Mikhail Kaufman, and youngest of the three by a number of years. During the chaos of Russian civil war his parents had taken him back to Poland,

The three Kaufman brothers—before the Russian Revolution.

Mikhail Kaufman collection

and a few years later he went to Paris for study. He corresponded with Mikhail, who attempted to give him cinematography instruction by mail. In Paris Boris was able to see a number of Dziga Vertov films, and he saw Dziga when the latter visited France. Boris inevitably gravitated toward cinematography, making admired film studies of the Seine and the Champs Élysées. These led to a collaboration with a brilliant young *cinéaste,* Jean Vigo.[4]

Jean Vigo (1905–34), son of a radical journalist of Basque descent who had died mysteriously in jail, was educated in various boarding schools. A siege of tuberculosis made him settle in Nice, a resort which fascinated and revolted him. He became assistant in a photo studio, and a leading force in the Nice cine-club. Corresponding with film experimenters far and wide to secure films for his cine-club programs, he became saturated with film theory and determined to make films of his own. In 1929 he invited Boris Kaufman to Nice to work with him, and the collaboration resulted in *On the Subject of Nice* (*À Propos de Nice*), released the following year.

Kaufman photographed, Vigo directed. Vigo often wheeled Kaufman up and down the boardwalk in a wheelchair; Kaufman had a camouflaged camera in his lap. Wheelchairs were common enough in Nice to pass unnoticed, and this facilitated catching action unaware. Kaufman and Vigo were both committed to this *Kino-Pravda* approach; if someone became aware of being photographed, they

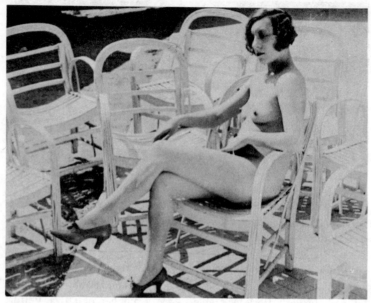

À Propos de Nice, 1930.

Cinémathèque Française

stopped instantly. At the same time, Vigo wanted a personal film—
point de vue documenté, he called it. The maker of such documentaries, Vigo later told an audience in Paris, should be "thin enough to
squeeze through a Romanian keyhole and shoot Prince Carol getting
up in his nightshirt"—if the spectacle proved interesting—and "small
enough . . . to squat under the chair of the croupier, the great god
of the Casino at Monte Carlo."

In Nice the collaborators did not succeed in squatting under the
croupier's chair, but they made up for it with ingenuity. Early in
their film is a device characteristic of city-symphony films. On a chess-
board, in evening clothes, we see some small dolls—somewhat like
those used on wedding cakes. Suddenly a croupier's rake sweeps
them away. This movement is at once followed by a matching movement in which a streetcleaner sweeps away rubbish: in Nice, each
batch of tourists becomes tomorrow's garbage.

À Propos de Nice has many similarities to other city films, but adds
an edge of biting satire. Vigo felt that he was portraying "the last
twitchings of a society that neglects its own responsibilities to the

point of giving you nausea and making you an accomplice in a revolutionary solution."

Vigo, with Kaufman at the camera, later directed two brilliant fiction films—*Zéro de Conduite* and *L'Atalante*. But his first film remained a documentary landmark. Vigo died at the age of twenty-nine.

The city symphonies, while initiated by a painter, represented a crossbreeding of all the arts. This was a natural outcome of the ferment of the cine-clubs, where the interrelationship of the arts was constantly discussed. The cine-clubs were in touch with each other, often propelling each other along parallel lines. Many film makers toured the cine-clubs with their films.

In the Belgian seaside town of Ostende, where many artists worked, a cine-club was founded by Henri Storck, son of the leading shoemaker. Sooner or later everyone came to the shoe store, so Storck as a boy already knew many Ostende artists and considered a painting career. But a store opposite the shoe shop was converted into a theater, and night after night he fell asleep to laughter and piano music from across the street; trips to the store-cinema soon saturated him in melodrama and comedy. Then a visit to Brussels and its cine-club—the first in Belgium—showed him films of other kinds. The program included Flaherty's *Moana,* and it was a revelation to him. His immediate response was the organizing of the Ostende cine-club, for which he recruited local painters, sculptors, writers, musicians, while seeking advice from other cine-clubs. He began an intense correspondence with Jean Vigo in Nice. Finally, in 1930, his own film *Images of Ostende (Images d'Ostende)* began the round of the cine-clubs. Storck visited some of them with his film, meeting many film makers. In Paris he got advice from Boris Kaufman. He also met young Joris Ivens, a moving spirit in the Amsterdam cine-club, the Filmliga, or film-league.[5]

Joris Ivens managed the Amsterdam branch of his father's photographic business while pursuing university studies. At the Filmliga his first enthusiasm had been for the abstract films sent to them—in some cases, *brought* to them—from Germany by Ruttman, Eggeling, Richter, and others. Ivens's own early work took a similar direction. In *The Bridge (De Brug,* 1928) he concentrated on the complex action involving a Rotterdam railroad bridge. Its middle section was raised and lowered to let ships pass underneath and trains pass overhead. As

Joris Ivens editing, 1928.

Nederlands Filmmuseum

it moved, counterweights moved in the opposite direction. These movements, plus those of streaking trains, chugging boats, billowing smoke, waves, and traffic in the city beyond, made the bridge "a laboratory of movements, tones, shapes, contrasts, rhythms, and the relations between all of these." Day after day Ivens, climbing on the bridge during lunchtime intervals, searched out expressive angles. He discovered the joy and rewards of prolonged viewing. "You will always discover something new, the countermovement of a gliding shadow, a significant trembling as the cables come to a halt, or a more telling reflection. . . ."

The Bridge prepared Ivens for his later film *Rain* (*Regen,* 1929), a gem-like study made with the writer Mannus Franken and with help from John Fernhout—later known as Ferno. It appears to portray a passing shower in Amsterdam, but the footage required four months of shooting. With extraordinary beauty and precision, Ivens portrays the patterns made by rain—at first gentle, later of mounting violence—falling in puddles, gutters, canals, rivers, running down windows, umbrellas, wagons, cars, bicycles, dripping from gutters, spouts, umbrella spokes, and limbs of statues. The film starts modestly but develops richness and complexity; we are seeing a great city

Filming *Rain*, 1929.

Nederlands Filmmuseum—Van Dongen collection

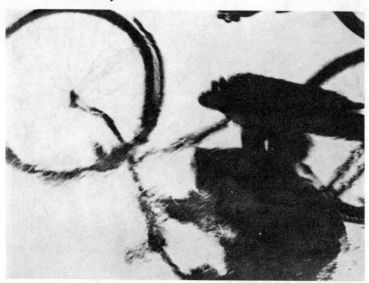

Rain, 1929.

Nederlands Filmmuseum

through the lens of rain. Made under the influence of the painter-as-documentarist genre, *Rain* was perhaps its most perfect product.[6]

The late 1920's produced other films in the genre, large and small: in Paris, Man Ray's *Emak Bakia* (1927), built on light patterns from rotating objects; in Belgium, Charles Dekeukeleire's *Boxing Match* (*Combat de Boxe,* 1927), in which boxing footage becomes raw material for editing experiments; in the United States, Ralph Steiner's *H_2O* (1929), a montage of water patterns; in Germany, Wilfried Basse's *Market in the Wittenbergplatz* (*Markt am Wittenbergplatz,* 1929), in which the erection and later dismantling of market stalls are dramatically compressed through time-lapse photography; in France, Eugene Deslaw's *The Electric Night* (*La Nuit Électrique,* 1930), a small symphony of Parisian illuminated signs. And the genre persisted.

But the painter-as-documentarist had only a brief moment of glory. There were reasons. His spurt of activity came at the last moment of the silent film. With the arrival of the spoken word, images were suddenly downgraded. Games of movement and texture were, for the moment, almost forgotten. Furious aesthetic battles over the uses of sound took their place.

This transition coincided with another: from prosperity to economic collapse and world-wide depression. The two transitions were not unrelated: the cinema transition to sound had been started as a desperate gamble by producers facing economic ruin.

To the documentary film the two transitions brought sharp change. During the 1920's explorer, journalist, artist, and others had experimented with the moving image in a spirit that was usually zestful and optimistic. Their films had seldom been contentious. But economic collapse brought tension and strife. Ideological combat began to dominate all media. Documentary film, acquiring the spoken word at this precise moment, was inevitably called on to join the battle. In the documentary field, the word-film became an instrument of struggle.

3
SOUND AND FURY
sempre staccatto

John Grierson.

Photograph by Virginia Leirens

Advocate

When John Grierson (1898–1972), son of a Scots schoolmaster and grandson of a lighthouse keeper, was studying at Glasgow University and earning distinction in moral philosophy, he was already thinking about film. He sensed that film and other popular media had acquired leverage over ideas and actions once exercised by church and school. These thoughts became the mainspring of his life.

A Rockefeller Foundation grant took him to the United States in 1924 for research in social sciences. While studying at the University of Chicago he crisscrossed the land interviewing film makers, scholars, politicians, journalists. Above all, he observed the American melting pot in action. And he began to feel—with Walter Lippmann —that expectations once held for democracy were proving illusory. Problems facing society had grown beyond the comprehension of most citizens; their participation had become perfunctory, apathetic, meaningless, often nonexistent.[1]

While Lippmann was pessimistic about all this, Grierson was not: he saw a solution. The documentary film maker, dramatizing issues and their implications in a meaningful way, could lead the citizen through the wilderness. This became the Grierson mission.

That this implied an assumption of leadership, of an elitist role, did not trouble Grierson. He believed in "the elect having their duty." They must not only explain, they must inspire. He was not frightened by the word "propaganda." He could even say: "I look on cinema as a pulpit. . . ."[2]

In the United States Grierson met Robert Flaherty, with whom he began a lifelong, stormy hate-love relationship, hailing Flaherty as the father of documentary while deploring his obsession with the remote and primitive. Grierson's determination was to "bring the citizen's eye in from the ends of the earth to the story, his own story, of what was happening under his nose . . . the drama of the doorstep." In this respect Grierson felt more drawn to the social relevance of Russian cinema. In New York, Grierson helped prepare *The Battleship Potemkin* for American audiences. This involved some tampering with the film, and months of struggle with New York State censors. The task gave him a detailed familiarity with Eisenstein's

Grierson: "I look on cinema as a pulpit . . ."

National Film Archive

editing techniques, which became a further major influence on his own film ideas.

Early in 1927 Grierson was back in England, visiting the Empire Marketing Board to call on its chief, Sir Stephen Tallents, who found him "brimming with ideas." The Empire Marketing Board was intended to cement the British Empire by promoting trade and a sense of unity among its various parts, and it was attempting this through posters, pamphlets, exhibitions. The next step, argued Grierson, must be film; Tallents already held the same view. But this required a meeting of minds with the Financial Secretary of the Treasury, Arthur Michael Samuel, who was considered the leading authority on the herring industry and who was flatly opposed to film. Grierson met this problem with a characteristic head-on approach. He came to the meeting recommending immediate production of a film on the herring industry. The result was an appropriation of £2500, with which Grierson produced and directed his first film, the fifty-minute silent film *Drifters,* photographed by Basil Emmott. It was premiered at the London Film Society late in 1929.

The society, a pioneer in the cine-club movement, had been formed in 1925. Programs of previous years had suggested an art-for-art's-sake orientation, with films like *Mannahatta, Berlin: Symphony of the City,* and *Rien Que les Heures.* The program of November 10, 1929, was representative of a shift. The main attraction was the Grierson version of *The Battleship Potemkin,* with *Drifters* as an added item. *The Battleship Potemkin* was, by British censorship decision, forbidden to theaters—but not to the London Film Society, a private group. As films grew more issue-oriented, this private status tended to make the society a place where forbidden films could be seen—usually leftist, sometimes Russian. The London Film Society, already tending leftward in its membership, became more so during the Depression years; the same was true of cine-clubs in many countries.

The *Potemkin* unveiling was a total triumph, and some London Film Society members were even more impressed with *Drifters.* Vigorously paced and imaginatively edited—some felt they saw an Eisenstein influence, but the style was less obtrusive—it brought the daily work of the herring fisheries to life in a way that astonished the audience. There was nothing doctrinally radical about it, but the fact that British workingmen—virtually ignored by British cinema except as

Shooting *Drifters,* 1929. Above, Grierson directing.

comedy material—were the heroes gave the film an almost revolutionary impact. In a British cinema grown stale with artificiality, it was a breath of salty sea air. The film went on to a successful run in theaters.

Drifters made clear the Grierson deviation from Flaherty. The herring fisheries, a subtitle tells us, used to be a thing of quaint old villages; the men still lived in the old villages, but the fishing had meanwhile become "an epic of steam and steel." Grierson gives only the briefest glimpse of the quaint old villages; his eye is on the steam and steel. Flaherty would have chosen otherwise. Amid churning sea and rolling ship, Grierson shows us in vivid detail "the teamwork of man and machine." Final scenes depict quayside auctioning of the catch and project the herring business into international trade—"a market for the world." Grierson must have had the Empire Marketing Board in mind in his final subtitle: "So to the ends of the earth goes the harvest of the sea."

The success of *Drifters* meant a new career for Grierson. Instead of directing further films, he became creative organizer; at the Empire Marketing Board he assembled untrained recruits and proceeded to turn them into a bustling EMB Film Unit, finding funds for them to function, goading them, teaching them—and meanwhile shielding them fanatically from bureaucratic interference. That all this called for a special kind of genius may be seen in the paradox of his position. His mandate and funds were from sources intent on consolidating the status quo and the British Empire. This was true of the Empire Marketing Board as well as of other entities, such as the Ceylon Tea Propaganda Board, that underwrote specific projects. Grierson's recruits, almost without exception, were socialistically inclined activists inspired by *Drifters* and *Potemkin*. After *Drifters* they flocked to the Grierson banner.

In a sense, all were learning together. The EMB Film Unit grew from a staff of two at the start of 1930 to over thirty in 1933. Most of the young recruits had little or no professional experience. For Edgar Anstey, Arthur Elton, Stuart Legg, the chief preparation had been London Film Society screenings. Paul Rotha, a Film Society member from the start, was already a film scholar and had written *The Film Till Now* (1930), but he had not produced or directed films. Basil Wright had done one avant-garde experiment, Vertov-inspired. All these men were in their early twenties. Grierson himself, with only *Drifters* behind him, scarcely had a start on the staff and was only a few years their senior. Yet he assumed at once an almost god-like position among them, dominating them with a "fierce benevolence." He was "the chief."

While handling sponsor negotiations, he managed to supervise all on-going projects. The viewing of rushes, or of an edited workprint, could be an intimidating occasion. The fledgling director would notify Grierson's aide, the soft-spoken J. P. R. Golightly, when the material was ready; then he would wait in the projection room. After a time Grierson would crash in and sit down. "Right. Shoot." His concentration on the film was total; then came a rapid stream of comments, which might range from lens choice to philosophical context. They were often a mixture of encouragement and stern reprimand. "Anstey, you've failed badly here." (He always used last names.) Identifying points of failure, he left solutions to the director; when the latter found a solution, Grierson gave full credit. "There, you've done it—pure genius." The staff, all tyros, seemed to welcome the tyrannical supervision, even when it was brutal.[3]

The atmosphere was strangely monastic. Working hours were limitless. Staff members got the impression that marriage was taboo, and the existence of girl-friends was kept from Grierson. Grierson himself fell for Margaret Taylor, sister of staff member John Taylor, and they got married, but Grierson did not mention it for eighteen months. She went to work at the unit, but they never arrived or left together. Harry Watt, who joined the unit in 1932, thought of Grierson as a "Presbyterian priest." Another recruit, William Coldstream, wondered whether the preference for film themes of work and corporate effort—never involving the intimacy of a Flaherty film—had something to do with Grierson's fastidiousness about personal matters. Yet Grierson and his staff spent hours at the pub together, drinking and talking. In a way these were seminars, heady and memorable, crammed with pungent observation.[4]

Beginning with mere scraps of equipment, the EMB Film Unit was confronted at once with problems of sound. To inspire and educate his staff, and to give the unit prestige, Grierson brought two celebrated names into the work. From France came the Brazilian Alberto Cavalcanti, who proved invaluable in sound experiments. From America came Robert Flaherty, to do photography for *Industrial Britain* (1933). Of his participation Grierson said later: "The amount of money put aside for Flaherty was £2,500, so I probably fired him by the time he spent £2,400. . . . We'd finish it within the £2,500 all right."[5] In fact, the group made several films from the Flaherty footage. All bore the Grierson rather than the Flaherty stamp.

Grierson importuned his staff to avoid the "aestheticky." He told them they were propagandists first, film makers second. Art is a hammer, not a mirror, he said. It was part of Grierson's genius that he could build an atmosphere of enthusiasm for necessary, vital propaganda without ever being quite clear about its aim, other than the general idea that it was citizenship education, looking toward a better and richer life. For many staff members it was enough that, like *Drifters,* their work was giving new dignity to the working man. "Every film we made," said Harry Watt, "had this in it, that we were trying to give an image of the workingman, away from the Edwardian, Victorian, capitalist attitudes." Looking at issues from a workingman's point of view, some films—such as *Housing Problems* (1935) and *Coal Face* (1936)—sounded a note of protest and of urgent need for reform. In this, Watt felt, they were suspect to many in government, and living on a razor's edge. "Not many of us were communists, but we were all socialists and I'm sure we had dossiers. . . ." For a time they were apparently observed by a secret-service operative in the guise of a trainee film-editor. All this kept them sharply aware of the political limits inherent in government sponsorship—a favorite subject of Grierson admonitions. Yet the emotional center of the output was pro-labor. They were giving the workingman his rightful place.

The sponsors had a different rationale. In later years Grierson explained it in these terms:

When it came to making industry not ugly for people, but a matter of beauty, so that people would accept their industrial selves, so that they would not revolt against their industrial selves, as they did in the late 19th century, who initiated the finding of beauty in industry? The British government—as a matter of policy.[6]

That their task was to nurture a more amenable labor force would have surprised the film staff. Grierson avoided such problems by putting himself firmly between sponsor and artist.

But the ambiguous relationship is implicit in many of the films. *Song of Ceylon* (1935)—directed, photographed, and edited by Basil Wright with the assistance of teenaged trainee John Taylor—is perhaps the most brilliant example.

The film is in four parts: (1) The Buddha, (2) The Virgin Land, (3) The Voices of Commerce, (4) The Apparel of a God. Wright was clearly enthralled by the Ceylonese people, and conveys his admiration throughout the film. The film was sponsored by the Ceylon Tea Propaganda Board, but the tea trade does not enter the film until the third part, when its activities are introduced on the sound track.

The first two parts, portraying the Ceylonese and their heritage, are of special interest. Accompanying scenes of extraordinary beauty, Wright uses passages from a travel book of 1680 written by Robert Knox. Thus the antiquity of Ceylonese culture is dramatically emphasized: we hear age-old words that were still applicable in British-ruled Ceylon. The words are linked with photographed action:

COMMENTARY: . . . But husbandry is the great employment of the people. In this the best men labour; nor is it held any disgrace to work for

oneself be it at home or in the fields; but to work for hire with them is reckoned for a great shame, and very few are here to be found who will work so. They are very active and nimble in their limbs and very ingenious, and all things they have need of, except ironwork, they make and do themselves, insomuch as they all build their own houses.

In the third part we continue to see handsome people, but commerce enters the sound track with a montage of voices: market quotations of tea prices, telephone orders, invoices, mail inquiries. The sequence ends with "faithfully yours . . . faithfully yours . . . faithfully yours." The overriding impression is of commerce intruding on a lovely, age-old environment.

In the fourth part commerce finally appears visually, in scenes of ships, docks, and loading operations. We see files of Ceylonese carrying cargo. Perhaps—perhaps not—we will recall the Robert Knox words: ". . . but to work for hire with them is reckoned for a great shame. . . ." Near the end of the film we return to a theme from the first part, extolling the beauty of the Buddha. But it is the beauty of the Ceylonese that the images compel us to contemplate.

Song of Ceylon exemplified the working atmosphere of the film unit, in which anyone could be enlisted for any sort of task. The "voices of commerce" heard in the sound track montage included voices of Cavalcanti, Grierson, Legg, and Wright.[7]

Like *Drifters, Song of Ceylon* won enthusiastic plaudits at the London Film Society and went on to successful theatrical showings. Perhaps the Ceylon Tea Propaganda Board was delighted with it: the film put the Board on record as fervently admiring the Ceylonese and their culture. It made clear the role of tea as an imperial link. To others it may have suggested exploitation. Without question, the film made the rising British documentary movement known throughout the world.

In 1934 the Empire Marketing Board was dissolved, and the film unit was moved bodily into the General Post Office to become the GPO Film Unit. *Song of Ceylon*, begun under EMB, was completed as a GPO project. The unit's task was now to "bring the post office alive." But the General Post Office was in reality a sort of communication ministry, which also had charge of the development of wireless in all its forms, including radio and television broadcasting. Grierson saw the situation as a mandate to explore the entire role of communication in modern society—a favorite Grierson topic.

Basil Wright.

From this emerged another of the most renowned works of the unit—*Night Mail* (1936), directed by Harry Watt and Basil Wright. Again the skill of workers and the importance of their role were dominant themes. As in *Song of Ceylon*, the sound track was an experiment; Cavalcanti as sound supervisor seems to have contributed much to this. A verse sound track had been tried in *Coal Face* with only minor success; the trippingly rhythmical *Night Mail* narration, written by W. H. Auden and scored by Benjamin Britten, was immensely successful, and became a model for numerous imitations. The film was edited to the rhythm of its sound track. A lyric poem celebrating the rushing of the mail to homes and businesses of northern England and Scotland, *Night Mail* is infectious in spirit and style—a cinema classic of lasting interest.

Another sound-track experiment, of a prophetic sort, was carried out in *Housing Problems* (1935), directed by Edgar Anstey and Arthur Elton. The Gas Light and Coke Company sponsored it, persuaded by Grierson that the demolition of derelict slums and their replacement by government-financed housing—a key demand of the socialistic Labour party—would inevitably bring modernization and increased use of gas. Thus the company financed a film of blunt and moving protest.

The method was novel. Instead of the commentator or narrator characteristic of Grierson documentaries, slum-dwellers appeared as spokesmen. In their rat-infested kitchens, unheated living rooms, crumbling hallways, they talk directly to the camera and provide a guided tour. Horror and humor merge for powerful impact. At least one of the spokesmen—a lady who tells of epic battles with a rat—had never seen a film—but sensed that she was having a chance to communicate her problems to a large constituency. Arthur Elton had used such direct testimony in an earlier GPO film for the Ministry of Labour, *Workers and Jobs* (1935). But *Housing Problems* more clearly demonstrated the potential values of the device—later used extensively in television.

As the film unit grew, it also proliferated, giving birth to a Strand Film Unit with Paul Rotha as production director; a Realist Film Unit under Basil Wright; a Shell Film Unit begun by Edgar Anstey; a Film Centre under Grierson himself, which provided an advisory service. Government support had been the starting point, but corporate sponsors were soon underwriting many of the films. The "movement" retained cohesiveness throughout the 1930's, continuing to look on Grierson as its godfather and to congregate and confer in pubs. Meanwhile films gushed forth in a steady stream: Elton's *The Voice of the World* (1932), Rotha's *Contact* (1933), Anstey's *Granton Trawler* (1934), Legg's *BBC: the Voice of Britain* (1935), Rotha's *Shipyard* (1935), Anstey's *Enough to Eat* (1936), John Taylor's *The Smoke Menace* (1937), Mary Field's *They Made the Land* (1938), Watt's *North Sea* (1938), Elton's *Transfer of Power* (1939).

The influence of the movement, at home and abroad, was fed by speeches and writing, especially by Grierson and Rotha. Rotha's book *Documentary Film* (1935) appeared in many translations. Such magazines as *Sight and Sound, Cinema Quarterly,* and Grierson's *World Film News* furthered the process.

At first, members of the film unit disagreed as to whether they should fight for a place in the theatrical film world or build an alternative system based on club, school, church, library, business firm. In the end they did both. Outstanding films such as *Song of Ceylon* and *Night Mail* got wide theatrical exposure; meanwhile nontheatrical

Night Mail, 1936.

Housing Problems, 1935.

distribution, encouraged by the rise of 16mm film, began to assume some importance.*

The divergence of the apostle Grierson from the master Flaherty was increasingly apparent, and often mentioned by Grierson. He liked to pay tribute to Flaherty, then follow with a comment cutting the master down. In a typical statement, Grierson wrote:

Flaherty has been one of the great film teachers of our day, and not one of us but has been enriched by his example and, I shall add, but has been even more greatly enriched by failing in the final issue to follow it . . .

Such comments became increasingly frequent—from Grierson and his followers—after the appearance of a new Flaherty film, *Man of Aran* (1934). Flaherty's visit to England had enabled him to make a new start via a contract with Gaumont British, giving him the freedom he needed and a topic to his liking. The setting was the bleak Aran Islands off Ireland, swept by storms and battered by incredible seas; the theme, the struggle for survival. As in Samoa, Flaherty had the help of his wife Frances and brother David, and assorted technicians. John Taylor, Grierson trainee, joined the unit. Laboratory work was done on the spot in an old stone wharf-house. The film was edited by John Goldman and scored by John Greenwood.

Flaherty and his group spent almost two years on the Aran Islands. What emerged was a film of far greater professional polish than *Nanook of the North* or *Moana,* and with epic grandeur. The "caressing" movements of Flaherty's camera over landscape and people won admiration from Paul Rotha, among others. With long-focus lenses Flaherty followed in detail the perilous maneuvers of small boats heaving in mountainous waves—often at distances of several hundred yards from his camera positions on the cliffs. Sound effects were later added to the film with telling effect. Fragments of dialogue were also post-synchronized. Almost lost in the roar of wind and wave, they were used with exceptional skill—almost as an additional sound effect. Along with these production values were familiar Flaherty elements. As in *Nanook* and *Moana,* he concentrated on a small group; again,

---

* The need for a less bulky alternative to 35mm was recognized early in film history. Manufacturers introduced 9½mm, 11mm, 15mm, 16mm, 17½mm, 21mm, 22mm, and 28mm equipment; in the competitive chaos, none could win a foothold. In 1923 Eastman, Bell & Howell, and Victor Animatograph agreed to standardize on 16mm and a nonflammable type of film; other companies followed suit. This enabled 16mm to begin a slow advance.

Man of Aran, 1934.

a child played an important part. There was once more a return to the past. The Aran islanders had not for many decades hunted the basking shark in small boats with harpoons; Flaherty brought in an expert to teach them how, and in the process exposed them to much danger, but they welcomed it. "God bless the work," they would say. Frances Flaherty later recalled: "They served us and the film hand and foot; they lived and died with us with the ups and downs of the film. It was a way Bob had." Pat Mullen, Aran islander who interpreted for them, put it this way: "He won me and won my soul out of me as well."[8]

Man of Aran won first prize at the Venice film festival and was hailed by many as a great film, and Flaherty's finest. Dissenters—especially Grierson and his group—asked how Flaherty could possibly have ignored, amid a world economic crisis, the social context in which Aran islanders carried on their bitter struggles. Was he unaware of the evils of absentee landlordism? With all its cinematic craftsmanship, the film seemed to Paul Rotha a "reactionary return to the worship of the heroic." He began to write of Flaherty's characters

Paul Rotha.

Photograph by Virginia Leirens

as "waxwork figures acting the lives of their grandfathers." He added: "Surely we have the right to believe that the documentary method, the most virile of all kinds of film, should not ignore the vital social issues of this year of grace." To many, *Man of Aran* seemed a hold-over from an earlier period.[9]

Grierson and his movement had in a few years changed the expectations aroused by the word "documentary." A Flaherty documentary had been a feature-length, close-up portrait of a group of people, remotely located but familiar in their humanity. The characteristic Grierson documentary dealt with impersonal social processes; it was usually a short film fused by a "commentary" that articulated a point of view—an intrusion that was anathema to Flaherty. The Grierson pattern was spreading.

In 1939, with war apparently in the offing, the Imperial Relations Trust dispatched Grierson to Canada to apply his organizing skills in another part of the empire; the National Film Board of Canada was the result. Later he went on similar missions to Australia and New Zealand.

He had already played a pivotal role in the British cinema, and one which, in a curious way, was richly representative of his time. He had presided over pro-Labour film production under Conservative sponsorship. "In that sense," thought Grierson years later in retrospect, "*Night Mail* and *Housing Problems* were the films of a Tory regime gradually going socialist. . . ." He would hardly have said so at the time.[10]

The politicizing of documentary was not a Grierson innovation but a world phenomenon, a product of the times. In Germany it took a different form, with very different results.

As soon as Hitler came to power in 1933, his thirty-six-year-old Minister of Popular Enlightenment and Propaganda, Joseph Goebbels, began steps to bring all media under his control. On political or racial grounds, countless workers were driven from their jobs; many went abroad. These were replaced by Nazi adherents. By October 1933 anyone with editorial duties had to be licensed by Goebbels. Proclaiming that censorship would be positive, not merely negative, he gradually took charge of all aspects of production, distribution, and exhibition.[11]

In Germany, as in a number of countries, cine-clubs had operated outside regular rules of censorship. Goebbels abolished the distinction, decimating the cine-clubs. There would be no independent cine-club movement in the new Germany.

As a result of these sweeping moves, films in Nazi Germany began a rapid, catastrophic decline. But there was an exception: the work of one genius who—due to unusual circumstances—flourished outside the Goebbels dominion.

Leni Riefenstahl was a dancer before turning to acting, and a screen star and pin-up beauty before becoming a director. As fiction-film star and director she was especially associated with "mountain films"—a German genre often compared to American westerns. The setting evoked heroism and virtue, and had mythic overtones. For a highly industrialized nation, the misty peaks and streams and crashing storms provided a sense of contact with primordial beginnings; the films sometimes reached back into Teutonic mythology. Among successes in which she appeared were *The Sacred Mountain* (*Die Heilige Berg*, 1926), *The White Hell of Piz Palu* (*Die Weisse Hölle von Piz Palu*, 1929), and *The Blue Light* (*Das Blaue Licht*, 1932), which she also directed.[12]

A prominent Riefenstahl admirer was Adolf Hitler. In 1933 she received a call from him. It was a few months after he had achieved dictatorial power, and just two days before the annual rally of the National Socialist German Workers party—the Nazi party. According to her account, he asked how she was getting on with the work. She asked, "What work?" He said that months earlier, he had ordered his propaganda ministry to have her make a film about the rally. She had heard nothing of this, but he insisted she proceed, doing whatever she could. Without time to prepare, she gathered equipment and a few assistants and rushed to the rally. There a succession of bureaucratic harassments—emanating, she thought, from a Goebbels resentful at being bypassed—made the experience a nightmare, but she completed the short film *Victory of Faith* (*Sieg des Glaubens*, 1933), financed by the Nazi party.

Exhausted, she left for Spain for work on a new feature, but there she collapsed, spending two months in a Madrid hospital—an aftermath, she was sure, of the sufferings Goebbels had caused her. Their mutual resentment grew into a feud.

On her return to Germany, Hitler got in touch with her again. He wanted her to make a film of the 1934 party rally, which was to be the largest ever staged—announcement and demonstration, to all the world, of German rebirth. For this film she must have all necessary time to prepare, and all resources would be at her disposal.

She demurred. She suggested Walther Ruttman, creator of the famous *Berlin: Symphony of the City*, and even discussed it with Ruttman. Though he had been considered on the left politically, he was eager to do the project and drafted plans. But Hitler insisted it must be Leni Riefenstahl. According to her account, she then agreed on condition that neither Hitler nor Goebbels nor anyone else would interfere, nor even see the film until it was finished. The film appears to have been made under these terms. An ample budget was set up by the UFA studio—Universum Film Aktiengesellschaft—which also distributed the film.

She got to work. Never had there been such mobilization and deployment of resources—men and gear. Before long she had assembled a staff of 120 people, including sixteen leading cameramen, their assistants, and supporting technicians. Thirty cameras and four sound trucks would be in operation. Twenty-two automobiles and their drivers were assigned to her, along with uniformed field police. She felt they must all live together in Nuremberg, location of the rally, for constant coordination through the week of scheduled events— September 4–10, 1934. But all hotels were booked. More than a million people were expected in Nuremberg, tripling its population. Leading Nazi official Julius Streicher owned a large Nuremberg building and offered it. Making an advance inspection, she was dismayed to find scores of empty rooms without furniture, water, light, or telephone. But within forty-eight hours miracles had been performed for her—bedrooms for all her 120 people had been fully furnished; offices, conference rooms, dark rooms stood ready; a telephone switchboard had been installed; kitchen and dining hall were being equipped and staffed.[13]

Meanwhile with relentless drive and sense of detail Leni Riefenstahl—then thirty-two years old—was plotting camera locations and movements with her staff, and the town of Nuremberg was constructing, to her specifications and on a scale without precedent, special bridges, towers, ramps. A 120-foot flagpole at the Luitpoldhain was being equipped with an electric elevator, which was to be able to take a cameraman to the top in seconds. Along Adolf Hitler Square a ramp was being built at second-floor level to allow a camera dolly to move with marching troops while photographing them from bird's eye vantage. She commandeered a fire department truck; atop its ninety-foot extension ladder, a cameraman would be able to soar over the gables and monuments of Nuremberg, high above marching troops and their banners. Other vehicles with extension ladders were put at her disposal by utility and streetcar companies.

Planning of rally events and of their film coverage went on together. On a field, huge parades of spade-carrying men—the Labor Service—were to march past Adolf Hitler, then line up in perfect order to hear his speech extolling labor. Wooden rails were laid out so that cameras would be able to photograph the men from within their ranks. A camera platform was built at the precise spot where they would give the Führer an "eyes right" salute. Camera positions were staked out on city rooftops, on church towers, and in road-side ditches. In meeting halls cameras would peer down through skylights and up from orchestra pits. All cameramen were given elite-troop uniforms; the Chief of Staff had expressed the opinion that the presence of cameramen in civilian dress would "mar the solemnity of the occasion."

As crowds began to descend on Nuremberg, Riefenstahl's cameramen were rehearsing on their fantastic ladders, ramps, and towers. A report on all these arrangements was later published, with a text credited to Leni Riefenstahl. It paid tribute to Hitler:

> The Führer has recognized the importance of cinema. Where else in the world have the film's inherent potentialities to act as the chronicler and interpreter of contemporary events been recognized in so far-sighted a manner? . . .
>
> That the Führer has raised film-making to a position of such pre-eminence testifies to his prophetic awareness of the unrealized suggestive power of this art form. One is familiar with documentaries. Governments have ordered them and political parties have used them for their ends. But the belief that a true and genuinely powerful national experience can be kindled through the medium of film, this belief originated in Germany.[14]

According to her own accounts, of then and later, Riefenstahl was at this time dazzled by Hitler, though disliking many around him. And he had put her as film maker in a position unique in film history.

She did not invent the actions captured by her cameras. She saw it as her task to bring them to the screen with maximum impact.

During the week of photography she coordinated her forces with an almost maniacal drive and discipline, mirroring the atmosphere of the events themselves. Then she gave months to editing. A score in Wagnerian style was provided by Herbert Windt. The final result, *Triumph of the Will* (*Triumph des Willens*), was premiered in March 1935 and was at once hailed as a masterpiece—inspiring to some, sinister and terrifying to others. The Venice film festival gave it a top award; so did a Paris festival.

The opening credits stated:

Produced by Order of the Führer
Directed by Leni Riefenstahl*

Triumph of the Will has no spoken commentary; she considered any commentator an "enemy of film." Verbalization of the message is left to speeches by Hitler and other Nazi leaders. But the almost phys-

---

* Various translations are possible. The original titles: "Hergestellt im Auftrage des Führers/Gestaltet von Leni Riefenstahl."

Triumph of the Will, 1935.

ical impact of the film derives much from her choreography of images and sounds: marching men, cheers, banners, swastikas, eagles, crowds, ancient German streets and towers, folksongs, clouds, oratory, uniforms, women, children—and above all, in a series of apparitions, the Führer.

The film opens with an amazing sequence—one that makes Hitler a sort of deity descending to earth to save the German people. This sequence uses subtitles, which Riefenstahl credited to Walther Ruttman. They were, according to her account, the only part of Ruttman's proposals used in the final film.[15] The sequence shows us a lone plane skimming over cloud tops; occasionally mists obscure it, but it re-emerges. Eventually the earth is seen: spires of Nuremberg, wrapped in mists. The shadow of the plane touches the city. Crowds are waiting, looking up. Finally the plane lands. A door opens. After a moment, Hitler appears. Deafening roars of vast crowds split the air.

The subtitles have set the stage:

On September 5
1934

20 years
after the outbreak
of the World War

16 years
after the start
of German suffering

19 months
after the beginning
of Germany's rebirth

Adolf Hitler flew
again to Nuremberg
to review the columns of his faithful followers

Triumph of the Will was considered an overwhelming propaganda success, rallying many to the Hitler cause. Some critics have felt that the role of Leni Riefenstahl in this success was unforgivable. But it is also pointed out that no film has been more widely used by opposition forces. Every nation ultimately arrayed against Hitler used huge segments of *Triumph of the Will* in its own propaganda films; nothing else depicted so vividly the demoniac nature of the Hitler leadership, and the scarcely human discipline supporting it. Riefenstahl's cameras did not lie; they told a story that has never lost its power to chill the marrow.

Amid ovations for *Triumph of the Will,* Riefenstahl proposed a new project to UFA: a long film on the Olympic games to be held in Berlin in 1936. UFA was dubious: the Olympic games had never been given feature-length treatment. The 1932 Olympics, held in Los Angeles, had been virtually ignored by Hollywood except as newsreel material. Besides, Riefenstahl wanted more than a year for editing; UFA felt the film would be obsolete when issued. However, Tobis—a smaller company than UFA—agreed to finance the film. She meanwhile negotiated with the International Olympic Committee, not mentioning her plan to Hitler; she wished to avoid official sponsorship.

The Olympic officials were cautious. Riefenstahl wished to prepare pits beside jumping areas, camera rails along running tracks, towers at the diving sites. Fearing that the outcome of contests might eventually be challenged on the ground of distraction, officials required

Making *Olympia*, 1936. Directing in pit, Leni Riefenstahl. The film was released in 1938.

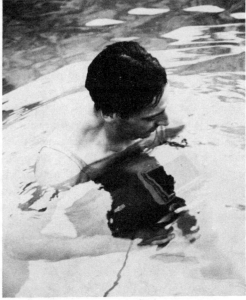

Riefenstahl-Film

Early morning training run—from *Olympia*, 1938.

her to obtain approvals from all national committees and from all contestants individually. At enormous effort, over many months, she secured these approvals.

Olympia eventually became two feature-length films, and another organizational achievement of amazing virtuosity. She was restricted to six camera positions on the stadium field, but supplemented these with cameras in grandstands and many elsewhere. She had the opening of the games photographed from the Zeppelin Hindenburg. Automatic cameras were sent aloft via free balloons, with attached instructions for returning the film to Leni Riefenstahl. The most startling photographic innovation involved diving; dives were followed through the air and then under water without a break. The start of the dive was photographed from the surface of the water; at the moment of impact the cameraman went under water with his special camera while changing focus and aperture. It took months to perfect the procedure. For boat-racing sequences, shots of a coxswain were made by an automatic camera placed in the boat during practice runs. Along race courses, photography by amateurs supplemented that of the professionals.

Most of the film was shot silent; sound elements were added later. Even footsteps of runners and jumpers were created and post-synchronized during the editing process. The state of technology, in Germany and elsewhere, discouraged sound recording on location, except for static sequences such as speeches.

While the Riefenstahl forces were at work, the Propaganda Ministry was producing its own Olympia film. Far from cooperating with her, Goebbels—still resentful—forbade leading cameramen to work with her; at one point, ministry employees tried to bar her from the stadium. Hitler is said to have ordered a ceremony of reconciliation to quiet scandal over this waspish feud.

The Riefenstahl *Olympia* has an extraordinary Wagnerian opening, reminiscent in its mythic overtones of *Triumph of the Will* and of Leni Riefenstahl's early "mountain film" career. We begin with shots suggesting a misty, primitive world. Soon we see a runner carrying a torch across rugged landscape; architecture and coastline tell us this is ancient Greece. We briefly see nude athletes and dancers training—one of them is Leni Riefenstahl. Then we see the torch handed from one runner to another, as they carry it from ancient Greece to modern Germany, and into a vast stadium presided over by Adolf Hitler. The sequence seems to tell us that the torch of civilization has been carried from its ancient center, Greece, to modern Germany, watched over by a pantheon at whose apex is Hitler.

While any such opening, placing Hitler at the center of international pageantry, was bound to suggest a dominant propaganda intention, the remainder gives a different impression. The first of the two films concentrates on track and field events, in which the high points are victories by nineteen-year-old Jesse Owens and other black athletes. It is said that Goebbels representatives pressed Riefenstahl to exclude these from her films, but that she declined. She accords these victories a dramatic buildup, and an admiration of muscular beauty, comparable to her treatment of other victors and victories. Many critics have stressed this fairness—often with expressions of surprise.

But she could not eliminate the historic context from the minds of audiences. Outside Germany it was widely reported that Hitler had left the stadium just before an Owens triumph, and had thus avoided witnessing a setback for the master race. This "snub" is not shown or mentioned in the film. To American screen writer Budd Schulberg the omission exposed Riefenstahl as a dedicated Nazi propagandist. But its inclusion would surely have damned her on similar grounds.[16]

The second of the two *Olympia* films suggests that her main obsession was not politics, but the magnificence of the body in action. Dropping earlier attention to victories and statistics, she composes sequences of unforgettable splendor—moving, as she explained to interviewer Gordon Hitchens, from "reality" to "poetry." The high point of this comes at the climax of the diving events, in a sequence based on a simple but brilliant editing idea. In a series of dives, she gives us only the flight through the air, eliminating the climactic splashes. We see a long succession of such dives, sometimes overlapping via dissolves. The impression is one of total victory over gravity, as body after body tumbles through the air, in choreographed patterns of stunning beauty, without ever being brought to earth. Few lovelier sequences have ever been put on film.

The *Olympia* films, released in 1938—two years after the event—won their quota of prizes, critical hosannahs, and box-office success. But amid world tension, they also met storms. Britain banned the films, using the footage for physical-education films for war training. During 1938–39 Leni Riefenstahl visited Hollywood to help launch American distribution. She was the guest of Walt Disney, but was ignored by most of the film colony. On the eve of war she returned to Germany, and to fiction films. She tried to organize a film to be titled *Penthesilea,* in which she was to appear as queen of the Amazons. But war brought a long hiatus in her work.

Among the cameramen she employed for the *Olympia* films was Heinz von Jaworsky—later, in America, Henry Jaworsky. He had worked on some of her fiction films, and she had tried to enlist him for *Triumph of the Will.* Being in part "non-Aryan"—Jewish—he told her it would be best for him to stay out of it. But she asked him again for *Olympia,* with possible risks to both, and he gladly worked on it. She continued to befriend him. When war broke out she told him Germany would lose the war. She apparently still believed in Hitler but felt he was surrounded by criminals—*verbrecher.* Her career as propagandist seems to have been a product of unique gifts for spectacle, and political ingenuousness. Her two major films stand as valuable documents of an age.[17]

Walther Ruttman, abandoning his early leftist bent, apparently became an ardent Nazi advocate. His films for the cause included the UFA short *German Tanks* (*Deutsche Panzer,* 1940). He is reported to have died of wounds received while making a film on the eastern front.

While Goebbels was snuffing out the German cine-clubs, another cine-club movement was on the rise. This was in the United States.

Cine-clubs arrived late in America, probably because it was home base of the leading film empire. Elsewhere Hollywood films were foreign culture, and challenged pride and the sense of identity. In the United States this nationalistic challenge was not a factor.

When cine-clubs did burgeon, it was as by-product of Depression unrest, which in the final days of the Hoover regime became almost revolutionary. Now the deprived experienced an identity problem: nowhere in the mass media did they find their plight represented.

President Hoover considered the Depression to be mainly a crisis of confidence; undermining confidence was therefore a public disservice, and optimism was statesmanship. The press, almost wholly Republican, tended to reflect this view; it constantly noted signs of upturn, even as the breadlines lengthened. Meanwhile radio concentrated on smooth music, fortune-telling, and advertising; it scarcely had the beginnings of a news service. Fiction films from Hollywood were in an opulent phase of Busby Berkeley choruses, and were beginning to seem as remote to many Americans as to Asians and Africans. And its "non-fiction" product, the newsreel, was perhaps even more irrelevant and bizarre—and was so by design.

To theaters throughout the world, major American studios were selling a contract service of 52 features, 52 shorts, and 52 newsreels per year. In this block-booking system—later altered by antitrust action—newsreels were only an item in an entertainment package. Studio executives generally felt that controversy could only bring troubles; its avoidance became hallowed principle. The attitude actually hardened in the early Depression. In 1931 the Fox Corporation issued a statement that none of its theaters would be allowed to show newsreels of a controversial nature.[18]

All this set the stage for the Workers Film and Photo League, which began in New York City in 1930 and spread rapidly. Within two years local Film and Photo Leagues (the "Workers" was dropped from the name) were in operation in major cities, loosely united in a National Film and Photo League. The years 1930–32 were a time of hunger marches and "Hoovervilles"—clusters of shacks thrown up in parks and along railroad tracks. Evictions, foreclosures, strikes, protests were epidemic. Members of the Film and Photo Leagues concentrated on documenting these phenomena. Exchanging material, they organized a *Workers Newsreel* which was circulated among members and successfully pressed on some theaters. Many of the groups participated in documenting the National Hunger March of December 1932; their combined footage grew into a feature documentary, *Hunger*.

The newsreel activity used silent film, mainly 35mm. The market value of silent projectors had collapsed with the coming of sound; thus the equipment was readily available to the League groups.

The New York Film and Photo League met in a loft at 22 West 17th Street. Its secretary was Thomas Brandon, later a pioneer distributor of foreign films. Sessions included screenings of such films, as well as current work brought by participants. Meetings welcomed members and nonmembers, still photographers and film makers, veterans and novices—all united by crisis.

Margaret Bourke-White and Berenice Abbott (both associated with *Fortune* magazine) were among the still photographers who came to the loft. So were Ralph Steiner and Paul Strand—photographers already deeply involved in film. Other participants were Leo Hurwitz and Herbert Kline, who were associated with the magazine *New Theatre,* which often reflected the Film and Photo League ferment. Willard Van Dyke, arriving from California with a reputation in still photography, was a later participant.[19]

The New York Film and Photo League issued its own mimeographed bulletin, *Filmfront*. It sometimes included translations of articles by European film theorists—the Russian Dziga Vertov, the Hungarian Béla Balász, the Frenchman Léon Moussinac.

In 1934 the Film and Photo Leagues joined in organizing a National Film Conference in Chicago, screening and discussing forty reels of film made the previous year. A report on the conference stated:

. . . in the same way as the Soviet cinema began with the kino-eye and grew organically from there on . . . the Leagues started also with the simple newsreel documents, photographing events as they appeared to the lens . . . exploited in a revolutionary cinematic way.[20]

The Film and Photo Leagues formed a loose movement, but their agitation generated organized production ventures. Notable among these was Frontier Films, which in 1935 began an impressive career of militant film making, involving a galaxy of talent—Paul Strand, Leo Hurwitz, Irving Lerner, Sidney Meyers, Jay Leyda, Willard Van Dyke, Harry Dunham, and many others.

But meanwhile the surge of protest activity was having high-level effect. After President Franklin D. Roosevelt took office in 1933, visual documentation of the sort fostered by the Film and Photo Leagues began to find broader support. An early example was the short film *Hands* (1934), by Ralph Steiner and Willard Van Dyke. Dramatizing the relief work of the WPA—Works Progress Administration—it concentrated on hands: idle hands, hands at work, and finally hands putting earnings (from government relief projects) back into circulation. Artful in its understatement, the film was underwritten and distributed by Pathé. But it was soon eclipsed by far more ambitious projects sponsored by RA—the Resettlement Administration, which concerned itself with dust storms and their human toll. In its information division was Roy Stryker, heading a photographic unit. Under him a group of extraordinary photographers—Walker Evans, Dorothea Lange, Carl Mydans, Ben Shahn, and others—began touring the land, photographing dust-storm victims, migrant workers, sharecroppers, and other rural derelicts. Through publications and exhibits they began to open the eyes of the nation to the unchronicled devastation of rural poverty. The head of the agency, ex-professor Rexford Guy Tugwell, wanted to extend this work to motion pictures. This ushered in the meteoric career—brief and brilliant—of Pare Lorentz.[21]

Born in 1905 and reared in the southern college town of Clarksburg, W. Va., Pare Lorentz had a home life saturated in the arts. After college he headed for New York and was soon writing film criticism for the humor magazine *Judge,* the sophisticated *Vanity Fair,* the New York *Evening Journal,* and other publications. Along with film screenings—commercial and experimental—he soaked up concerts, opera, theater, and married the actress Sally Bates. Fascinated by the social role of cinema, young Lorentz collaborated with civil-libertarian lawyer Morris Ernst in the book *Censored: the Private Life of the Movies,* published in 1930. His interests were gradually shifting to politics. In 1933 he published *The Roosevelt Year: 1933;* he had hoped to use the material for a film but, unable to raise film funds, he turned it into a book full of photos of protests, breadlines, farm riots, dust storms, accompanied by a lucidly written text. The book won him an offer from King Features, syndication arm of the Hearst publishing empire, to write a political column. Thus *Washington Sideshow* began appearing in 1934, but when Lorentz in an early column praised the New Deal farm program, he was promptly fired via telegram by Hearst from his headquarters in San Simeon, California. Lorentz was out of a job, but was already trying to promote a film about the dust bowl. It was just what Rexford Guy Tugwell wanted.

Lorentz had never made a film, but he gave an impression of extreme competence. He was handsome, articulate, and seemed to know everything about film. He was resolved to make a film that could win theater distribution and reach a wide public. Few government films had achieved this, but he felt it could be done. Asked if he could do it for $6000, he said he could.

Lorentz realized that government film production was, to many in Hollywood, an outrage—in fact, "socialism." He hoped to overcome this attitude. But with his absurdly minuscule budget he knew he must, for the moment, stay away from Hollywood. He turned first to the experimental talent of New York, on the margins of the film world. As cameramen he engaged Ralph Steiner, Paul Strand, Leo Hurwitz. All had been associated with the New York Film and Photo League; all had films to their credit. Paul Strand had recently completed *The Wave,* a widely praised semidocumentary film about a Mexican fishing village, sponsored by the Mexican government.

The group began photography in Montana and moved southward to Texas—following dust storms that were rapidly turning millions of acres of farmland into desert. Amid the choking blizzards Lorentz searched for images of the sort he wanted, but he had no precise script. This sometimes annoyed his cameramen and finally brought an "ultimatum." Strand and Hurwitz presented Lorentz with a proposed shooting script; if Lorentz would adopt it as basis for further shooting, they would continue. Lorentz refused. The crisis represented a division such as Grierson had also had to contend with. The dissidents saw the dust storms not just as a catastrophe of nature, but as a consequence of the misuse of land by a rapacious social system. Perhaps—to an extent—Lorentz did too. But in the context of government sponsorship his task was conservation, not iconoclasm. The impasse involved questions of tactics, as well as philosophical orientation. Lorentz managed to hold his crew together, but tension continued.

The crew was not the only source of trouble. With completion of the dust-storm sequences Lorentz disbanded his group and headed for Hollywood. He hoped to depict the historical background of the dust-bowl crisis by means of stock footage, such as the major studios make available at a standard price per foot. But the companies had apparently adopted a policy of noncooperation with government—or at least with the Roosevelt administration. The stock film libraries refused to serve Lorentz.

Lorentz had expected Hollywood opposition, but scarcely at this stage. Fortunately some leading Hollywood artists—notably King Vidor—were angered at the studio policy and, *sub rosa,* acted as intermediaries to get Lorentz the footage he needed. Later Lorentz obtained 1917–18 war footage from the Signal Corps in New York.

His troubles were only beginning. His $6000 budget had been spent. He hired a girl to teach him the mechanics of film editing and made himself an editor. Then he achieved a crucial coup. The composer Virgil Thomson, moved by the material Lorentz was assembling, agreed to work with him for whatever funds Lorentz might scrounge. They began their collaboration as Lorentz pressed Washington for additional appropriations.

The Lorentz-Thomson teamwork became a key element in *The Plow That Broke the Plains.* They shared enthusiasm for folk-music themes, rich in association, and abhorrence for "mickey-mousing" scores—those which regularly underline points made by word or image. Thomson's music constantly supplied added dimensions. An example was his music for a 1917–18 wartime sequence. To meet world demand for wheat, farmers were being pressed to turn grazing lands into wheatlands. As we see tractors coming over a hill, we hear

The Plow That Broke the Plains, 1936.   Museum of Modern Art

Library of Congress

a strain from *Mademoiselle from Armentières*—marching song of American troops. It provides momentary emphasis that farmers are becoming part of a war machine. For Lorentz and Thomson, editing and composing became a unified process. Neither wanted a score imposed on a finished film, or vice versa. The commentary written by Lorentz evolved as part of the same process. Eventually read by Thomas Chalmers, a former Metropolitan Opera baritone, it became a kind of *recitatif*. It sometimes addressed people seen on the screen: "Settler, plow at your peril. . . ." The score was finally recorded by performers from the New York Philharmonic under the baton of Alexander Smallens—recruited by Virgil Thomson.

A series of previews early in 1936 soon made it known, in and out of government and film circles, that *The Plow That Broke the Plains* illuminated a national problem with strong documentation, and with emotional power and beauty. This was its glory, and the nub of its further problems. Government film activity had been going on unimpressively for almost three decades: the Department of Agriculture had been making demonstration films of sorts since 1908; the Department of the Interior had used films to announce availability of western lands; Signal Corps cameramen had documented practice maneuvers and battle action. As long as these and other projects had special functions, or were ineffectual, they raised few problems. But films addressing a general audience with overwhelming impact were another matter. This was government competition with Hollywood; besides, it was controversy threatening to disturb temples sacred to Entertainment. In Congress the power of the film agitated opponents of Roosevelt farm policies; they saw it as New Deal propaganda—an election-year stab in the back. Some politicians felt their states had been irreparably damaged by being depicted as wastelands.

At the same time Lorentz was in trouble with his own agency. His $6000 project had become a $19,260 film. He had paid many bills en route from his own resources, and arrived in Washington with receipts—some written on scraps of wrapping paper and backs of envelopes. This did not suit government protocol: in the end, much of the surplus cost had to be defrayed by Lorentz—who had earned $18 per day for his work on *The Plow That Broke the Plains*—and by his actress wife. Amid these crises the Resettlement Agency itself was in trouble; it was declared unconstitutional by the U.S. Court of Appeals. Litigation continued, but plans were afoot for transferring the work, or part of it, to the Department of Agriculture.

The united-front opposition of the film industry was, once again, broken by a man with an independent spirit. Although the major distributors had rejected *The Plow That Broke the Plains,* the urbane Arthur Mayer, former Paramount executive who had become manager of New York's important Rialto Theater, decided to show the film. What is more, he resolved to capitalize on the industry's opposition. Opening it on May 28, 1936, he called the film "The Picture They Dared Us to Show!" His advertisements quoted critical eulogies obtained via previews, then added: "Yet Hollywood has turned its manicured thumb down!" From the Rialto came word that audiences were cheering at every performance. Theaters in other major cities—Philadelphia, Boston, Washington—followed the Rialto example; then came an explosion of bookings. Some 3000 theaters eventually showed the film—without benefit of major studio distribution.

Lorentz had lived through months of unrelieved, almost inhuman pressures, and felt he had had enough. In mid-1936 he visited the office of Tugwell—by then in the Department of Agriculture—to announce his resignation, but stayed to urge a new film idea—*The River.* "You people," he told Tugwell, "are missing the biggest story in the world—the Mississippi River." Within days this discussion seemed to produce miracles. The suggested topic reached into numerous issues of concern to the New Deal: flood control, hydroelectric power, soil conservation, rural electrification. At home Lorentz received a phone call from Tugwell, saying he had talked with the President; Roosevelt was providing a budget of $50,000 for *The River.* This time Lorentz would get $30 per day. A fiscal expert would accompany the unit to handle finances. They were to begin at once. By the fall of 1936 Lorentz had completed research and hired several cameramen: Willard Van Dyke, who with Ralph Steiner had made *Hands;* and Stacy and Horace Woodard, nature-film specialists. The Woodards left the project early but were replaced by Floyd Crosby, cameraman for the Murnau-Flaherty film *Tabu,* who had been recommended by King Vidor. By January 1937 the planned shooting was done and the crew was disbanded, when it became clear that a flood along tributaries of the Mississippi was about to produce a thousand-mile catastrophe. Lorentz hastily recalled Crosby and Van Dyke. The Department of Agriculture provided additional

The River, 1937.

funds. The cameramen, improvising as they went, were in action for one of the greatest of film climaxes—and momentous ammunition for the New Deal.

Again the music of Virgil Thomson and the sonorous voice of Thomas Chalmers became part of the project. This time narration took an incantatory style, reminiscent of Walt Whitman—and also of the film *Turksib,* known to all the participants. There was constant use of cadenced catalogues—of the names of places, rivers, trees. In a review of the insensate destruction of primeval forests—

NARRATOR: . . . Black spruce and Norway pine; Douglas fir and red cedar; scarlet oak and shagbark hickory—we built a hundred cities and a thousand towns, but at what cost!

Repetition was part of the style. The words "we built a hundred cities and a thousand towns" were used as a refrain. Lorentz sometimes called the film an "opera."

On completion of the film late in 1937, Lorentz once more built up interest through previews in major cities, as well as special screenings along the Mississippi. This time a historic breakthrough was achieved: Paramount offered to distribute *The River.*

When President Franklin D. Roosevelt saw the film at a screening at his home in Hyde Park, N.Y., he turned at once to Lorentz and said: "That's a grand movie. What can I do to help?" This led to talk of a U.S. Film Service, to make such films for various agencies.

During the months that followed, *The River* won several prizes, including best-documentary award of the Venice festival. In August 1938, as *The River* was showing unexpected box-office pull for Paramount, the U.S. Film Service was established by presidential order, under the National Emergency Council. The herculean labors of Pare Lorentz now seemed to win success after success. A film on unemployment—tentatively titled *Ecce Homo*—was begun with funds from federal relief agencies. Shortly afterward a film on infant mortality was begun—a fiction film with professional actors, under Public Health Service auspices, also using relief funds. At the same time the Rural Electrification Agency contracted for a film, eventually titled *Power and the Land.* Concurrently the Department of Agriculture decided to back a film on soil conservation, *The Land,* which Robert Flaherty agreed to direct. There were discussions with the State Department about a film on Latin America. Lorentz seemed to have achieved a status comparable to that of Grierson, watching over a spreading documentary empire. But Grierson was a skilled politician who knew how to keep his fences mended; Lorentz was not. Lorentz was in the field, trying to maintain artistic control over diverse enterprises. In the midst of his whirlwind efforts, he received a shock: the appropriations committee of the House of Representatives had scuttled the U.S. Film Service budget.

Desperate efforts were made to save the situation. But opponents had united in a deadly strategy. In using relief appropriations for "movies," they said, the U.S. Film Service was violating the law. The appropriation bill had not mentioned "movies."

President Roosevelt did not press the battle. His attention was shifting to international crises and defense needs. In mid-1940 the U.S. Film Service died. Some of its projects had already been abandoned; others had been transferred to the sponsoring agencies. The leadership the government had briefly assumed in documentary production was being relinquished. The spotlight shifted back to private entrepreneurs.

The atmosphere of cinema had meanwhile changed. With such films as *The Grapes of Wrath* (1939), Hollywood was following where Lorentz and others had led. Even newsreels seemed to be yielding to the times—mainly under the impact of *The March of Time*.

Launched in 1935, *The March of Time* was not a newsreel in any accepted sense. It used actuality sequences but combined these with freewheeling dramatizations. Events were re-enacted not only by participants—this had often been done—but by professional actors in scenes scripted, directed, edited, and scored by professionals, in a manner established in a radio series also titled *The March of Time*. Thus the ambiance of events as depicted on *The March of Time* was often entirely a *Time* creation, and hardly of a "documentary" or "newsreel" character. *March of Time* executives had no difficulty rationalizing this: their probing of events simply went beyond elementary newsreels. Henry Luce, head of the *Time* organization, proclaimed the style "fakery in allegiance to the truth."[22]

In content as well as style, *The March of Time* broke with newsreel tradition: it set out to be provocative. Sometimes it provoked liberals, sometimes conservatives. Through its narration, delivered in an apocalyptic tone by Westbrook Van Voorhis, the Voice of Time, it took editorial positions. The style of the series has been aptly described by Raymond Fielding in his book *The American Newsreel 1911–1967:*

> The static camera and nervous editing, the *vox e sepulchro* strained with alarm, the posture of omniscience, and the calculated air of fearlessness— all combined to delight a contemporary audience otherwise bored with the inanities of intermission travelogues and farces. *Time* editorialized openly, infuriating its enemies and oftentimes alienating its friends. And it did all this with vigor, artistry, arid showmanship which shamed its less-daring competitors.[23]

In 1937 *The March of Time* received an Academy Award for having "revolutionized" newsreels. Some industry elements deplored the award and the trend. It meant the destruction, warned the *Motion Picture Herald,* of the theater as "the public's escape from the bitter realities, the anguishes, and the turmoil of life." But newsreels seemed, at least for a time, to enter a more adventurous phase. RKO later (1942) started a monthly release, *This Is America,* competitive with *The March of Time* but working on a less panoramic scale. It tried to "relate the small cog to the big wheel instead of showing the big wheel"—as *The March of Time* did.[24]

Meanwhile the New York film makers whose activism had started the documentary upturn of the 1930's were not resting. In 1939 they produced one of the most impressive films of the period—*The City,* directed by Ralph Steiner and Willard Van Dyke. Sponsored by the American Institute of City Planners, it was based on a brief outline by Pare Lorentz, elaborated by Henwar Rodakiewicz. Lewis Mumford wrote the commentary, which was read by Morris Carnovsky. Like other ambitious documentaries of the time, the project enlisted a major composer—Aaron Copland. The film was produced for use at the 1939 New York World's Fair, which became a significant documentary showcase. *The City* was full of experiments, some highly successful. A stylized lunch-counter montage was a triumph of satire; traffic jams provided memorable sequences. Choral voice montages—as in concurrent radio experiments by Norman Corwin and in several British documentaries—were occasionally used. Concealed cameras in a suitcase on a counter, or on a street behind a military recruitment poster, yielded rich moments. On a crowded street we see a man discarding a newspaper into a trash barrel; a second later another recovers and examines it. Children playing irrepressibly amid filth and

Willard Van Dyke.

traffic congestion provide fascinating vignettes. *The City,* as impressive as the Lorentz films in developing its thesis, has the advantage of streaks of humor that are lacking in Lorentz. As an exposition of the urban crisis, *The City* was notable. The film *Valley Town* (1940), directed by Willard Van Dyke and edited by Irving Lerner, with a score by Marc Blitzstein, applied similar techniques to the problems of an industrial town.

The most prolific documentary production group of these years was the hard-hitting Frontier Films, formed by veterans of the Film and Photo Leagues. Its *People of the Cumberland*—about the Highlander Folk School promoting unionization among Cumberland Mountain people—represented a rich array of talent. Photographed by Ralph Steiner, it was written by Erskine Caldwell, with music by Alex North and Earl Robinson, conducted by Elie Siegmeister. In a manner reminiscent of *Housing Problems,* it featured a sequence foreshadowing television. A farmer working in a field is suddenly asked a question by a disembodied voice. Stopping his work, he considers the question for a moment, then answers. A final sequence offers a number of such "at-work" statements—clearly not life caught on the run, but a highly stylized device, deliberately discarding illusion.

The City, 1939.

Museum of Modern Art

Another Frontier Films production, *Native Land,* by Paul Strand and Leo Hurwitz—narrated by Paul Robeson with a score by Marc Blitzstein—dealt with civil rights violations cited in government hearings. The film used dramatized reconstructions. Since few civil rights violations were occurring on camera, the film makers felt no more difficulty than did *The March of Time* in justifying dramatizations: they were going beyond surface truth. Years in the making, the film was not released until 1942. Meanwhile public concern, and that of Frontier Films, had shifted to the international arena, and here Frontier Films did its most notable work.

The "civil war" that erupted in Spain in 1936 was, more precisely, a rehearsal for world war. An insurrection under General Francisco Franco against the elected Spanish government was aided with arms and troops by Hitler's Germany and Mussolini's Italy. This went on in blatant violation of a "nonintervention" pact they had proclaimed, along with France and Britain—which nations nonetheless observed the agreement, refusing to sell or give arms to the combatants. The United States meanwhile had its hands tied by an arms embargo law, passed by Congress after revelations of vast profits made by American "merchants of death" during the 1914–18 World War. With arms withheld by France, Britain, and the United States, the elected Spanish government—the "loyalist" forces—depended mainly on limited supplies arriving from the Soviet Union, and seemed ultimately doomed. The "nonintervention" thus seemed to guarantee a Hitler–Mussolini–Franco victory, and this aroused indignation through much of the world. Volunteers by the thousands began to arrive in Spain to fight for the loyalists in an International Brigade, or to assist it through medical or relief work. Fund-raising to support these efforts, and propaganda to end the "nonintervention" and arms embargo, occupied artists and writers in many countries. For the moment, it was a cause that united liberals, socialists, communists, anarchists. Among numerous film makers who arrived on the scene was a young Russian, Roman Karmen, whose vivid film reports from Spain laid the basis for a long and notable documentary career. His reports provided the nucleus for a feature-length compilation titled *Spain (Ispaniya,* 1939), edited by Esfir Shub. Another early arrival in Spain was the American Herbert Kline, who collaborated with the Hungarian photographer Geza Karpathi to document a shining fragment of history: the work of Dr. Norman Bethune, dapper Canadian society physician who had suddenly given up his Montreal practice in order to join the loyalist forces, and who in their service invented the blood bank. The footage by Kline and Karpathi was turned over to Frontier Films; edited and amplified by Paul Strand and Leo Hurwitz, it became *Heart of Spain* (1937).

Another Frontier Films production proved even more newsworthy —and prophetic. The Japanese war on China had flared intermittently since 1931, when Japan had seized Manchuria. While China was being nibbled away, it was also ravaged by civil struggle, which was the subject of many rumors, seldom reliable. Most news dispatches centered on—and emanated from—Chiang Kai-shek and his Wellesley-graduate wife, Madame Chiang, who were depicted as unifiers of China. But there were also reports of another force, which had somehow made its way in an epic march—in the face of incredible hardships, and attacked and pursued by Chiang Kai-shek forces —from eastern China to a remote, mountain-locked stronghold in the northwest—under one Mao Tse-tung and the military leader Chu Teh. The first American observer to reach this stronghold was the journalist Edgar Snow, who wrote of his findings in the book *Red Star Over China,* published in 1937. But before its appearance another American, Harry Dunham—a ballet dancer turned cameraman, who had published pictures in *Life* magazine—made his way through the chaos of China to Mao's domain and—even more miraculously— was able to bring hundreds of feet of film back through China and to the United States, reportedly in Chinese ginger jars. The film became *China Strikes Back* (1937), completed for Frontier Films by the scholarly Jay Leyda with Irving Lerner and Sidney Meyers, who were among the busiest of film editors, and the poet and screen writer Ben Maddow. For the mysterious Harry Dunham, who apparently explored numerous arts, it was the one major contribution to cinema; he died during World War II.

China Strikes Back shows us the youthful Mao Tse-tung, Chu Teh, and other early associates. It reveals to us the rugged Yenan area adopted as their base. It makes clear that Mao has set aside an orthodox Marxist principle, at least for China: he sees in the Chinese peasantry—not in a city-based proletariat—the power base from which a new China is to emerge. The film makes clear Mao's emphasis on guerrilla struggle against the Japanese, on close relations with the

Roman Karmen filming Mao Tse-tung—Yenan, 1939. The expedition resulted in the feature *In China*, released 1941.

Karmen collection

peasant population, and on punctilious cleanliness and respectful dealing. The revelations in *China Strikes Back*, meshing with Snow's report in *Red Star Over China*, won attention as far away as Moscow, which until then had apparently had little communication with Yenan. According to Jay Leyda, Stalin had referred to Mao's forces contemptuously as "margarine communists." But a Moscow screening of *China Strikes Back* persuaded young Roman Karmen—back from Spain in 1938—to propose a film expedition to Yenan. The result was another notable series of film reports, culminating in the Russian feature documentary *In China* (1941).[25]

It is significant that those who completed *China Strikes Back* for Frontier Films—Lerner, Leyda, Maddow, Meyers—used pseudonyms. The film brought news that ran against prevailing tides of doctrine, which made Chiang Kai-shek savior of China. As war clouds gathered, unorthodox ideas increasingly stirred suspicion. In segments of Congress and the press, a witch-hunting atmosphere was developing. The men of Frontier Films, veterans of the Film and Photo Leagues, had had an impact on the history of American documentary. But as war approached, some of its leaders found themselves working in increasing isolation.

Something of the same sort was happening in Japan, but with more drastic results. As in other countries there had been a cine-club movement, which leaned leftward under the impact of economic crisis.

One of its leaders was Akira Iwasaki. While studying German literature and philosophy at Tokyo Imperial University in the late 1920's, he found his interest shifting to cinema, and he took up film criticism. He saw foreign films whenever he could—American, German, French. Few Russian films were admitted to Japan, but he did see *Turksib* and *Storm Over Asia*. He became part of a group calling itself the Proletarian Film League, or Prokino—formed in 1929. Like the Film and Photo Leagues in the United States, Prokino members met to screen films and went on to make them—newsreels and longer documentaries. Working with meager funds, they generally used 16mm reversal film. This meant that original films could be used for projection, and they usually were; when these wore out, nothing remained. Like the Film and Photo Leagues, Prokino organized its own distribution system, holding screenings for labor unions and farm groups over a widening area.

Among youthful Prokino recruits was Fumio Kamei. Originally a painter, he had visited the Soviet Union to study industrial arts. There the work of Pudovkin and Blyokh especially excited him, and weaned him from painting to film. On his return to Japan he fell under the influence of Akira Iwasaki and the Prokino group. Work on public-relations films won him his first film earnings and led to a job in the documentary unit of Toho, one of the major Japanese studios.[26]

The documentary had been slow to develop in Japan, but military expansion on the Asian mainland became a subject of frequent newsreel items and of occasional documentaries. These adhered to a special foreign-policy vocabulary. The 1931 seizure of Manchuria and a concurrent ferocious attack on Shanghai were introduced with such subtitles as "Manchurian Incidents" and "Movements in East Asia." When conquered Manchuria became Manchukuo, it was the occasion for rituals prominently featured in newsreels: the founding of Manchukuo, the crowning of its Emperor, and his state visit to Japan. In western news media Manchukuo was a "puppet state"; in Japanese newsreels it was part of the "new order in Asia" and of an Asian "co-prosperity sphere."[27]

In 1937 Japan renewed its war on China in full force with drives on Shanghai, Soochow, Nanking, Peking. The rising pitch of events gave the documentary new standing. With the fall of Shanghai, Toho sent young Fumio Kamei to film the occupation of the city. The result was the feature-length *Shanghai*, a Toho release made with army cooperation—a film of fascinating ambiguity.

The film shows no battle action; the battle itself had received exceptionally strong newsreel coverage, mainly from the vantage of the international settlement. But Kamei invited Japanese officers of varied rank to explain, on camera, how they had achieved their victory. This they do, fulsomely and proudly, with occasional reference to maps. Meanwhile Kamei occasionally cuts away from them to shots in which the camera travels over battlefield devastation and over city ruins teeming with uprooted humanity. On the battlefields we see innumerable Japanese graves, suggesting that the Japanese paid a higher price for the victory than news reports have suggested. Within the city, the shots of conquered people are unforgettable. We see endless lines at a water pump. In scenes of Japanese soldiers trying to make friends with Chinese children—through pats on the head, gifts of candy, and donkey rides—the confused faces of the children are haunting.

The film, released by Toho, appears to have infuriated army officials, and to have made Kamei a marked man. His film *Fighting Soldiers* (*Tatakau Heitai*), about the life of soldiers, completed for Toho in 1939 and released, was banned the following year, and its negative destroyed. His script for a Toho short on the geology of Mt. Fuji was vetoed on grounds that Fuji symbolized the empire and must not be examined scientifically. The fate of the completed *Kobayashi-Issa,* a lyric tourist film released in 1940, was especially curious. It dealt with the haiku poet Kobayashi, but more particularly with the rugged part of the country where he grew up. His poems were used by Kamei as the commentary—occasionally sardonic. The region consists largely of unarable land, so that farmers toil endlessly on small hillside strips. Hence the climactic haiku:

> Spring has come
> but my happiness
> is moderate.

Fighting Soldiers—released 1939, banned 1940.

Toho

The opening of the film tells us:

> Three things are important
> here: the moon, Buddha,
> and noodles.

The film was denounced for excessive concern with poverty.

In 1939 Japan, following the German example, decreed that films could be directed only by those with government licenses; Kamei was denied a license. A preventive detention law was adopted, permitting arrest of those suspected of dangerous tendencies. Kamei was arrested in October 1941 and remained in prison for almost two years.

Prokino had been outlawed. However, interest in documentary was on the rise. It was stimulated by a Japanese edition of Paul Rotha's *Documentary Film,* which was translated by a young woman, Taka Atsugi, and appeared in 1938. In 1940, as a war measure, the showing of *bunka eiga*—cultural films, including documentaries—was made compulsory for all theaters in major cities; the following year the rule was extended to other areas. The newsreels were consolidated into one official newsreel, Nippon Eiga Sha—often shortened to Nichiei. Newsreel and documentary began to root themselves firmly in Japanese cinema. But it became a highly controlled movement, having no room—at least for the moment—for a Kamei or Iwasaki.

Asia, Europe, America—in diverse places, documentary film continued to show parallel developments. During the 1930's these involved not only the rise of advocacy—subtle or overt—and such phenomena as the guerrilla pressure of cine-clubs, suppressed in some places; it involved also matters of form. The typical film of advocacy was shot like a silent film, with "voice-over" narration added. This had almost become the standard documentary form. Even the Spanish Luis Buñuel, associated with surrealism, made a voice-over documentary, the sardonic *Land Without Bread* (*Tierra Sin Pan* or *Las Hurdes,* 1932), banned in Spain for its horrifying portrayal of a Spanish village. Voice-over was also the technique used in the Belgian film *Easter Island* (*L'Ile de Pâques,* 1935), a Henri Storck production shot in the South Pacific by John Ferno, a former co-worker of Joris Ivens. Its portrait of an island dominated by monuments of a civilization whose inhabitants had virtually exterminated each other in warfare—the camera showed scraggy remnants living in squalor—seemed to carry a warning to a world increasingly dominated by strife. There were voice-over passages, accompanying newsreel material, in Jean Renoir's *Life Belongs to Us* (*La Vie est à Nous,* 1936), a semi-documentary tract for the French *Front Populaire.*

In the voice-over format, some narrators were characterized but most were abstract voices. Some were calm but most were resonant with authority, and backed by impressive music. These were becoming documentary clichés.

Reenactments played a part in some documentaries—and these, as in *The March of Time,* occasionally involved actors. There was little public discussion about the validity of such techniques.

The parallel developments were furthered by traveling documentarists. From the start, the documentary had been represented by artists moving from continent to continent: the Lumière cinematographers; then Flaherty, Grierson, Cavalcanti, Karmen, and others. The film of advocacy produced an especially striking example, in a single career linking nations, genres, and eras. This was the leading film maker of Holland, Joris Ivens.[28]

Although his early films *The Bridge* and *Rain* had been experiments in design, social issues were already important to him. He had been a student activist. Later, in the mid-1920's, he had worked in a German camera factory and had marched in protest against working conditions. When the marchers were fired on by police, he felt he had

Easter Island, 1935.

been involved in an early battle against spreading fascism. Then, in Amsterdam, the Filmliga provided continuing political stimulus. Its showings of foreign films included films forbidden to Dutch theaters. The right of artists to view such films in privacy had been upheld after a stormy 1927 incident in which police had tried to stop a screening of Pudovkin's *Mother* (*Mat,* 1926)—apparently the first Soviet film to reach Amsterdam. The libertarian victory had given the Filmliga its initial organizing impulse and helped it to grow dramatically.

Unlike similar groups elsewhere, Ivens and his friends did not produce newsreels, but they contrived a provocative equivalent. In the Netherlands, cinemas were closed on Sundays; during this weekend interval newsreels were borrowed from cooperative projectionists, then retitled and rearranged for totally revised, left-wing impact. Having relished the results and used them for discussion meetings, the *cinéastes* restored the films to their original form for the Monday theater showings.

The rapid growth of the Filmliga enabled it to institute meetings at which prominent film makers were invited to discuss their work. From France came several, including Alberto Cavalcanti and René Clair. From the Soviet Union came Sergei Eisenstein, Vsevolod Pudovkin, Dziga Vertov. While Russian studios were being converted to sound, their directors were encouraged to make such travels.

The Pudovkin appearance brought a turn in the life of Ivens. Netherlands authorities, nervous about Pudovkin's visit, allowed him to be on Dutch soil not more than twenty-four hours before, and twenty-four hours after, his Filmliga appearance. But during those hours Pudovkin saw several films, including *The Bridge* and *Rain,* and he said to Ivens: "It might be a good thing for us if you would come and visit us in the Soviet Union." Three months later a letter from Pudovkin brought a specific follow-up: "Why don't you come now? Your expenses from the frontier will be paid. Be sure to bring your films." In December of 1929 Ivens headed for the Soviet Union.

During the following months he gave scores of lectures, with screenings of his films. Shunted from place to place with an interpreter, he answered questions about film, social conditions, and his own life and background. And he saw films: at the Ukraine studio Dovzhenko showed him his new film *Earth* (*Zemlya,* 1930); at the Georgia studio Mikhail Kalatozov showed him the recently completed *Salt for Svanetia.* Then, to his astonishment, Ivens was invited to direct a film, on a topic of his choosing. He chose a new steel center at Magnitogorsk, which was being built and organized largely by youth brigades. The film eventually became *Song of Heroes* (*Pesn o Gueroyakh,* 1932).

Before he could start production, he made a return trip to the Netherlands, where in a short time he improved his financial situation by making two industrial films, including one for Philips Radio. Working in its almost luxurious plant he made *Industrial Symphony* (also known as *Philips-Radio,* 1931), a film of great technical beauty, with emphasis on textures and patterns of movement—as in *The Bridge.* (He had suggested photography in workers' homes, but the idea was vetoed by the company.) Returning to the Soviet Union, he launched into his other factory film: here, on the frontier between Europe and Asia, he lived in log-house barracks, working sometimes in a sea of mud, sometimes in incredible cold. Equipment was scant, and all film production material—like every other kind of material—was in short supply. Yet Ivens later wrote in his memoirs: "It was the first time in my life that I felt integrated with my work, a part of my environment."

On completing *Song of Heroes,* he returned to the Netherlands in time for the climax of something he had begun years earlier: a continuing film record of the draining of the Zuider Zee. But the completion of this engineering feat, designed to create new wheatlands, brought an unexpected, bitter irony—which became the final point of his film. In 1933 wheat was being dumped into the seas to maintain its price on international markets. Ivens expressed his anger in the jolting finish of *New Earth* (*Nieuwe Gronden,* 1934). In a sudden change of mood, accented by Hanns Eisler's music, the film indicts a system placing wheat prices above the hunger of millions.

Meanwhile the Belgian Henri Storck was in touch with him. Storck was outraged over the problems of coal miners in the Borinage section of Belgium, and the violent police action used to quell their strike, which had been precipitated by wage cuts. Ivens joined Storck to make *Borinage* (1933), financed by the Brussels cine-club, Club de L'Écran. To elude the police they worked in extreme secrecy, living in miners' homes, moving frequently from home to home. Recent evictions, demonstrations, and clashes with police were reenacted with the help of miners. It was virtually "underground" film making, shadowed by secret police.[29] Censors banned the completed film in both Belgium and Netherlands, but it had substantial cine-club circulation.

Ivens was becoming a celebrated man of causes. He was invited to the United States. A group of prominent writers and artists—Herman

Borinage, 1933.

Shumlin, Lillian Hellman, Dorothy Parker, and others—proposed to raise funds and form a corporation, Contemporary Historians, Inc. They wanted Ivens to go to Spain to make a film about the antifascist struggle. Ivens cabled young John Ferno to join him on the Spanish project. Both would contribute their services to the cause. Ernest Hemingway joined the project, writing and speaking the narration. In Spain they found Roman Karmen of the Soviet Union at work on his film mission. For both Ivens and Ferno, it was the first filming of war. In a village they saw Caproni planes coming and bombs descending—smooth, shining brilliantly in the sun. Then came the crash of bombs and silence all over the village, followed by the cries of the wounded. Then, amid the dust of the explosions, women began to emerge, bewildered, not yet knowing what had happened. Ivens and Ferno followed them, with cameras in action. Two women picking up a baby. Ivens found himself thinking, how can I possibly be so brutal? But he was determined to keep shooting, and did. They kept on for weeks. Hemingway said they took "too many chances" and would be killed. The editing was done in New York by Ivens's editor, Helen van Dongen, who came from Holland for the project. Irving Reis, director of the experimental CBS radio series *Columbia*

Spain, 1936: Roman Karmen, Ernest Hemingway, Joris Ivens.

Karmen collection

Workshop, worked with her, adding sound effects to the silent footage. For their bombardment effect they found the sort of solution not unusual for this period: they appropriated a sequence of earthquake noises from the film *San Francisco* and ran it backwards. The effect was found triumphantly authentic. Virgil Thomson and Marc Blitzstein culled music from recordings of Spanish folk tunes. President Roosevelt saw a preview of *The Spanish Earth* at the White House and asked questions about the Russian tanks. Mrs. Roosevelt asked about the chances of a loyalist victory. The film was premiered in 1937. Some critics said Ivens had turned from art to propaganda. The *Motion Picture Herald* said it was "too stark, bitter and brutal to please the general audience." But many felt they had seen a classic. *Time* said:

Not since the silent French film, *The Passion of Joan of Arc,* had such dramatic use been made of the human face. As face after face looks out from the screen the picture becomes a sort of portfolio of portraits of the human soul in the presence of disaster and distress. These are the earnest faces of speakers at meetings and in the villages talking war, exhorting the defense. These are faces of old women moved from their homes in Madrid for safety's sake, staring at a bleak, uncertain future, faces in terror after a bombing, faces of men going into battle and the faces of men who will never return from battle, faces full of grief and determination and fear.

For those most concerned with the loyalist cause, Ivens was a hero of the hour. He had become one of the great names of documentary film. Pare Lorentz, making plans for a U.S. Film Service, wanted him for a project—the film he was planning on rural electrification. But there were more urgent topics, such as the war in China. The artists and writers who had sent Ivens to Spain wanted him now to film the Chinese-Japanese war. They formed a new corporation—History Today, Inc. Luise Rainer, who had starred in *The Good Earth,* headed the fundraising. The Chinese ambassador was helpful. Early in 1938 Joris Ivens and John Ferno—they were co-directors on this project— were on their way; Robert Capa of *Life* went with them, to make stills. Footage would go—via Hollywood laboratories—to Helen van Dongen in New York for editing. They devised with her a cable code. The message JOHNNY VERY ILL would tell her: "Get us out of this country as soon as possible—tangling with the Japanese army or occupation authorities."[30]

But there were problems besides the Japanese. A Colonel Huang, assigned by the Chiang Kai-shek government to advise them, seemed to be in charge of making obstacles. Every move of the film group was apparently reported to Madame Chiang. In Hankow, temporary capital, the group encountered a new censorship system.

Every time I took a shot, one of the Chinese censor people took exactly the same shot with a 16mm camera. The 16mm print was sent to Hong Kong, developed there by Kodak, flown back to Hankow and seen by the censor before we were allowed to send the identical 35mm film to Hollywood.

Ivens asked for permission to visit the Mao Tse-tung Eighth Route Army—but without results. Guerrilla units, they were told, could be found anywhere. All requests and inquiries concerning the Yenan forces precipitated a runaround. Ivens and Ferno tried, nevertheless, to make their way to the northwest; their efforts were watched, and a telegram from Hankow brought warning:

MADAME WANTS ME TO INFORM YOU CHINA HAS ONLY ONE ARMY UNDER GENERALISSIMOS COMMAND IN YOUR PRODUCTION YOU ARE CAUTIONED NOT TO PUBLICIZE ANY PARTICULAR UNIT BUT GIVE PROMINENCE TO THE CHINESE ARMY STOP JULY AND AUGUST VERY HOT FOR HANKOW FILMING HOPE YOU TAKE FULL ADVANTAGE OF JUNE WEATHER HERE.

The Four Hundred Million, 1939.

China, 1938: John Ferno, Joris Ivens and Chinese associate—at work on *The Four Hundred Million*.

The film, *The Four Hundred Million,* scored by Hanns Eisler with a narration written by Dudley Nichols and read by Fredric March, was premiered in 1939, and was both acclaimed and attacked. As an explanation of the upheavals in China, the film had limited value. As testimony on the horrors of modern war, it provided unforgettable moments.

From *The Bridge* through *New Earth* to *The Four Hundred Million,* Joris Ivens had moved long distances. At first it had been a matter of patterns in motion; then of social problems; now it seemed mainly a matter of loyalties. Ideological debate was being drowned by bombs. Ivens had moved on into a time when film makers, surrounded by the rumble of explosions, would not be asked to probe issues, but to sound the call to action.

Bugler

When German armies drove into Poland in September 1939, they plunged also into the film genre that was to dominate documentary production throughout World War II: the bugle-call film, adjunct to military action, weapon of war. The film maker's task: as to the faithful, to stir the blood, building determination to the highest pitch; as to the enemy, to chill the marrow, paralyzing the will to resist. In all these tasks, German war films made a glittering start.[1]

The importance attached to the work was evident. In the advance on the Polish city of Gdynia, the attack is said to have been delayed so that cameramen could take positions ahead of the assault troops, so as to document the full impact. In the later conquest of Norway, which made unprecedented use of parachute troops in coordination with naval landings, 300 German cameramen were said to be in action. Many German cameramen were killed during the war.

The accumulating battle footage was processed into expanded newsreels in the *German Weekly Review (Deutsche Wochenschau)* series—it often ran to forty minutes during the early part of the war—and into long documentaries. Captured footage, stirring music, animated maps, and highly emotional narration were important additional elements. While the overwhelmingly dynamic action riveted attention, speech and music were used to impose specific meanings and values on the events. The viewer was word-regimented.

Among films emerging from the footage on Poland, *Baptism of Fire* (*Feuertaufe,* 1940), made for the German Air Ministry and featuring an exultant epilogue by its chief, Hermann Göring, seems to have had the widest impact. Directed by Hans Bertram, himself an air ace, the film had music by Norbert Schultze, composer of the song "Lili Marlene." *Baptism of Fire* glorified the role of air power in the smashing of Poland, and was aimed partly at England—as a softening-up tactic. Its narration had an impetuous lyric quality, taking sensuous delight in aerial action and embroidering it with fanciful figures of speech. As planes complete a triumphant mission and veer homeward, the narrator tells us: "Like noble greyhounds, our pursuit planes gambol over the conquered area." Narration alternates with passages of song:

High up, we feel in the east wind the day's brave venture.

We reach for the sun, leaving the earth far below.
Comrade, comrade, all the girls must wait.

Comrade, comrade, the order is clear, we're ready to go!

Comrade, comrade, you know the slogan: on, to the enemy! On, to the enemy! Bombs on the land of the Poles![2]

But in the end, Britain is the film's target. Her pledge to support Poland, made by Prime Minister Neville Chamberlain, is pictured in *Baptism of Fire* as the most heinous of war crimes, in that it encouraged the Poles to try to defend unfortified Warsaw. The film displays vividly the resulting rain of annihilation—and accompanies it with lyric and self-righteous exultation.

NARRATOR: Warsaw . . . the drama of a town nearing its end. . . . The wind carries the curtain of smoke eastward. The glare of the sun is reflected on the sheer-white cumulus which, lifted by the heat of the flames into bizarre tower-like shapes, soars up like a gigantic mountain range. Down below, hell. . . . Thirty-six hours later, Warsaw surrenders. . . . We fly over the town once again, this time without bombs. Mr. Chamberlain should be of the party. . . . What have you to say now, Mr. Chamberlain? Here you find conclusive evidence of the catastrophe you brought about in the Polish capital. Do you fear the curse of a betrayed people? . . . All this is your work, yours is the guilt, and you will have to answer for it at the last judgment. And remember one thing: this is what happens when the German Luftwaffe strikes. It will also know how to strike at the guiltiest of the guilty.

The final moment of the film brings a reprise—with a variation—of the film's exuberant refrain:

Do you hear the password? On, to the enemy! . . . Bombs, bombs, bombs on England!

The Polish footage gave birth also to *Campaign in Poland* (*Feldzug in Polen*, 1940), which demonstrated Nazi ground warfare in equally shattering fashion. Dynamically animated maps, depicting pockets of resistance encircled and choked by German tank divisions, convey an almost physical sense of strangulation. Like *Baptism of Fire*, the film pictures German destruction as a sword of retribution. The hour of reckoning is at hand for sinful nations.

Campaign in Poland was the first major work of Fritz Hippler, who also directed *Victory in the West* (*Sieg im Westen*, 1941), celebrating with similar impact the defeat of Norway, Denmark, Holland, Belgium, and France. Hippler was a rising force in the Goebbels regime. Having studied sociology and law at Heidelberg University, he had joined the newsreel division of the Propaganda Ministry in 1935. But it was the war years that propelled him into prominence. He came to be considered, according to David Stewart Hull in his *Film in the Third Reich*, the "evil genius" behind a number of Nazi film projects. The most notorious of these was *The Eternal Jew* (*Der Ewige Jude*), released late in 1940.

In that year several anti-Semitic films appeared, apparently to set the stage for Hitler's "final solution of the Jewish problem." Except for *The Eternal Jew*, they were fiction films. Goebbels assigned to Hippler the task of producing an anti-Semitic "documentary," and he complied in spectacularly odious fashion.

Like other Hippler films it relied heavily on narration—in this case a compendium of anti-Semitic invective, linked with images of many kinds including "degenerate" art, pornography, and slaughterhouse scenes allegedly illustrating Jewish ritual.

In one respect, the film was another by-product of the crushing of Poland. Hippler supervised photography in the Warsaw ghetto, where hundreds of thousands of Jews were herded by the conquerors into pockets of indescribable misery. His footage showed half-starved, unshaven creatures caught in pathetic acts of barter—a pair of socks for a scrap of food. Such footage is used in *The Eternal Jew* as showing Jews "in their natural state." The audience is warned that Jews have elsewhere learned to hide their nature behind a veneer of civilization; but now German audiences can see them as they are, an unclean, cheating, parasitic species.

The Eternal Jew then embarks on a "history" of the Jew, purporting to show how his true nature shows through the acquired veneer. The story is here "documented" through footage from *fiction* films. A selection from *The House of Rothschild* (1934) shows a rich Rothschild—played by George Arliss—putting on old clothes to fool and cheat a tax collector. Another excerpt purports to document the role of Jews in international finance and the starting of wars. Then we are told: "The Jew is interested instinctively in everything abnormal and depraved." This aspect is illustrated via an excerpt from *M* (1932), the Fritz Lang film starring Peter Lorre—"the Jew Lorre," as the narration puts it, "in the role of a child murderer." We get a snatch of its original dialogue.

LORRE: . . . it burns within me. I must go the way that I am driven. . . . Who knows what is going on inside me? How I must do it—not want, *must!*

The end of the film tells us that under the Führer Germany dedicates itself to the cause of racial purity.

The idea of "documenting" a thesis with fiction excerpts was not entirely new. A Grierson film of the Empire Marketing Board period, *Conquest* (1930), used footage from the 1923 feature *The Covered Wagon* as though it were history; its "documentary" look made this a tempting though dubious action. And according to Jay Leyda, the scholarly Esfir Shub in her compilation film *Spain* used a brief battle shot from the 1930 feature *All Quiet on the Western Front*. Inclusions of this sort may be made unwittingly; filing anomalies in stock-shot libraries have made this an increasing possibility. But this was hardly the case with Hippler, who used a questionable device in a particularly unscrupulous manner.

Hippler's film career ended when he was captured by the British. After the war he was employed as translator by the United States army. Film historian David Stewart Hull later found him working as a travel agent in Berchtesgaden.

Although high-pitched lyricism and invective were especially characteristic of Nazi war films, there was also occasional use of irony, as in the short film *Gentlemen* (1940). This shows us Churchill, Chamberlain, Halifax, and Eden as British leaders brought up in the code of "gentlemen." It then demonstrates via foreign newsreel footage how "gentlemen" behave. Eden travels far and wide to try to get Indians, Egyptians and others to fight Britain's war so as to save the gentleman's way of life. Meanwhile Britain has deserted France, her chief ally, pulling troops out of the continent in helter-skelter evacuation. In doing so, the British blow up French bridges and buildings and drop bombs on towns and roads, not caring that they meanwhile kill countless French people, create masses of refugees, and destroy hospitals, schools, and cultural treasures. In contrast, the German advance is pictured as liberation. German troops rebuild bridges, care for the wounded, and give people food and gasoline to help them return home. The French, says the film, are beginning to see that their hope is with Germany and not with "gentlemen."

In similar vein, *Round the Statue of Liberty* (*Rund um die Freiheitsstatue,* 1941) takes an ironic look at the United States, contrasting pretensions with actualities via footage of gang wars, race riots, strikes, slums. No wonder, says the commentary, that the Statue of Liberty turns her back on America.

Nazi film strategies appeared to yield success as long as the armies advanced. When reverses began, the lyric campaign films dwindled, then ceased. Newsreel issues shortened, and tended to fill up with examples of home front devotion and sacrifice, Hitler's visits to military units, and orations by Nazi leaders. One of the most extraordinary newsreel issues, released in 1943, consisted of a "total war" speech by Goebbels—apparently staged for camera purposes, since it addresses the world at large. To dispel any speculation that Germany might weaken, Goebbels says he has invited representative Germans to join him in the Berlin Sportpalast, to answer his questions about their state of mind. Those arrayed before him include members of the Nazi hierarchy, scientists, artists, wounded war veterans, munitions workers, housewives. They respond to him in chorus.

GOEBBELS: The English maintain that the German people are resisting the government's measures for total war.

CROWD: Lies! Shame!

GOEBBELS: They do not want total war, say the British, but capitulation.

CROWD: Sieg heil!

GOEBBELS: Do you want total war?

CROWD: Yes!

GOEBBELS: Do you want a war more total and more ruthless than we could ever have first imagined?

CROWD: Yes!

GOEBBELS: Are you ready to stand with the Führer as a phalanx of the homeland behind the fighting Wehrmacht, to continue the struggle unshaken and with savage determination, through all vicissitudes of fate until victory is in our hands?

CROWD: Yes! . . .

GOEBBELS: You have proclaimed to our enemies what they need to know to prevent them from indulging in false dreams and illusions. . . .

German newsreel issues regularly reached opposing governments through non-belligerent nations, especially Spain, Portugal, and Turkey. *Deutsche Wochenschau* issue No. 651, the Goebbels Sportpalast speech, must have convinced them with its vehemence that thoughts of defeat were troubling Germany.

In Britain as in Germany, the start of war brought a concentration on bugle-call films. The GPO Film Unit became the Crown Film Unit; war films were its task. Their purpose was similar to that of the German films, but the styles were different.

The Grierson years had prepared Britain well for a documentary war. Many of "Grierson's boys" were by now seasoned film veterans; eager to serve war needs, many made valuable contributions—Cavalcanti, Watt, Rotha, and others. But as in Germany, the war brought forth new names, most notably that of Humphrey Jennings (1907–50).[3]

A Cambridge graduate interested in painting, poetry, and drama, Jennings had worked in and around the GPO Film Unit since 1934 as scene designer, actor, editor—generally on other people's films. Grierson considered him a dilettante. But with the outbreak of war he directed—with the collaboration of Harry Watt and Pat Jackson— a modest short film titled *First Days* (1939) that somehow caught the spirit of the moment. Its style was precise, calm, rich in resonance. He developed the style further in *London Can Take It* (1940) —again with Harry Watt—and in *Listen to Britain* (1942), which earned Jennings a world-wide reputation. With *Fires Were Started* (1943), generally considered his masterpiece, he became virtually a wartime poet-laureate of the British screen. His later films included *The Silent Village* (1943), *The 80 Days* (1944), *A Diary for Timothy* (1945).

Humphrey Jennings, at left.

National Film Archive

In many ways, the Jennings style was at odds with connotations of "war film," and this was a reason for his impact. The war provided him with a melodramatic backdrop. *The First Days* shows us at once a world full of threat. As people gather round radios to listen to the announcement of Britain's declaration of war, the city around them is undergoing grotesque changes. Monstrous barrage balloons hang overhead. Millions of sandbags are being piled against buildings. Tanks sit in the shadows of trees. Gunners are on the alert. There are searchlights and sirens. In the National Gallery we see room after room hung with empty frames—the art treasures have been removed to safety. The historic Thames, winding its way through the city, is now seen as a threat. "The gleaming river may betray London yet," says the commentary.

It is against this background that Jennings performs his specialty: the vignette of human behavior under extraordinary stress. The films are crowded with small, unspectacular moments: humorous, touching, curious. In the midst of the surrealist madness of war, they form a tapestry of men and women behaving in a human way, and somehow confirming our faith in humanity. They are carrying on. Jennings was credited with catching the mood of the British in crisis, but he may have done more: perhaps he helped set a pattern for crisis behavior.

The Jennings war films never explain, exhort, harangue. They *observe*. Some critics, admiring them, wondered if this was enough. Among these was John Grierson, a man with faith in explanations—who, in Canada, continued to foster work in a different vein, usually vigorously articulate. But the response of the British people to the work of Jennings left no doubt. Seeing themselves in his film tapestry, they discovered they were quite wonderful people after all.

The moments are diverse, and almost always brief. There are incongruities—never pushed to extremes. Emerging from shelters after a night of sirens and crashing bombs, Londoners briefly survey the wreckage, as though checking the weather outlook, then set off to work with their umbrellas. A woman enters a shop via its smashed front window. A mother remarks how quiet it is since the children were evacuated. Though all is askew, familiar things are seen and heard: snatches of popular song, radio broadcasts, street signs, well-known buildings. They represent a stream that cannot be stopped or diverted.

A remarkable aspect of the Jennings films is the absence of hate-the-enemy incitements—which did crop up in British newsreels. In *Fires Were Started* we see members of the Auxiliary Fire Service—a group not of heroic demeanor—at work during the air blitz, coping with an incredible holocaust and surrounded by death and disaster. Yet—as the critic Jim Hillier points out—the blitz is treated almost as a natural disaster. The firemen show no interest in "the enemy" as such, nor does Jennings. He was, in this sense, uncompromising. He seemed to be saying that time was short for humanity; that being human could not be postponed until some postwar era.

This spirit is carried out in the musical selections that permeate the films. The sound track of *Listen to Britain* gives us an anthology of the sounds of Britain at war—juxtaposed with characteristic Jennings vignettes. The sounds include the music of Beethoven, Brahms, Mozart. We see the pianist Myra Hess playing Mozart in lunchtime concerts for war workers in the midst of the ruined city. Britain is preserving culture—including German culture—from disaster.

The films seem simple, but the editing weaves complex patterns.

The music played by Myra Hess is carried on over scenes of ordinary people in various parts of the city, and touches them and their activities lightly with an aura of nobility. Sound effects established in one setting are constantly carried over into others, creating thought-provoking resonances and associations. Jennings was an avid sound-track experimenter. He used narration sparsely. He used dialogue—usually in brief snatches, improvised on the spot—more often than most contemporary documentarists.

Listen to Britain and *Fires Were Started* are among the few war films that can be seen decades later without embarrassment. In these, nothing of humanity has been sacrificed for assumed strategic needs. They are films of affirmation. In his final war film, *A Diary for Timothy* (1945), a disturbing note enters. It relies on narration—written by E. M. Forster—more heavily than do most Jennings films. The narration takes the form of a "diary" written for a baby born late in the war, when victory seems assured. It is to let him know of the fearful Armageddon that has set the stage for the world he will inherit, and to pose questions he must ultimately answer, as to what to do with that world. A dissolve symbolically shows the baby emerging from the flames of war. In spite of lifting rhetoric, the film has a sense of foreboding. It is as though Jennings has been certain all along that Britain would see its way through the war, but has deep fears about the peace.

Jennings continued film-making in the postwar years, but never with his wartime success. It is as though his gentle vignettes needed the violent backdrop. None of his postwar films added to his reputation. In 1950, while setting up a shot on a cliff in Greece, he lost his footing and fell to his death.

He has been called by director Lindsay Anderson "the one real poet" of British cinema. It is curious that Jennings, so unwarlike, should have found his voice in the most ferocious of wars.

His works were defensive. In one way or another, all of them said that England could "take it"—the keynote of the early years of war, but less appropriate later. It was a relief to many Britons when Harry Watt emerged with *Target for Tonight* (1941), filmed on a bombing mission over Germany. Marking a shift to the offensive, it initiated the films of victorious action that took the spotlight in the later years of war. Of special brilliance among these was *Desert Victory* (1943), directed by Roy Boulting—a lucid and breath-taking exposition of the

Desert Victory, 1943.

National Film Archive

North African campaign that chased Rommel's Afrika Korps 1300 miles from El Alamein to Tripoli. The film crew suffered losses—killed, wounded, and captured. But it is said that a film unit actually took Tobruk, arriving before the troops. The *Desert Victory* success paved the way for Boulting's similarly impressive *Tunisian Victory* (1944)—made with United States collaboration—and *Burma Victory* (1945). Each of these had elements of the Jennings spirit: emphasis on small human moments within the vortex of war. Finally came *The True Glory* (1945), a climactic British-American war report directed by Carol Reed and Garson Kanin, with voice-over narration by General Eisenhower and numerous anonymous soldiers.

Like the Germans, the British occasionally attacked with irony. One of the most satisfying moments of the war was provided by Alberto Cavalcanti in the opening of *Yellow Caesar* (1940), a compilation of Mussolini footage. We first see a street organ-grinder; then, as his music continues, there is a dissolve from his rotating hand to the rotating hand of Mussolini, emphasizing his oratory with circular flourishes. It took genius to note, in the Mussolini footage, the possibility of such a dissolve, and the mordant effect of hurdy-gurdy music

Alberto Cavalcanti, at right.

National Film Archive

as Mussolini leitmotif. Another moment beloved by audiences was provided by an unidentified film editor in *Swinging the Lambeth Walk* (1940). Again, a simple trick is the basis: German military marchers are recut, with backward and forward motion, to a popular English tune; Hitler himself is made to jig back and forth. The reduction of the grandiose to the absurd by this simple device held fascination for years.

In late stages of the war, film played a part in British communication with underground groups on the continent. Cavalcanti made the film *Three Songs of Resistance* (*Trois Chansons de Resistance,* 1943) specifically to be parachuted to partisans. Some footage reached England from underground groups. The Danish underground operated a camera truck in Copenhagen throughout the war, with a Nazi-uniformed driver at the wheel, documenting Nazi activities and its own occasional acts of sabotage. Some footage of this sort came to England via Sweden, and was used in English newsreels and documentaries.

The Danish underground made daring use of films—those from England and its own. It made an occasional commando-type raid on

The Danish underground at work—in footage shot by the underground. The footage reached England during the war, and was used in the postwar Danish feature *Your Freedom Is at Stake* (*Det Gaelder Din Frihed,* 1946), compiled by Theodor Christensen.

a theater, forcing the projectionist to show underground films. Guarding the entrances, the commandos told the audience to sit and enjoy. Afterwards they took the films and vanished. It was under such circumstances that Danes saw *Swinging the Lambeth Walk.* The extraordinary risks were apparently felt justified by a moment of savage anti-Hitler ridicule.[4]

When Hitler, chafing over the stalemate with Britain, wheeled his main attack eastward—Russian oil and wheat were among the incentives—it became the turn of the Soviet Union to jolt audiences with its war films. It was soon able to offer the world a closer look at war than other nations could give, for its war experience was to be unique.

Beginning with retreat, the Russians yielded vast areas to the Nazi advance, falling back to the very rim of Moscow—and Leningrad, and Stalingrad—but leaving pockets of partisans, including cameramen. In the rubble of frozen cities the defenders made agonizing stands, then counterattacked. As units advanced, retaking villages, Soviet cameramen began to show something the world had not seen: captured Nazi soldiers, weary and disheveled, trudging through Russian mud and snow. The cameras also began to show, in recaptured areas, atrocities at first scarcely credible. In Russia the war was shot in painful close-up.[5]

Fiction-film studios were evacuated eastward—to Alma-Ata and elsewhere—but newsreel and documentary activities retained a Moscow base. In darkness and cold, within the sound of artillery and bomb explosions, laboratories processed incoming film. It came from everywhere, by all conceivable routes. Sometimes it arrived—astonishingly—from cameramen who had seemingly vanished into oblivion. Moscow often wondered how they had obtained film.

In charge of assembling the combat newsreels—the sort of job Vertov had held during revolutionary struggles, but on a hugely expanded scale—was Roman Gregoriev. He had begun film work in the Ukraine studios, to which Dziga Vertov and Mikhail Kaufman had been sent in the 1930's. Gregoriev, writer and editor, became a Vertov admirer and documentary devotee. Called to Moscow as newsreel editor, he was on the job in 1936–37 as Roman Karmen's Spanish war footage came in—and later, his Yenan footage. By the time the Nazi–Soviet clash moved into high gear, footage of some 400 cameramen was converging on Moscow editing tables. As elsewhere, the footage was turned into newsreels and more structured documentaries.

Soviet cinema, in decline during the 1930's, began a renascence during the war, with documentary leading the way. Its hold over audiences, in a land where virtually all families lost members in combat, was incalculable; documentaries and newsreels often seemed the only link with distant loved ones. For many years after the war, on May 3 of each year, a woman in Tashkent laid flowers at the screen of her local cinema. It was where she had had her last glimpse of a son.

In stations of the Moscow Metro—used, like the London underground, as air raid shelters—film projectors were set up. In cinemas, documentaries began to outdraw fiction films.

Individual battles and campaigns became the subject of feature documentaries—many of them war-film classics. The first of these were directed by documentary veterans. Leonid Varlamov (1907–62), who had begun documentary work as an assistant cutter in 1929, teamed with the *Kino-Pravda* veteran Ilya Kopalin on the triumphant *Defeat of the German Armies near Moscow* (*Razgrom Nemetzkikh voisk pod Moskvoi*, 1942). It became *Moscow Strikes Back* in an American version, winner of a 1943 Academy Award. Varlamov then directed a film that caused global astonishment—*Stalingrad* (1943), documenting one of the great turning points of World War II and including the surrender of Field Marshall Friedrich von Paulus and vast, bedraggled columns of Nazi troops.

Roman Karmen was among numerous cameramen whose footage appears in the Moscow and Stalingrad films, and he also directed a film that matched them in power and drama—*Leningrad at War* (*Leningrad v Borbe*, 1942). Its survival story involved new, strange sights: a midwinter lifeline of supply vehicles threading across frozen Lake Ladoga in the dead of night, continuing through spring thaws as trucks sloshed over perilously thinning layers of ice; meanwhile the melting of the ice in the fuelless city, and a chance to bury thawing corpses in the finally thawing ground. The imagination of fiction could not match the scenario.

Leading fiction directors began to turn to documentary—Alexander Dovzhenko with *The Fight for Our Soviet Ukraine* (*Bitva za Nashu Sovietskoyu Ukrainu*, 1943) and *Victory in the Ukraine* (*Pobeda na Provoberezhnoi Ukraine*, 1945); Sergei Yutkevitch with *Liberated France* (*Osvobozhdjennaja Franzija*, 1944), composed of foreign footage including captured German material; and Yuli Raizman with the climactic *Berlin* (1945), showing capture of the city in street-to-

Surrender of Fieldmarshall Von Paulus—from *Stalingrad*, 1943.

Karmen collection

Staatliches Filmarchiv der DDR

Victory in the Ukraine, 1945—directed by Dovzhenko.

street, house-to-house combat. Again, unthinkable vistas: amid the rubble, as tanks and troops push on, we see a German gentleman cutting meat from a horse killed in battle.

The director Mikhail Slutsky supervised an unusual project: *Day of War* (*Den Voiny,* 1942)—for which all footage was shot on one day—June 13, 1942—by over 200 cameramen at "filming points" throughout the Soviet Union. The project was modeled on a prewar film, *Day in a New World* (*Den Novovo Mira,* 1940), which is said to have originated as a suggestion by Gorky. *Day of War,* in shortened form, became a *March of Time* issue titled *One Day in the War.*

The film coverage of the war was the stuff of legends. More than 100 Soviet cameramen died in action; their ranks were readily and eagerly filled. The state film academy—founded in 1919 in the midst of revolution—added combat photography to its curriculum; diplomas were earned in part through front-line action. Combat cameramen won many awards. During an air battle a cameraman left his camera, took a gun position and shot down a German pursuit plane. He won an award for valor, and a reprimand from his studio.

The accumulated war footage of one cameraman, Vladimir Sushinsky, is shown in the film *Cameraman at the Front* (*Frontovoj Kinooperator,* 1946), compiled by Maria Slavinskaya and depicting the cameraman's own death. Film was moving through his camera as he was shot, and we see the footage blur into a spiral as he falls. Another cameraman saw him fall, filmed his final moments—and also died in action.

Wartime film activity sowed seeds of postwar relationships. Polish and other national detachments fighting with the Russian advance had their own documentary units, Soviet-equipped. Film equipment and supplies were dropped to Yugoslav partisans. Roman Gregoriev, asking for a field assignment away from executive duties, covered the link-up with Bulgarian partisans and the expulsion of the Nazis from Bulgaria—in *Entrance of the Red Army into Bulgaria* (*Vstuplenije Krasnoj Armii w Bulgariju,* 1944).

Soviet war films were credited with strong impact in the United States. American opinion of the Soviet Union had been at low ebb after the Hitler-Stalin nonaggression pact of 1939; many felt that the pact had irrevocably discredited the Stalin regime and the entire communist cause. When Hitler later attacked Russia, early collapse of the

Soviet Union was widely predicted—often with satisfaction. The heroic stands at Moscow, Stalingrad, Leningrad—all vividly documented in film—brought a change. Division of sentiment remained, but anti-Soviet expressions tended to become muted. Admiration for the Soviet war effort was widely voiced. And its films elicited ecstatic admiration from critics and Hollywood executives. After Pearl Harbor, Soviet war films became a major source of material for war films of the American government.

The Japanese attack on Pearl Harbor, followed by the German declaration of war on the United States, made it America's turn to plunge into bugle-call films. Its need was crucial and had special aspects, producing a film strategy different from those of other belligerents. As exemplified by the celebrated *Why We Fight* films, America's early war films were the most eclectic, relying heavily on combat footage of other nations—friend and foe—as well as on diverse other sources. They were also marked by an unusual emphasis on history.[6]

There were reasons for all this. Isolationism had deep roots and remained strong. Reluctance to spill blood "to save the British Empire" or "to save communism" was great. Disillusionment over the results of World War I and American participation in it remained a factor. And there was little feeling of threat to the homeland—in spite of heavily promoted air raid drills. The devastation inflicted by the Japanese at Pearl Harbor did stir war fever, but it lacked historic context, and was inclined to be racist. It did not relate itself readily to the European war. On the whole, the U.S. War Department found draftees confused and divided about the war, and massively ignorant about its background.

A few weeks after Pearl Harbor, Hollywood director Frank Capra —he had suddenly become *Major* Capra and was in spotless new uniform—found himself seated opposite General George C. Marshall, Chief of Staff—gray, sober, admired. The place was a new building, the Pentagon. The dialogue was later recounted by Capra in his memoir, *The Name Above the Title*.

"Mr. Capra—allow me to call you that for a moment—you have an opportunity to contribute enormously to your country and the cause of freedom. Are you aware of that, sir?"

Capra, usually brash, found himself acting more like the shy, fumbling heroes of his *Mr. Deeds Goes to Town* (with Gary Cooper) and

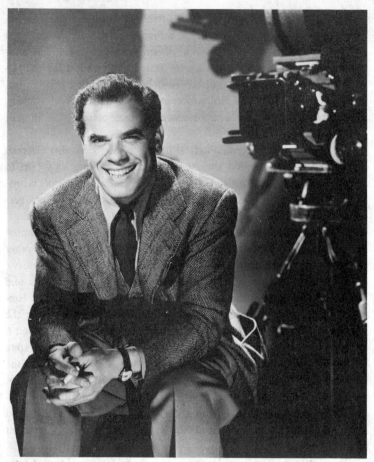

Frank Capra.

Museum of Modern Art

Mr. Smith Goes to Washington (with James Stewart). He said: "Well, General Marshall, I—I mean if you're asking me does it scare the heck out of me, I'll have to say, yessir. It does!"

The General explained that in the American army, civilians would soon outnumber professional soldiers by fifty to one. Germans and Japanese were sure, the general said, that these American boys would be too soft for modern war; but Marshall felt they would fight like tigers—*if* told clearly why they were in uniform. "Now Capra, I want to nail down with you a plan to make a series of documented, factual-information films—the first in our history—that will explain to our boys in the Army *why* we are fighting, and the *principles* for which we are fighting."

"General Marshall, it's only fair to tell you that I have never before made a single documentary film. In fact, I've never even been near anyone that's made one."

"Capra, I have never been Chief of Staff before. Thousands of young Americans have never had their legs shot off before. Boys are commanding ships today who a year ago had never seen the ocean before."

"I'm sorry, sir. I'll make the best darn documentary films ever made."

Capra felt he should at once learn something about documentaries, and he asked the War Department to show him Leni Riefenstahl's *Triumph of the Will*—which he discovered to be "blood-chilling." He had to have special "security clearance" before being allowed to see it, and this seemed preposterous to him. The more he contemplated his own reaction to the film, the more he felt it was a key to his problem. If American soldiers could see *that,* they would surely know why they were fighting. When he discovered that the Alien Property Custodian had hundreds of wartime newsreels and documentaries from Germany, Italy, Japan, he arranged—it took adroit jurisdictional maneuvering—to have them transferred to his control. Then he felt he must also get material from America's war allies, so he got in touch with the Soviet embassy. Here his campaign took a sudden detour.

At the War Department's Office of Internal Security—to which he was abruptly summoned—he found himself confronted by a bespectacled colonel. A "faceless" male stenotypist took notes. The colonel informed Capra that he was under arrest for violation of the Articles of War and would be held incommunicado, pending an inquiry. The colonel then produced a photo, which Capra recognized as a picture of himself, with his hands in his pockets, standing in front of the Soviet embassy.

Capra said, "Hey, that's me, Colonel, standing in front of the Soviet embassy. By golly . . . !"

The "admission" was noted. "By whose authorization did you consort with representatives of a foreign power?"

It was a perfect Capra scene. Mentioning that he was making films under direct orders from General Marshall, he said: "And damn it all, Colonel, if you insist on keeping me from carrying out the orders of the Chief of Staff, I demand a certified transcript of this nonsensical interrogation." He said he knew a columnist—Drew Pearson—who would probably print it verbatim.

Capra was permitted to walk away—and he got his Soviet and other newsreels. Out of his labors emerged the seven films of the *Why We Fight* series: *Prelude to War* (1942), *The Nazis Strike* (1942), *Divide and Conquer* (1943), *The Battle of Britain* (1943), *The Battle of Russia* (1943), *The Battle of China* (1944), and *War Comes to America* (1945). The unit he organized also launched a newsreel for troops, *Army-Navy Screen Magazine,* and made several additional films, including *The Negro Soldier* (1944) and films on the themes "know your enemy" and "know your ally." It was also the Capra unit that cooperated on the British–American production *Tunisian Victory.*

The *Why We Fight* films became a required part of military training. Some were shown to civilians. Translated into other languages, most were shown abroad. In terms of their basic purpose, the films achieved dramatic successes. Opinion studies among American draftees showed a sharp reduction of anti-British sentiment after their viewing of *The Battle of Britain;* weeks later, the changed opinion seemed to hold. Since most draftees at the time were headed for Britain, the change was considered a valuable accomplishment.

In form, the films were emotionalized history lessons—word-dominated, like many war films. The illustrative footage was largely culled from existing material, from a great variety of sources. A few sequences were staged for the films. Animated maps, made at the Disney studios under the supervision of novelist Eric Knight—who also participated in the writing of the scripts—contributed powerful moments. For the spread of aggression, black ink oozed menacingly

". . . smack up against a rock called Britain." Animated map by Disney studios
for *Divide and Conquer*, 1943.

National Archives

across maps. Maps were used to dramatize such lines as: "World
conquest was impossible, without running smack up against the rock
called Britain." While hearing these words of commentary—from *Divide and Conquer*—we see a black, solid-looking arrow punching out
from the black area under Nazi control, and then crumpling like an
accordion. An animated sequence showing one hemisphere in darkness, the other in bright sunlight, was used to depict the war as a
struggle between a "slave world" and a "free world."

The style of commentary was muscular and down-to-earth. While
the screen showed Hitler, Mussolini, Hirohito as "slave world" leaders, the narrator said: "Take a good look at this trio. Remember
their faces. . . . If you ever meet them, don't hesitate. . . ." (*Prelude to War*). The style favored aphorisms: "For free men are like
rubber balls. The harder they fall, the higher they bounce. . . ." (*Divide and Conquer*).

Most of the work of assembling the films was done at abandoned
Twentieth Century-Fox buildings on Western Avenue in Hollywood,
which became Capra headquarters—and a bustling, hard-driving film-

production factory—after his initial Pentagon struggles. Leading Hollywood artists—Carl Foreman, Walter Huston, Anatole Litvak, Alfred Newman, Lloyd Nolan, Leonard Spigelgass, Dimitri Tiomkin, Tony Veiller, and many others—came here for anomyous work as editors, writers, composers, conductors, narrators, directors. No personal credits appeared on the *Why We Fight* films.

Documentarists Robert Flaherty and Joris Ivens were for a time brought into the work of the Capra unit, but without notable result. Neither could fit himself into the mass-production atmosphere.

The unit examined and catalogued huge quantities of footage. Selected fragments came from newsreels of practically all nations, from documentaries of Hippler, Ivens, Jennings, Riefenstahl, Varlamov, Watt, and others—and from fiction films. The *Why We Fight* films were attempting a vast panorama: a short history of modern times, with passages on traditions of various countries. Where the commentary could not be supported by actuality footage, the editors looked to fiction. Since most were fiction-film practitioners, this probably seemed a matter of course.

The result was a strange amalgam. *Divide and Conquer* showed a very real combat-footage war plus bits of European history from Twentieth Century-Fox's *Viking Trails,* Warner's *Escape from Crime,* Paramount's *The Avengers,* Artkino's *The Girl from Leningrad,* and Columbia Pictures' *The Commandos Strike.* In *The Battle of China* the actuality war had a history rooted in moments from Goldwyn's *Marco Polo,* David Selznick's *Ku Kan,* and Metro-Goldwyn-Mayer's *The Good Earth.* In *War Comes to America,* the very real war had a historic background depicted via moments from Griffith's *America,* Twentieth Century-Fox's *Drums Along the Mohawk* and *The Roaring Twenties,* Metro-Goldwyn-Mayer's *The Big Parade,* and Warner's *Confessions of a Nazi Spy.*[7]

The films were, like most war films, simplistic in interpretation. This was felt necessary. In depicting all allies in "free world" terms, many unpleasant problems were simply ignored. This helps account for the immense popularity of the films among our allies: *The Battle of Britain* was shown widely in Britain, on Churchill's orders; *The Battle of Russia* was shown widely in Russia, on Stalin's orders. America's own problems were similarly swept under the rug. In writing glowingly of "the idea of freedom . . . the idea that made us the people we are" (*War Comes to America*), the scriptwriters were aware they were addressing a racially segregated army, and the fact disturbed them. But they hoped the stress on proclaimed ideals would influence the actuality. This was the essence of wartime strategy, and the use of fiction excerpts probably dovetailed with it. Myth became, for the moment, history. Something of the sunny spirit of Mr. Deeds and Mr. Smith shone through the *Why We Fight* films.

Not all films of the Capra unit were well received. *The Battle of China,* depicting China as resolutely unified under Chiang Kai-shek, seemed so dubious that it was soon withdrawn. *Know Your Enemy: Japan*—on which Joris Ivens worked with his editor, Helen van Dongen—was completed in 1944, but was not distributed. It was full of the generalizations promulgated early in the war, but not easily believed even then. Concerning the Japanese soldier, the commentary—written largely by Carl Foreman—warns American draftees:

NARRATOR: He and his brother soldiers are as much alike as photographic prints off the same negative. . . .

To the Japanese their Emperor is the most holy of holies, their visible god. . . .

If you are Japanese, you believe you have been commanded by heaven to conquer all other races and peoples. . . .

That's why mothers and wives accept the ashes of their dead soldiers without grief or sorrow . . . for the dead are warrior gods who live on beside them to be cherished and cared for, to be given food and drink, and a lighted cigarette to smoke. . . .

If you are Japanese, you believe these things implicitly.[8]

According to Ivens, the demise of *Know Your Enemy: Japan* was caused by its depiction of Emperor Hirohito as a war criminal. The *Why We Fight* films had also done so, but there had been a policy shift. It was now felt that the Emperor should be kept after the war, as an aid to maintenance of order.

The Negro Soldier was made to allay agitation over segregation in the armed forces. Neither segregation nor agitation against it are mentioned in the film, although segregation is shown, as an apparently benign and accepted institution. In form the film is a sermon by a black minister speaking from his pulpit in a crowded church—plus flashbacks. The flashbacks—using, like the *Why We Fight* films, a mixture of actuality footage, fiction footage, and staged scenes—deal with the war, the Negro's participation in it, his heroism in previous wars, and his contributions to American life. We also follow a black soldier through his military experience. The film was widely praised for dignity and sincerity, but seemed unable to extricate itself from stereotypes. Ultimately condescending, unrelenting in religiosity, it ends with black soldiers marching off to war to the tune of "Joshua fought the battle of Jericho."

One significant aspect of the Capra unit—and of the *Why We Fight* films—received little comment at the time. For the first time in history, the army was undertaking the political education of millions of Americans—who were, for the time being, a captive audience. It was called a "morale" service, but the crystallization of attitudes on a wide range of issues—national and international—was very much a political matter. If this new role of the military stirred little opposition, it was partly because it was wartime, and because the highly respected General Marshall led the way. Civil libertarians who might have objected did not do so, perhaps because they were surprised and pleased by the films. The first film released, *Prelude to War,* took a liberal-socialist view of the Spanish war—pro-loyalist, anti-Franco. It denounced isolationism in a way that delighted liberals. *The Battle of Russia* was so friendly to the Soviet Union that it seemed to augur a new era of international amity. All this was surprising, and welcome to many. But the persuasive power so suddenly—for military reasons —mobilized behind a particular set of ideas could as suddenly be switched. Attitudes of the moment masked more shifty realities—as Capra's encounter with the Office of Internal Security, and Ivens's troubles over the Japanese Emperor, must have suggested.

In later months of the war the spotlight shifted, as elsewhere, to filmed reports of victorious campaigns. As in the Soviet Union, leading figures of the fiction-film world were drawn into this work: John Ford with *The Battle of Midway* (1944); William Wyler with *Memphis Belle* (1944). But the most impressive recruit was John Huston, who directed three war documentaries. The first, *Report from the Aleutians* (1942), was routine; the others were unique.

The Battle of San Pietro was made in 1944 to explain "why we hadn't swept over Italy" as rapidly as had been expected. In carrying out the assignment, Huston conveyed unforgettably the foot soldier's experience of battle and awareness of his expendability, in a slaughter of uncertain value. After the fighting we see the dead put into sacks; in his original version, Huston used the voices of the dead men, as recorded before battle, over shots of their dead bodies—an extraordinarily poignant use of the sound track. The military hierarchy was horrified. Cuts were ordered, and even then release of the film was delayed until the war was almost over. Huston later recounted dialogue at a Pentagon screening. One general said: "This picture is pacifistic. It's against war. Against *the* war. Against war." Huston replied, "Well, sir, whenever I make a picture that's *for* war—why, I hope you take me out and shoot me." Yet Huston insisted his main purpose was not to condemn war but to express his deep feeling for the men.[9]

This motivation carried over into *Let There Be Light,* shot in 1945. The army wanted a film to demonstrate to industry that "nervous and emotional casualties were not lunatics." The aim was to facilitate their employment. For this purpose, Huston filmed the process of rehabilitation at an army hospital, using concealed cameras to cover individual and group therapy. The viewer becomes witness of moving triumphs, as when a man who has lost the power of speech finds he can talk again. In astonishment he says, "Why, I can talk, I can talk! Listen! I can talk! Oh God, listen, I can talk. Oh, there's nothing wrong. Oh God, listen!" Few more moving climaxes have been filmed.

John Huston. United Artists

Huston looked back on this project as "the most hopeful and optimistic and even joyous thing I ever had a hand in. I felt as though I were going to church every day out in that hospital." All patients portrayed in the film approved its release. But the army—with various explanations—banned it except for showings to psychiatrists. One explanation was that the film was not the sort of film that had been intended; that Huston had "pulled a fast one." Another was that the War Department wished to avoid raising false hopes for incurable cases. But perhaps Huston had again brought the viewer too close to war and its human toll.[10]

Although the most celebrated American war films were made for the armed forces, impressive work was also done in the film division of the OWI (Office of War Information) Overseas Branch. Many of its films—directed to audiences abroad—were likewise war-related, but usually with home-front emphasis. *The Cummington Story* (1945), directed by Helen Grayson, recorded touchingly the sometimes painful integration of a group of war refugees into a Connecticut town. *Toscanini: Hymn of the Nations* (1945) portrayed the great conductor on and off the podium, with stress on his anti-fascist activities. It was made in celebration of the liberation of Italy, and was directed by Alexander Hammid, a refugee from Czechoslovakia —where as Alexander Hackenschmied he had been a pioneer documentarist. It was produced, like many OWI films, by Irving Lerner. Unlike the army films, the OWI films were dominated by veteran documentarists, largely from the New York film world.

The war years, even more than other periods of documentary history, produced global migrations of film makers. The mobile armies took and drove them everywhere, with lasting effects on the film map. Film production had clustered in major centers; the war irrevocably dispersed it. This was significant for Asia, where crisscrossing armies planted film production in countless new areas. The Japanese assaults scattered China's Shanghai film enterprises in various directions: some moved south to Hong Kong and beyond, to Singapore; some followed the Chiang Kai-shek government when it moved inland to Chungking; some film makers and equipment also found their way to the northwest, to Yenan, enabling the Chinese Red Army to begin its own documentary record of the war. Jay Leyda mentions *Yenan and the Eighth Route Army* (*Yenan ho Ba Lu Chun,* 1939) as its first formal film.[11]

Dr. Norman Bethune, with the Eighth Route Army, China. After his work with the loyalists in Spain, Dr. Bethune joined the Mao Tse-tung forces in 1938, and died in their service. Footage of his final days, shot by Eighth Route Army cameramen, was later made available to the National Film Board of Canada for its biographical film *Bethune,* 1964.

National Film Board of Canada

Japanese forces were not only goads; they served also as documentary missionaries. In Japan as elsewhere, documentary and newsreel had won new status as cohesive forces in a widely dispersed war. Recognition of a soldier-son in Nippon Eiga Sha newsreels was a momentous experience. The theater customarily presented the family with a still from the newsreel. Japanese film makers were producing their own stirring reports of victories in the field, such as *Malayan War Record* (*Marei Senki,* 1942); *Divine Soldiers of the Sky* (*Sora no Shimpei,* 1942), about parachute troops; and *Sunk Instantly* (*Gochin,* 1943), shot largely from a prowling submarine. Meanwhile the Japanese in almost all areas coming under their control—Korea, Manchuria, the Philippines, Indochina, Indonesia, Malaysia, Burma—introduced their film equipment and knowhow, and involved the conquered in "co-productions." This was in furtherance of their proclaimed Asian "co-prosperity sphere." It was done—according to Anderson and Richie, in *The Japanese Film*—in the spirit of "an older brother to one slightly younger." The aim was Japanese hegemony, but the activity unquestionably stirred nationalistic feelings among the conquered, and a determination to express them through film.[12]

The war produced numerous migrations of individual film makers. Boris Kaufman, brother of Vertov, left France as a refugee and spent the war years partly in the United States, partly in Canada—where, at the National Film Board, he helped John Grierson build a strong documentary movement. In the war series *The World in Action* (1941–45), supervised by Stuart Legg, the NFB soon showed remarkable vigor and artistry.

Perhaps the most bizarre of individual migrations was that of Paul Zils, who began as an UFA employee and Goebbels favorite. As a teenager he had won a film prize, which resulted in an UFA apprenticeship at Neubabelsberg, starting in 1933. He rose rapidly; blond, handsome, with full Aryan credentials, he found favor with Goebbels. UFA frequently made him an intermediary to secure script approvals from Goebbels. (Goebbels once asked him: "Would it help your career if I approve this script?") The position of trust enabled Zils to attend a 1937 festival in Paris, where he defected. A donation from an English lady enabled him to board a freighter eastward for South Asian ports, hoping to reach the United States. Obsessed with Asia since reading Herman Hesse's *Siddharta,* he stopped off in In-

Boris Kaufman.

Photograph by Virginia Leirens

John Grierson, in early days of National Film Board of Canada.

National Film Board of Canada

dia, Singapore, and Indonesia—at that time known as the Netherlands
East Indies—earning money by taking odd jobs en route. He was
especially enamoured of Bali, and drafted plans for a feature-length
documentary about it. In Tokyo he got a tourist visa for the United
States and so reached Hollywood. With other German refugees he
taught at Max Reinhardt's School of the Theater on Sunset Boulevard, while finding film employment difficult. But his Bali proposal
caught fire at Paramount, which decided to finance it. With a budget
he headed back to Bali and was hard at work on the film when, on
May 10, 1940, he was arrested. Germany had invaded Holland, so
3500 German nationals in Indonesia were imprisoned in a Sumatra
jungle stockade. The following year brought a sudden change. The
Japanese, having devastated Pearl Harbor, were moving rapidly on
Indonesia. Many of the German prisoners were experts on Indonesia; to keep them out of Japanese hands, it was decided to move them
to India on three transports, one of which was torpedoed and went
down. The survivors, along with German prisoners and internees
from Ceylon and elsewhere, were herded to a large prison camp in
Bihar. Some were anti-Nazi, some pro-Nazi, some just "good Germans." Zils found there were forty musicians in the camp; also a conductor, composers, writers. He began to organize shows—a major
production each month. All instruments were made by prisoners. A
ballet was organized, scenery built. Sometimes as many as 150 people
were working on a production. They were rigid about schedules, première dates, and curtain time. Month after month the guards
watched in astonishment as the productions grew more ambitious.
The British were so impressed that they approached Zils with an
offer. They would release him if he would go to work for Information
Films of India—a newsreel and documentary unit organized by the
British to win Indian cooperation in the war effort, against the opposition of the Indian National Congress. In 1945 Zils went to work as
a British propagandist. When war ended the unit closed, but he decided to stay in India. Ardently pro-independence, he came to play a
role in documentary films of independent India—and later, even more
prominently, of Ceylon.[13]

A still more dramatic odyssey was made by the inveterate traveler,
Joris Ivens. Shortly after his service with Capra, he was invited by
the Netherlands government to become Film Commissioner for Indonesia. A contract defining his duties, and government press re-

Joris Ivens.

Photograph by Virginia Leirens

leases announcing the appointment, featured dedicated rhetoric. A government release said the Dutch were ready to "shed their blood" for the liberation of the East Indies, not for a return to prewar status. The contract spoke of "the great western ideal of freedom and democracy (*het grote westelijke ideaal van vrijheid en democratie*)." As Film Commissioner, Ivens would begin by documenting the liberation. He received a substantial budget to buy equipment in the United States. Well provided, he headed for Australia, where a liberation armada of Dutch and English ships was gathering. Awaiting the day, Ivens recruited Australian film personnel. Camerawoman Marion Michelle joined him from the United States, where she had done her first film work during Depression days in the Chicago Film and Photo League.[14]

In August 1945, as the ships stood ready, word came that an independent Indonesia had been proclaimed in Indonesia itself, under Achmed Sukarno. The news seemed to bring consternation to the "liberation" fleet. A first group of ships sailed, apparently not to assist the new Indonesia but to nip the development. The Dutch spoke of Sukarno as a Japanese agent and of his government as a Japanese puppet regime. The fleet would bring "order." Plans were made to blockade the islands.

It had been assumed in all plans that Film Commissioner Ivens and his crew would go with the first ships to photograph the liberation. But they were not allowed aboard.

At this juncture Ivens held an indignant press conference. He said he had been engaged to film the liberation of the islands, but since the Netherlands government itself had made this impossible, he considered his contract void.

Events moved rapidly on the Australian waterfront. Javanese crew members walked off ships destined for the islands, and numerous Australian labor unions acted in support. A ship with largely Indian crew left port, but a speedboat went in pursuit for the unions; from its deck, by bullhorn, appeals were shouted to the Indian crew—and won the day. The Indians forced the return of the ship. "The ship that didn't sail" became the theme of *Indonesia Calling* (1946)—a film made by Ivens and his group in support of the new Indonesia. Its opening proclaims:

The Waterfront Unions of Australia
present
INDONESIA CALLING

The Ivens action was front-page news around the world. Netherlands newspapers called him a traitor. He was accused of making *Indonesia Calling* with Dutch government equipment, but denied it. Having handed in the equipment when resigning, he had made *Indonesia Calling* mainly with an old Kinemo—the camera he had used for *The Bridge* in 1928.

The film was partly a documentation of events shot on the run, partly a reconstruction of very recent events. The climactic pursuit of "the ship that didn't sail" could be reproduced photographically by having the speedboat pursue a transport—any appropriate transport. In the speedboat, a man stood up with a bullhorn and was seen to shout. The shouted bullhorn words were added during the editing process.

In spite of its air of feverish improvisation, *Indonesia Calling* had strong impact. Australia banned the film, then reversed itself, evidently in deference to the popularity of the Indonesian cause. In the Netherlands the film was taboo, and Ivens no longer welcome. Sailing ships carried two prints of *Indonesia Calling* through the blockade to the Indonesian islands; there they had many night showings for independence forces, who had to fight until late in 1946 against Dutch and British "liberation" troops.

The sequence of events, and the attention it received in the world press, suggests the status the documentary film had acquired during war years. Film makers had become accustomed to dwelling near the center of power. They looked forward to having similar importance in the postwar world. But first another war-related task awaited documentarists.

Prosecutor

Among film men of advancing armies, closing in on Germany and Japan, an activity receiving urgent attention was the documenting of war crimes. Almost all belligerent armies were involved.

As Yugoslav partisans overthrew the Nazi puppet regime in Croatia, their film makers documented its concentration-camp atrocities in the film *Jasenovac* (1945), the work of Gustav Gavrin and Kosta Hlavaty. Their own footage was supplemented by captured material, including documents and still photographs. *Jasenovac* became the first film approved for showing in postwar Yugoslavia, and the contents served as evidence in war-crimes trials.

The events were paralleled in Poland. The film unit of the Polish contingent moving with Soviet troops was headed by young Aleksander Ford and Jerzy Bossak. Both had been members of a left-wing cine-club called Start, which they had helped to form in the early 1930's. In Poland's pre-war film world they had been outsiders, angry young critics publishing manifestos and occasionally making films, but not welcomed by the commercial industry they assailed. As they returned, producing a newsreel for Polish troops—titled *Fighting Poland (Polska Walczaca)*—they became the nucleus of a postwar film industry. Their first major task faced them when they came on the Nazi extermination camp Majdanek. They had heard rumors of atrocities, but could scarcely believe what they found there. Ford and Bossak made the Polish film *Majdanek* (1944)—scenes of unspeakable grief as people found corpses of friends and relatives stacked like wood, and such relics of other lives as half a million pairs of shoes and mountains of human hair and teeth and eyeglasses. This footage, too, became evidence at war-crimes trials.[1]

The advancing American, Russian, British, and French troops had special evidence-gathering units. In the American forces these were OSS (Office of Strategic Services) teams, usually consisting of a cameraman, a German interpreter, and an information specialist. Film evidence came to them from many sources, often in fragments. A house that had been occupied by a Nazi officer yielded some 8mm reels—"home movies" that, it turned out, included footage of a 1941 episode in Stuttgart in which a dozen or more Jews were pulled from their homes, beaten, stripped, and dragged by their hair through the street—a pogrom witnessed without interference by bystanders. The sequence lasted a minute and a half. By reproducing each frame, the action was slowed to make a three-minute sequence. In this form it was used at the Nuremberg trials of Nazi leaders.[2]

Allied research teams were astonished at the care with which Germans had documented their crimes and preserved the record. Outside Munich a tank unit found a villa that had been used by Heinrich Himmler; a 35mm projector was threaded and ready to show a reel of medical experiments carried on in prison camps. In the home of an eastern front veteran, searchers found a sequence apparently filmed as a demonstration of resourcefulness. Troopers were shown leading a man and a boy, half starved, into a small blockhouse. The camera then showed the troopers arranging a hose from an automobile exhaust to a small aperture in the wall, and starting the motor.

In the film archives at Neubabelsberg, a half-flooded bunker yielded the Nazis' own documentation of their extermination of the Warsaw ghetto. Much of this material eventually appeared in the Polish film *Requiem for 500,000* (*Requiem dla 500,000,* 1963), by Jerzy Bossak and Waclaw Kazimierczak. Among the curious findings on various fronts were souvenir albums left by dead Nazis in which, along with the usual family snapshots and scenic wonders, were mementos of the Nazi reign of terror. Were they kept with nostalgia, or pride? In later years such material yielded such films as the Polish *Fleischer's Album* (*Album Fleischera,* 1962), by Janusz Majewski, and *The Every-day Life of Gestapo Officer Schmidt* (*Powszedni Dzien Gestapowca Schmidta,* 1963), by Jerzy Ziarnik.

Extensive war-crimes footage and many still photographs were presented in evidence at the Nuremberg trials. Such wide use of pho-

Jerzy Bossak.

Wytwórnia Filmów Dokumentalnych

The Every-day Life of Gestapo Officer Schmidt, 1963.

tographic evidence was apparently without precedent. The trials themselves were filmed in full, and the combined material became the basis for two historic—yet little-known—feature-length documentaries, one Russian, the other American. The Russian film, *Judgment of the Nations* (*Sud Naradov* in Russian, *Gericht der Völker* in German, 1946), was directed by Roman Karmen and edited by Yelizaveta Svilova, wife and long-time editor of Dziga Vertov. The American film, *Nuremberg* (*Nürnberg*, 1948) was initiated by Pare Lorentz, who supervised footage searches in American archives—mainly at Astoria, Long Island, where an old Paramount studio had become the Signal Corps Pictorial Center—but was completed in Germany by Stuart Schulberg, a member of one of the OSS evidence-gathering teams. The film was a production of the American military government. The Soviet Union's *Judgment of the Nations* was shown in theaters throughout Russian-occupied areas of Germany and in the Soviet Union, where it was reissued in 1962. America's *Nuremberg* had a two-year run in theaters in American-occupied areas of Germany, and was also shown in British areas, but was never released to American theaters—apparently in deference to pleas by Chancellor Konrad Adenauer of West Germany. The U. S. Department of Defense withdrew the film from all circulation in 1950.[3]

These two films, based on trials, were in themselves a kind of show-trial through which the German people were invited to contemplate a scarcely believable record of horror. Even without compulsion, theaters were filled for months.

Obsession with evidence to be unearthed from film archives lasted longer in eastern Europe than elsewhere—a not surprising consequence of the calamitous events it had witnessed. The interest persisted especially in East Germany, location of copious Nazi film archives. Seized by the Soviets, these archives were turned over to East German control in 1955, and became the basis for an unusual career —that of the film-making team Andrew and Annelie Thorndike. For years they combed through the massive accumulations of film—much of it still uncatalogued decades after the war. They came to epitomize the documentarist-as-prosecutor.[4]

Andrew Thorndike, of German-American descent, was born in Berlin in 1909. His father was a member of the Krupp board of directors, and Andrew began his film career making promotional films for industry at the UFA studios. But he reacted against his establishment background. Early in the war, charged with anti-Nazi activity, he was dispatched to the eastern front as a punitive assignment. He was captured and spent four years as a Soviet prisoner. Returning in 1948, he resumed documentary work at UFA, which had meanwhile become DEFA, the East German state film organization. While making a film about a new school, he became interested in the young teacher who had founded the school, and married her. They became a film team specializing in historic compilations—in the manner of Esfir Shub, but with a difference. Esfir Shub had exposed a defunct monarchy; the Thorndikes were concerned with the persistence in power of living Nazis—not in East Germany, but in West Germany.

In their first major compilation, *You and Many a Comrade* (*Du und Mancher Kamerad*, 1955), they recounted modern German history, warning that alliances of military and industrial leaders (including Krupp) had twice brought Germany to war and disaster. Such alliances, said the film, were no longer possible in East Germany; but the film warned that military-industrial groups representing the same interests were again moving into control in West Germany. It detailed the Nazi careers of various West German leaders.

The film, assembled with impressive skill, had enormous impact in East Germany, and probably helped consolidate the East German regime. It also had important film consequences. It persuaded the East German government of the importance of its film possessions and of their proper storage, preservation, and cataloguing. The facilities that were subsequently developed for this purpose—at Wilhelmshagen, near Berlin—soon became the envy of film archivists throughout the world. A steady procession of archivists and documentarists came to inspect the subterranean labyrinths, with their arrangements for rigid temperature and humidity control, and the intensive cataloguing efforts.

All this encouraged further archive films. The Thorndikes pursued their successful theme in two films—more were originally intended—titled *The Archives Testify*. . . . The films open with a traveling shot along cans of film in the DEFA vaults. The first target of their accusation, in the film *Holiday on Sylt* (*Urlaub auf Sylt*, 1957), was one Heinz Reinefarth, who after the war had settled in the West German town of Westerland, on Sylt Island in the North Sea, and become its mayor. The film shows him relaxing there in benign splendor. Then, through a mass of archive footage, stills, and clippings, the

Du und Mancher Kamerad, 1955.

Staatliches Filmarchiv der DDR

Andrew and Annelie Thorndike.

Thorndikes identify him as a brutal officer in charge of wartime executions in Warsaw. They use the technique of freezing a frame at this or that crucial point and superimposing an arrow, to pinpoint significant detail.

Their next film dossier, *Operation Teutonic Sword* (*Unternehmen Teutonenschwert,* 1958)—the second in the series *The Archives Testify* . . . —was aimed at Hans Speidel, a leading military official of NATO—the North Atlantic Treaty Organization. The film accuses him of a long, lurid career of Nazi secret-service activity involving assigned murders of "communists and Jews" in France and "devastation duties" in the Soviet Union. Again masses of archive footage, with frozen frames, relentless arrows, clippings, stills, and maps, are offered in evidence.

While the Thorndikes had made some use of reconstructed events in *You and Many a Comrade,* they foreswore such methods in their later work. Archive material had become their passion. Their concern was to document—not illustrate—their accusations.

In a similar spirit of indictment, the East German director Joachim Hellwig followed the Thorndike lead in *A Diary for Anne Frank* (*Ein Tagebuch für Anne Frank,* 1958). The film begins deceptively in fiction-movie fashion: a girl runs home excitedly to tell her mother she got the part, she will play Anne Frank! But the film switches abruptly to more grisly matter. Tracing the route of Anne Frank from Amsterdam to her extermination-camp death, the film poses the question: what happened to those who supervised her arrest, deportation, and death? It finds them—again via massive archive material—alive and in influential positions in West Germany.

These films were made at a time of considerable traffic between East and West Germany. A number of West German critics came to see the films, and their comments precipitated wide discussion in West Germany. The films reflected the bitter antagonism between the East and West German regimes, and made their contribution to the bitterness. They also put continued pressure on West Germany for action against war criminals.

In Japan agitation over war guilt was less persistent, for good reason. In Europe the horror of the extermination camps had provided the emotional center for prosecutions. In Japan all horrors were overshadowed by the war-ending horrors of Hiroshima and Nagasaki, where two small atomic bombs had incinerated a vast population and cast a shadow of genetic damage over generations. Even as war-crimes trials brought execution to leading Japanese militarists, the atomic holocaust haunted men's minds.

In Japan, war-guilt issues produced curious and dramatic reversals. While events had discredited and crushed the military, they had brought new dignity to men who had been early and avowed anti-militarists. In the film field this included men like Akira Iwasaki, a leader in the prewar Prokino group, and Fumio Kamei, who had angered the military with his film *Shanghai* and later gone to jail. Even before the American occupation force arrived on the scene, Iwasaki won new standing: he was commissioned by Nippon Eiga Sha, the government newsreel monopoly, to produce a documentary on the effects of the two atomic bombs. In spite of chaos and the breakdown of transportation, Iwasaki managed to have cameramen at work at Hiroshima and Nagasaki as the occupation arrived; this brought him into immediate contact with its headquarters staff.

Americans took control of the project; then, for fear of its impact, declared the footage *secret* and impounded it in Washington, where it remained for almost a quarter of a century. But occupation headquarters was clearly impressed with Iwasaki's anti-militarist credentials, and appointed him to a committee of twenty charged with the task of identifying rabid militarists in the Japanese film industry. Such a list was drawn up and the individuals suspended—most of them for short periods. Meanwhile Iwasaki also received a go-ahead from headquarters for a major project—a compilation film to be titled *The Tragedy of Japan (Nihon no Higeki)*. Iwasaki chose Fumio Kamei to direct the work.

It was to be a history of modern Japan and—like the East German *You and Many a Comrade*—an indictment of the forces that had led the nation to war and ruin. Responding to the "democratization" order of the American occupation, it was meant to help eradicate feudalism and militarism from Japanese society.

Unfortunately, segments of American headquarters worked at cross-purposes. Plans for *The Tragedy of Japan* were approved by CIE—the Civil Information and Education Section, which was largely staffed with academicians and writers, very serious about "democratization." They also liked the resulting film, which was completed in 1946 and won strong applause at preview showings. But all films, before their general release, needed a go-ahead from CCD—the Civil

Censorship Division, dominated by army career men, strongly conservative. They promptly banned *The Tragedy of Japan*. The film makers looked on the Emperor as a war criminal, whereas the CCD was intent on maintaining his sacrosanct status: this had become occupation policy. *The Tragedy of Japan* was declared by CCD to be "communistic." Amid vast changes—in Asia as in Europe—old patterns reasserted themselves.[5]

Documentarists specializing in war-crimes indictment films were not many, and the movement could not last. Too many new problems confronted film makers.

Yet the ghosts of World War II were not easily exorcised. Documentarists would return for decades to records of this war—more often, as time went on, in the spirit of historian, or elegist, than as prosecutor.

Of all documentaries born of war horror, the most admired was unquestionably *Night and Fog* (*Nuit et Bruillard*, 1955), directed by Alain Resnais. It was a searing indictment—but with a shift in aim. Resnais made brilliant use of a simple device: frequent shifts between black-and-white archive footage of the extermination camps, and sequences in warm color filmed in the verdant surroundings of a former camp. These alternations, bringing us again and again from postcard colors of a postwar tourist world to the black-and-white staring eyes, the barely stirring skeletons, the line-ups of the naked, and the ovens, give the film a greater impact than any other such film had achieved. The impact is intensified by a quietly reflective, powerful commentary written by Jean Cayrol. At the end of the film, in a color sequence, the camera moves along crematorium ruins, twisted wires, broken watchtowers, and blocks of cracked concrete.

NARRATOR: The crematorium is no longer in use. The devices of the Nazis are out of date. Nine million dead haunt this landscape. Who is on the lookout from this strange tower to warn us of the coming of new executioners? Are their faces really different from our own? Somewhere among us, there are lucky Kapos, reinstated officers, and unknown informers. There are those who refused to believe this, or believed it only from time to time. And there are those of us who sincerely look upon the ruins today, as if the old concentration camp monster were dead and buried beneath them. Those who pretend to take hope again as the image fades, as though there were a cure for the plague of these camps. Those of us who pretend to believe that all this happened only once, at a certain time and in a certain place, and those who refuse to see, who do not heed the cry to the end of time.[6]

Night and Fog, 1955.

There was peace—with many uncertainties. In a world heaped with ruins the documentarist saw challenges. But what role he would play in meeting them, he could not tell.

For a decade and a half he had been concerned with war: the threat of war, the war, the aftermath of war. Almost nothing else had seemed to matter.

During those years the documentary had seldom been subtle or profound, but it had had power, and had assumed central importance. It had often outdrawn the fiction film. The documentarist had moved among world leaders. He saw no reason why he should not continue to do so.

His audience had grown vastly—not only in theaters but in other outlets: army camps, clubs, schools, churches, libraries, offices, factories. For war purposes, hundreds of 16mm projectors had been spread around the globe. The 16mm film had grown up in war.

The documentarist felt he had achieved importance. But he also had a feeling that peace had left him dangling in mid-air. Armies had been his sponsors; who would take their place? For what objectives? On what terms? He peered ahead—in search of a role in a world he could not possibly know.

4

CLOUDED LENS
poco ritardo

N.Y., N.Y., 1958.

Museum of Modern Art

Poet

Several trends emerged as the smoke of battle cleared. One was toward documentary-like fiction. The widespread ruins of war helped set this trend in motion: they served as invitation to reconstruct the war experience and at the same time to mythologize it. Thus an environment of devastation gave birth to the Italian *Open City* (*Roma, Città Aperta,* 1945) by Roberto Rossellini, and Vittorio de Sica's *Shoeshine* (*Sciuscià,* 1946), based on a script by Cesare Zavattini—films that launched a "neorealist" movement. The trend was widely followed: in France with *Railway Battle* (*Bataille du Rail,* 1945), by René Clément; in Germany with a number of "rubble films" including *The Murderers Are Among Us* (*Die Mörder Sind Unter Uns,* 1946), by Wolfgang Staudte; and in the Swiss production *The Search* (1948), directed by Fred Zinnemann. All depended heavily on location-shooting. While they showed the influence of war documentaries, they were really a step back into the latitudes of fiction.[1]

That these were called "documentaries" probably reflected the wartime status won by documentaries. It also reflected the fact that leading documentarists, who were experiencing a shrinkage in documentary sponsorship, were participating in the trend. Thus the haunting film *The Quiet One* (1948), shot in various parts of Harlem and at the Wiltwyk School for disturbed children, was directed by Sidney Meyers, a Film and Photo League veteran who had edited many war documentaries for government agencies, but suddenly found himself unemployed. Written by James Agee, it was a group production made on a shoestring; Meyers himself appeared as a psychiatrist. Its fictional case study of a troubled black boy was so sensitively presented and so authentic in detail that the term "documentary" has clung to it. But in the postwar years the term was even applied to such films as the spy thriller *The House on 92nd Street* (1946), produced by *March of Time* veteran Louis de Rochemont. Using New York exteriors, it had somewhat the air of a *March of Time* reconstruction. *On the Waterfront* (1954), directed by Elia Kazan and shot in New York locations by Boris Kaufman, was also referred to as a "documentary."

Another trend was toward poetry; some documentarists became

Fred Zinnemann filming *The Search*—released 1948.

Praesens

makers of short film odes, contemplating with wonder the world around them—a not surprising reaction to years of slaughter.

The trend had actually begun during war, in neutral and occupied countries. Several factors had encouraged it. Sweden, surrounded by war, maintained a nervous neutrality; authorities scanned films for anything that might provoke—or be used to justify—intervention by belligerents. When a twenty-three-year-old youngster, Arne Sucksdorff, made his film debut with two short items which he called "hymns to the Swedish summer"—*August Rhapsody* (*Augustirapsodi,* 1940) and *This Land is Full of Life* (*Din Tillvaros Land,* 1941, with text by Swedish poet Harry Martinson)—they seemed the perfect product for a wartime neutral. The important Svensk Filmindustri became his backer and distributor. With a series of masterly short films—mostly of nature, wildlife, and man's relation to it—Sucksdorff became a major figure in Swedish cinema. He eventually expanded into feature-length work. After the war his films swept the globe.[2]

He had unique preparation for his career. As a boy he spent long, solitary periods in woodland exploration, and was regarded as a prodigy in taming animals—foxes, otters, and others. The family home bordered an area rich in wild animals, and they learned to have no fear of the boy who was always among them, feeding and befriending them. His parents encouraged him to create, at their villa, a small zoo—a home for his wild-life friends.

A childhood dedicated to such pursuits seemed, at first, to pose a vocational problem. He considered study of the natural sciences, but leaned toward the arts. He tried painting, and went to Berlin to study theater at the Reimannschule. But on a trip to Italy he took photographs that won prizes in a Stockholm exhibition, and this turned him toward photography, then cinematography. Soon he was back in his woods with a camera, and with the help of his forest friends developed wildlife dramas. Humans, especially children, appeared in a number of the films, but Sucksdorff seemed more at home with the animals.

His first film for Svensk Filmindustri, the enormously popular *A Summer's Tale* (*En Sommarsaga*, 1941), followed a fox on his adventures and depradations. It has moments of enchantment and, like most Sucksdorff films, of cruelty—depicted without comment or judgment. Sucksdorff's editing shows a rare rhythmic sense. The photography is rich in the texture of grass, leaves, ferns, and patterns of light playing on and through them. The extreme close-ups of animal eyes and fur are full of sensuous excitement.

Short films of similar style followed in rapid succession, notably *Wind From the West* (*Vinden från Väster*, 1942) *Reindeer Time* (*Sarvtid*, 1943), *Gull!* (*Trut!*, 1944), *Dawn* (*Gryning*, 1944), *Shadows on the Snow* (*Skuggor över Snön*, 1945), *A Divided World* (*En Kluven Värld*, 1948). Ironically, their remoteness from war did not always keep these films from ideological suspicion. The film *Gull!*, in which we watch ruthless plundering by an egg-stealing species of gull, was widely interpreted as a parable of Nazism. Sucksdorff denied such an intention, but did not protest the interpretation. A film that is not open to interpretation, he said, is a dead film.*

The postwar period brought digressions in Sucksdorff's work. In *People of the City* (*Människor i Stad*, 1947) he studied the rhythms of city life, but not with the passion he brought to woodland subjects.

---

* The Danish film *The Wheat is in Danger* (*Kornet er Fare*, 1944)—Nazi-approved, warning farmers of a troublesome weevil and urging preventive measures—likewise acquired a rumored anti-Nazi meaning, which in this case may have been intended. The weevils were animated and had strange voices.

Arne Sucksdorff, camera, and friend.

Sucksdorff collection

A trip to India resulted in the short films *Indian Village* (*Indisk By,* 1951) and *The Wind and the River* (*Vinden och Floden,* 1951)— films of impeccable craftsmanship and beauty, but lacking the exceptional insight of his wildlife films. In his first feature-length film, *The Great Adventure* (*Det Stora Äventyret,* 1953), he returned to his early themes and settings, and produced a masterpiece.

More than two years in the making, *The Great Adventure* focuses on a boy, an otter, a fox, and numerous other animals; it appears to be strongly autobiographical. It is narrated by an adult who looks back to the time when, at ten, he "woke up to the life all around me" in the forest. He awakes to the struggle for survival, with its cruelties; to the momentous flux of the seasons; and to sex. He witnesses —and we with him—various mating confrontations, including the clamorous mating of grouse—"like a coupling of prehistoric dragons." *The Great Adventure* reflects an idea also expressed in *A Divided World:* the world of nature and man's world are incompatible. Both men and animals kill, but animals do so for survival. Only men kill for other reasons and camouflage their reasons, always regarding themselves as instruments of morality and justice. Children are more attuned to the animal world. In *The Great Adventure* the boy aligns himself with the animal world, rescuing an otter his father has determined to kill. In the Sucksdorff films, children have virtues that are later stamped out by society.

The Great Adventure exemplifies methods used by Sucksdorff to achieve extraordinary scenes. Some of the animals we observe so intimately were wild animals, and some were tame animals from his collection, whom he took into the forest with him. They were free to roam or leave but generally stayed near him, enabling him to record their activity at leisure. Under these circumstances we see a remarkable romping sequence in which a fox teases an otter. Sucksdorff insisted that their actions were in no way foreign to their nature; foxes, he said, are inveterate teases.

Elsewhere in the film, we closely observe an owl sitting on a branch. He suddenly swoops down to the ground to seize and devour a dormouse, while the camera nimbly follows the action. It is the kind of shot for which others might have waited in hiding for days, without success. Sucksdorff did not have to wait. The owl—a wild one— was an old friend, whom he had often fed. The owl had no reason to move as Sucksdorff approached. Sucksdorff set up and adjusted his camera, then took from his pocket a dormouse he had brought from his collection. Tossing it to the foot of the tree, he knew precisely what action to expect and could follow it with his camera.

Because of such sequences, Sucksdorff was accused of a streak of sadism: cruelties shown in the film were often precipitated by him. But he defended the actions as natural: he had set the stage for them but had in no way controlled them. His method was not unlike that of Flaherty, who likewise—as in his walrus sequence in *Nanook of the North* and shark sequences in *Man of Aran*—had set the stage for conflict, then let it take its course. Sucksdorff saw cruelty as an essential ingredient in the world he was portraying. He loathed sentimental depictions of nature, such as those of his Swedish contemporary Gösta Roosling, whose work had a concurrent vogue.

Sucksdorff, like many other documentarists, took to world-wandering. Eventually settling in Brazil, he became deeply concerned with the threatened extinction of its forest-dwelling aborigines. For a time he directed a Brazilian film school. His work became increasingly fictional. But the poetic documentary he had launched in wartime had meanwhile found echoes in other nations—including Nazi-occupied lands, which had their own reasons for the trend.

Film makers remaining in occupied areas—like Henri Storck—could acquire raw film rations only by proposing projects satisfactory to allocation officials. The beauties of rural life, particularly farm life, were a favored topic. While diverting attention from war aggravations, it had additional values. Belgium needed increased farm produce to replace what was normally imported; there was therefore new interest in honoring the farmer. Thus when Storck proposed a series of films celebrating the passage of the seasons on a Belgian farm, to be titled *Peasant Symphony* (*Symphonie Paysanne* or *Boerensymfonie*, 1944), he got approval and raw film.[3]

In France a parallel project was launched during the war by Georges Rouquier. He had taken up film at an early age under inspiration of the work of Flaherty; his first film, *Vendanges* (1929), appeared when he was only twenty. But he discontinued film-making for financial reasons and became a printer. During the Nazi occupation he gave up printing and returned to the family farm—named Farrebique—where he had spent part of his childhood, and resumed highly personal film experiments. These culminated in the film *Farrebique* (1946), which, like the Storck film, follows farm life through

Farrebique, 1946.

International Film Bureau

the seasons, with minute observation of detail: movements of insects and lizards, the daily journey of shadows, the decay and growth
of living things. These are occasionally shown in speeded sequences
of time-lapse photography, which are like sudden lyrical cadenzas.

After the war, short films in a personal vein provided the starting
point for many young film makers. Such films were often conceived,
photographed, and edited by a single artist—a reaction against the
assembly-line projects of wartime. Instead of reasons of state, the individual sensibility became the point of departure. Economy was also
a crucial factor.

Bert Haanstra, born in 1916, son of the headmaster of a Dutch village school, had st ıdied photography before the war in hope of a
film career. But he had to wait till after the war—at the age of thirty—
to make his first film. Starting modestly with simple means, he at
once showed astonishing technical finesse and originality. To make
audiences see the familiar anew, he experimented with several devices.[4]

In *Mirror of Holland* (*Spiegel van Holland,* 1950) he began with
a familiar shot: the upside-down reflection of a building in a canal.
The image wobbles with the rippling of the water. Then Haanstra

Bert Haanstra

Photograph by Virginia Leirens

turns the frame upside down so that we see the building upright—but still with ripples. Now he proceeds to travel to many parts of Holland, showing many characteristic Dutch buildings in this same way—upright, but rippling with watery movements, sometimes gentle and sometimes agitated. Seldom has the familiar won such compelling attention.

In *Panta Rhei* (1951)—a Greek title suggesting that "everything flows"—he shows us the movement of clouds, speeded; then rushing water, slowed. As the one dissolves into the other, we sense a surprising identity between their rhythmic patterns. By similar use of slowed and speeded movements, Haanstra reveals a number of such identities. Leaves scurrying before an autumn wind suddenly become a flock of birds taking wing. The sparkling pattern of reflections on a beach, as surf recedes, turns into a flower bursting into bloom. Ocean waves crashing into a rock become clouds bouncing sharply off a mountain peak.

Haanstra began with such experiments because—as he later explained—he did not feel ready to cope with people. From the start his role was that of the perceptive observer, coaxing the viewer into sharing his vision.

His experiments brought an offer from a glass manufacturer, who wanted Haanstra to make a documentary about his factory. The manufacturer, with misguided enthusiasm, brought a detailed script complete with a prolix narration—the antithesis of the style Haanstra was developing. But Haanstra agreed to make the film as specified, if he could at the same time make a film of his own, which the manufacturer would not see until its completion. The manufacturer would have the option to make use of either, or both, but Haanstra would own the second film. This resulted in the birth of *Glass* (*Glas,* 1958), one of the most celebrated of all short films, an Oscar winner ultimately shown throughout the world.

Glass—Haanstra's version—plays subtly on mixed audience emotions toward industrialization. After a sequence on the traditional glass blower at work, we see how his skills have been mechanized in an automated assembly line. We cannot help marveling—but with uneasiness. Then the assembly line has a catastrophe: a broken bottle disrupts its rhythm, so that one of the machines methodically smashes a succession of bottles, sending glass crashing in all directions. Audiences howl with exhilaration. Ultimately order is restored on the assembly line. Haanstra here used, as an emotional "payoff," a calamity any sponsor would have excised from a film. Yet in the end the manufacturer came to prefer the Haanstra version to his own. To film poets of the postwar period, the sound track was supremely important. In *Glass,* action is so synchronized with music that the viewer can hardly escape the feeling that the glass blower is producing the music.

Like other trends, the short film poem—Haanstra called *Glass* a *ciné-poème*—erupted in many lands. A number of young Polish film makers, including graduates of the new state film school at Łódź, began work in this genre: Andrzej Munk with *A Walk in the Old City* (*Spacerek Staromiejski,* 1958); Kazimierz Karabasz with *Musicians* (*Muzykanci,* 1960); Jan Lomnicki with *A Ship is Born* (*Narodziny Statku,* 1961.) Economy and personal control were among the attractions of the genre. Dedication to intensified observation, and aversion to explanations, were its characteristics. Generally eschewing narration, the film maker preferred to stimulate question and inference.

The postwar decades marked, in many countries, a swing to urgent industrial development. In the "cold war" between capitalist and socialist blocs, both sides put increasing stress on "productivity." Film poets—on both sides—offered glimpses of the human reaction to this pressure. In *The Musicians* Karabasz opens with a cacophony—almost unendurable—of a factory at work. At closing time there is sudden silence as the workers head homeward. In the evening we see some of them reassemble with musical instruments for an amateur orchestra rehearsal: they make ensemble music. In a closing shot, as their music continues on the sound track, the camera pans across silent factory machines whose cacophony has opened the film.

In Yugoslavia young film poets often focused on an individual at work or play in an atmosphere of pressure. This seems to be the theme of Mića Milošević in *Gymnastic Performance* (*Končertogimnastiko,* 1962) and *The Green Table* (*Za Zelenim Stolom,* 1965), and of Vladimir Basara in *Hands and Threads* (*Ruke I Niti,* 1964). This last film shows in fascinating detail the activity of a rug-weaving workshop. Throughout much of the film, the sound track is dominated by the staccato clatter of the shuttles, as we watch the fingers of women at work. But their plucking of the threads is not unlike

A Walk in the Old City, 1958.

Musicians, 1960.

A Ship Is Born, 1961.

the action of harp-playing, and in the final moments harp music, perfectly synchronized with the plucking fingers, takes the aural spotlight. In a sequence perhaps inspired by Haanstra's *Glass,* we get the feeling the rug-weaver is making celestial music.

Many of the film poets of the postwar period pursued technical experiments. Some of these dealt with the sound track, which was entering a new era through the development of magnetic recording. Invented in Denmark in 1898 by Valdemar Poulsen, this form of sound recording had been virtually ignored for decades, but was brought to a high state of perfection in Germany during World War II. Advancing armies pushing into Germany were astonished to find radio stations broadcasting tape-recorded messages that seemed indistinguishable from "live" broadcasts. Such tapes could apparently be "dubbed"—duplicated—with hardly noticeable loss of quality. Best of all, editing of sound elements—speech, music, sound effects—became possible, and technically simple, to an extent unimagined before the war. All this, as the equipment became available, had a revolutionary effect on film technology. Interest in virtuoso sound track effects thus distinguished postwar experimenters from the "avantgarde" film makers of the silent era, who had been influenced predominantly by traditions of painting.

But the postwar period also brought developments in film stock, cameras, lenses. In the United States the documentarist Francis Thompson, in *N.Y., N.Y.* (1958), performed dazzling experiments with distorting mirrors, lenses, prisms. In his images the familiar skyscrapers and city crowds acquire a surrealistic quality. In one sequence, processions of identical images—of commuters, cars, buildings—move in lockstep across the screen, creating Busby Berkeley choruses of urban phenomena, beautiful and nightmarish. In *To Be Alive!,* made with Alexander Hammid, Thompson applied similar techniques to a multiscreen project, launched at the 1964 New York World's Fair. Shirley Clarke, in *Bridges-Go-Round* (1959), worked in the same vein, with emphasis on color experimentation.

In this tradition of the symbolic use of technical device was the remarkable *Necrology* (1968) of Standish D. Lawder. It shows masses of men and women on an escalator, closely packed. The photography, via telephoto lens, appears to slow the action and to confine it so that we do not know for some time that the people are on an escalator. Because Lawder reverses the movement, something quite

To Be Alive!—1964 World's Fair.

Francis Thompson

different is suggested: the massed people, though facing forward, move backward and upward. By accompanying this with funeral music, Lawder suggests that they are being wafted slowly up into some latter-day Valhalla. The title reinforces this impression, as do the mask-like faces of the men and women drifting upward. Actually they are commuters moving down an escalator in Grand Central Station, New York City, after the day's work, and their expressions are presumably their daily expressions during this ritual. Lawder here presents a daily phenomenon, generally unnoticed, in a way to provoke attention and thought.

The work of the poet-documentarists forms a thin, persistent thread through the postwar decades. A product of individual perception and innovative spirit, it was never important in terms of the film market. Many theaters that had been packed in wartime were in decline; short films, especially experimental films, were among first casualties.

Television, developing rapidly after the war, was one of the factors causing the decline; but television itself, reaching in most countries for mass audiences, offered only a limited market for experiments regarded as avant-garde. The poet-documentarist, in the tradition of poetry, lived marginally. Other documentarists struggled closer to the center.

Chronicler

The stream of documentary production, after flowing forcefully in wartime, had split into several channels. One channel, which soon appeared to widen and deepen, was that of the historic chronicle.

For a role as historian, the documentarist had a priceless resource: a half-century of newsfilm footage. The importance of such footage had been foretold in the Lumière era, demonstrated by Shub and others in the 1920's, then largely forgotten in the 1930's. Most documentarists of that time had concentrated on current crises; and the major newsreel companies, which controlled the principal footage archives, considered them of minor value. They tended to look on old news footage as comedy material.

A technical factor encouraged this. During the silent era most film had been shot at approximately sixteen frames per second. Because this was too slow for acceptable sound quality, the sound era adopted the speed of twenty-four frames per second. Old footage projected at this speed often looked ludicrous. Notables out of yesterday's newsreels moved in a jerky fashion which, with help from tinkly music and facetious commentary, was good for a hearty chuckle. This possibility produced innumerable short items with such titles as *Ye Olde Time Newsreel*. An industry that believed strongly in progress, and always saw the latest achievement as the culmination of all that had gone before, probably found it comforting to see the past in comic terms.[1]

But intensive wartime use of historic footage, and experience in "stretching" it via additional frames,* rekindled interest in archive material—not as weapon, not as comedy, but as raw material of history. The historic "compilation film" acquired new status.

For some time, the war remained a principal area of interest, especially when previously unknown footage came to light. But meanwhile film makers in many countries dug deeper and found unsus-

---

* The usual method has been to repeat every second frame, so that sixteen frames become twenty-four frames. The process usually provides an acceptably smooth motion, but is time-consuming and involves expense.

pected treasures. In France Nicole Védrès, with *Paris 1900* (1947), astonished audiences with a detailed portrait of Parisian life and culture in the years before World War I. No one had guessed that such rich and diverse material existed. It inspired a comparable Italian work, *Cavalcade of a Half Century* (*Cavalcata di Mezzo Secolo,* 1951), by Carlo Infascelli and others, which likewise surprised many with its contents, and even more with its popularity. Similarly in the Soviet Union, Ilya Kopalin, assembling *The Unforgettable Years* (*Nesabyvajemyje Gody,* 1957) for the fortieth anniversary of the revolution, caused amazement over footage he unearthed. George Morrison of Ireland, producing *I Am Ireland* (*Mise Eire,* 1959), a series of short films on the long struggle for independence from Britain, likewise found footage whose existence had scarcely been guessed. His experience was paralleled in Peking, where Fu Ya and Huang Bao-shan assembled a record of the evolution of the People's Republic of China in *A Spark Can Start a Prairie Fire* (*Hsing Hsing Chih Huo Keyi Liao Yuan,* 1961), drawing material from numerous sources, in China and abroad. The Thorndikes of East Germany, for their compilation *The Russian Miracle* (*Das Russische Wunder,* 1963), found material in Soviet archives that had eluded Soviet researchers. In India Satyajit Ray, in *Rabindranath Tagore* (1961), wished to pay tribute to the recently deceased poet, but the film grew into a wondrous epic of his era. And the compilation *Mahatma* (1968), by Vithalbhai K. Jhaveri, brought to light voluminous footage of Gandhi, including invaluable sequences long banned by the British.[2]

Meanwhile continued rummaging in war archives produced new revelations in two impressive films by Erwin Leiser—*Mein Kampf* (1960), made under Swedish auspices and originally titled *Den Blodiga Tiden,* or *Bloody Times;* and *Eichmann and the Third Reich* (*Eichmann und das Dritte Reich,* 1961), a Swiss production—and in Paul Rotha's *The Life of Adolf Hitler* (*Das Leben Adolf Hitlers,* 1961), made under West German auspices. The roots of the war were movingly re-examined in *To Die in Madrid* (*Mourir à Madrid,* 1962), by the French director Frédéric Rossif, which provided much documentation on the rise of General Franco, and in *Ordinary Fascism* (*Obyknovennyj Faschism,* 1965), in which the Russian director Mikhail Romm surveys the phenomenon of Nazism from various points of view, with particular attention to the non-protesting bystander. The footage produced by Akira Iwasaki at Hiroshima and Nagasaki in 1945, and long impounded by the Pentagon, finally made its appearance a quarter of a century later in *Hiroshima-Nagasaki: August 1945,* compiled at Columbia University.[3]

During these years television became an important source of support for compilation films; in many countries, the first television documentaries were of this genre. In the United States, the National Broadcasting Company achieved such success with its twenty-six-part series *Victory at Sea* (1952–53), chronicling the naval warfare of World War II, that the producing group was maintained as the Project Twenty Unit, carrying on with other compilation films such as *The Innocent Years* (1957) and *The Jazz Age* (1957). The rival Columbia Broadcasting System launched the competing series *Twentieth Century* (1957–66), at first devoted entirely to compilations. Television systems in many parts of the world started similar projects.

Working from film archives, film chroniclers necessarily began with concentration on the twentieth century. But in 1957 the National Film Board of Canada, releasing *City of Gold,* virtually created a new genre and opened another century. Its directors, Colin Low and Wolf Koenig, were planning a film on Dawson City, center of the Klondike gold rush of the 1890's, when they learned of a collection of some 200 glass-plate negatives, eight by ten inches, that had been found in a sod-roof house during its demolition some years earlier. These were largely the work of A. E. Haig, a photographer who had reached Dawson City in 1898, at the height of the gold rush. The photos comprised an incredibly vivid record of a bizarre moment of history. When enlarged, they were found to contain a minuteness of detail of which the photographer himself may have been unaware: an area one inch in width could be used to fill an entire motion picture screen. The photos thus allowed enormous scope for camera movement. More Haig photos were discovered in Seattle, and the collection gradually "took over the film."[4]

Material of this sort had often been used in films in an incidental way, but had generally been considered uncinematic. Koenig and Low harbored other views. Koenig was a still-pictures enthusiast who had long wanted to experiment with their use in film. Low, a former art student, had entered the National Film Board via its animation unit, and had experience in the plotting of camera movement in relation to graphics, such as maps. The use of camera movement in *City*

"Paradise Alley"—from *City of Gold,* Canada, 1957.

National Film Board of Canada

of Gold—toward significant detail, from detail to larger context, from detail to detail—is one of the special triumphs of the film. The movement is always meaningful, and human in rhythm, and achieves a brilliant interplay with the narration, which is in the form of a personal reminiscence by the writer Pierre Berton. The film won an Academy Award and at once opened new vistas to film chroniclers. Documentarists the world over began to ransack photographic files. In the United States, at the National Broadcasting Company, *City of Gold* inspired two projects that became television classics: *The Real West* (1961), narrated by Gary Cooper and illuminating the westward push of the 1880's and 1890's; and its sequel, *End of the Trail* (1965), narrated by Walter Brennan, telling the same story from the point of view of the Indian. Produced by Donald Hyatt and written by Philip Reisman, Jr., both films were based on tens of thousands of photographs assembled by researcher Daniel Jones from historic societies and private attics in a score of states.

While still photography was luring film chroniclers into the nineteenth century, their horizons were extended further by another development, set in motion by French documentarists. The film *1848,* directed by Victoria Mercanton in 1948, seems to have provided the main impetus. It recounted revolutionary upheavals of 1848 through skillful use of contemporary engravings, Daumier cartoons, etchings, paintings, and.posters, combined with a sound track rich in quotations and songs. Art works had in previous years been photographed mainly for films about art; here they became fragments of history, instruments of historic narrative. In *Images Médiévales* (1950), William Novik used illuminated manuscripts in the same way, to evoke the pattern of life in the Middle Ages. Roger Leenhardt used images of the Bayeux tapestry to chronicle the eleventh-century invasion of England by William the Conqueror, in *The Norman Conquest of England* (*La Conquête de l'Angleterre, 1955*). Precise, meaningful camera movement played a role in all such ventures.

This genre, too, circled the world. In India the director Bimal Roy, using diverse art works, told the story of the Buddha in the Cannes award winner, *Gotama the Buddha* (1956). In Egypt, Saad Nadeem made *A Tale from Nubia* (1963) from art work relating to the Nubian tribe—a subject of interest because its 50,000 members were being relocated for the Aswan Dam. In South Korea, Chung Sil Lee created a fascinating historic vignette in *The Magistrate's Boat Trip* (1965), using a three-panel eighteenth-century watercolor, a genre painting crowded with witty detail. And children's drawings were used tellingly as reflectors of social history in the Japanese film *Children Who Draw* (*Eo Kaku Kodomotachi, 1955*), by Susumu Hani, and in the Soviet film *Children of our Century* (*Deti Nashego Veka,* 1971), a chronicle of the history of children since the Russian revolution by Igor Bessarabov and Alexander Novogrudsky.

But the chronicler was meanwhile discovering still other resources. A feature film about Michelangelo, made in Italy before World War II by the Swiss director Curt Oertel, remained almost unknown until after the war. One reason was that it had begun its distribution in Nazi Germany and had eventually been seized by the United States Alien Property Custodian. Long negotiations led to its American release in 1950 under the auspices of Robert Flaherty, with a narration by Fredric March, and titled *The Titan*. Its form was unique. No human being was seen. The viewer's imagination—prodded by words, sounds, and music of the sound track—was allowed to construct events of Michelangelo's life as the camera moved through piazzas, palaces, landscapes. At various times, Michelangelo's sculptures, architecture, and other works moved into the spotlight with stunning impact. That such materials could be used as narrative in-

Iwanami

Children Who Draw—Japan, 1955.

Central Documentary Studio

Children of Our Century—Soviet Union, 1972.

Roll Call–Yugoslavia, 1964.   Jugoslovenska Kinoteka

Archaeology–Poland, 1967.   Wytwórnia Filmów Dokumentalnych

struments was the revelation made by *The Titan*. Again, the technique had echoes. An example was the Yugoslavian film *Roll Call* (*Apel,* 1964), in which the director Vera Jocić evoked the experience of a World War II concentration camp. Her materials were sculptures of Veda Jocić—no relation—who had taken up sculpture during her imprisonment, using mud of the concentration camp. After the war she had become a celebrated sculptress, making figures whose agonizing beauty maintained the look and texture of her concentration camp work. It was as though she could never shake off the terror. The film suggests this in one sequence, in which a number of her sculptures stand in darkness in a row. A searchlight then moves across them, as though from atop a wall, and briefly scans each of the silent human wreckages.

In the first two postwar decades, the film chronicler learned to consider almost any historic relic or artifact a potential narrative instrument. In a film by Poland's Andrzej Brzozowski, titled *Archaeology* (*Archeologia,* 1967), we see members of an archaeological group digging. Articles are found and carefully laid aside: a tin cup, a doll, a comb. We hear digging sounds, but no word is spoken. We are at first mystified by the accumulation of articles, but gradually a horrifying meaning emerges. We are on the site of a Nazi death camp—revealed as Auschwitz.

The ultimate application of such an approach was a film made in China in 1971 by the Peking Scientific and Educational Film Studio, titled *2100 Year Old Tomb Excavated*. Its focus was the body of a woman, found in Hunan province at a depth of sixty feet, enclosed in six caskets, one inside the next, with many artifacts. The corpse was extraordinarily well preserved, no doubt because of the multiple protection and depth of burial. The body even retained moisture. Under scrutiny of film cameras an autopsy was conducted, to discover what could be learned about a life of 2100 years ago. Specialists in archaeology, anatomy, pathology, biochemistry were in attendance. The woman was found to have been about fifty years old. She had given birth. She had type A blood. Lack of bedsores suggested sudden death, perhaps of a heart attack. Coronary symptoms supported this, as did melon seeds in the stomach and intestines—evidence of a meal taken before death. There were signs of tuberculosis in one lung. Pinworm and whipworm ova were in the rectum and liver. Silk fabrics and burial accessories demonstrating astonishing workmanship suggested that she belonged to the ruling class. She was tentatively identified as the wife of a potentate of the Western Han Dynasty. She had lived a life of luxury—at the expense, the Chinese narrator suggests, of the common people.

In the documentarist's approach to history, the multiplication of techniques and resources tended in the postwar years to displace scripted scenes using actors. Most postwar documentarists foreswore such reconstructions, which were felt to belong to historical fiction. For most documentarists, reconstructions were now acceptable only in such projects as trial reenactments, for which precise transcripts could provide a firm documentary anchor—as in a brilliant BBC-TV reconstruction, *The Chicago Conspiracy Trial* (1968).

While documentarists were utilizing a widening range of archive resources, film archives were also being augmented at an accelerating rate. For a while the reverse appeared to be true, as major theatrical newsreels and news-related series expired. In the United States *The March of Time* and *This Is America* gave up in 1951; *Pathé News,* which had become a Warner Brothers subsidiary, ended operations in 1956; *Paramount News* stopped in 1957; *Fox Movietone News* in 1963; the MGM-Hearst *News of the Day* and *Universal News* expired at the end of 1967.

But their functions and personnel had meanwhile been transferred to television, and to government news operations in many countries. The chronicling of current history was, in fact, assuming vast proportions. Growing like a chain explosion, it took many forms. Camera crews for television systems of all major powers—and some minor ones—were on the move on all continents. Their work swelled available film archives.

It took the form also of documentary film eruptions in new places —in Senegal, in the revealing work of Ousmane Sembene; in Argentina, in the work of Jorge Preloran; in Ceylon, in the work of Lester James Peries. Travels of veteran documentarists helped stimulate the process. Alberto Cavalcanti returned to his native Brazil (1949–54) to launch a documentary film movement. John Grierson dispatched Stanley Hawes from the National Film Board of Canada to Australia (1946–70) to help launch its Commonwealth Film Unit. Joris Ivens aided awakening film activity in Bulgaria (1947), Poland (1948), China (1958), Mali (1960), Cuba (1960), Chile (1963). Lothar Wolff, veteran of the *March of Time* and various Louis de Rochemont

"eruptions in new places . . ."
Tauw, 1970, by Ousmane Sembene, Senegal.
National Council of Churches

documentaries, went to Indonesia (1954) to aid its film development. Roman Karmen (1954) visited the Ho Chi Minh forces in Vietnam jungles in time to photograph the defeat of the French at Dienbienphu, and to aid Vietnam film beginnings; a few years later (1959) he was in Cuba for the Castro take-over, and was on hand for the birth of ICAIC—Instituto Cubano del Arte e Industria Cinematograficos—an organization soon bursting with energy.[5]

A film unit had become an expression of nationhood, a chronicler of achievement. In India the Films Division of the Ministry of Information and Broadcasting kept the nation informed about new power plants, steel plants, dams. Egypt in 1962 launched a series of sixty short films on the Aswan Dam; directed by Salah El Tohamy, they appeared in theaters as monthly progress reports on a project that was expected to transform Egypt's economy. The harnessing of waters was likewise the theme of the Chinese documentary *The Red Flag Canal (Hong Chi Chu,* 1969), perhaps the most spectacular of the genre. High hopes hung on such ventures.

The series of explosions also included more specialized forms of film chronicle. Film reporting by anthropologists grew dramatically after the war, stimulated in part by war experience. One of its leaders was Jean Rouch. Born in Paris, trained as an engineer, he had been a member of a World War II road-building unit in the French colony

Roman Karmen with Ho Chi Minh, 1954.   Karmen collection

Roman Karmen with Fidel Castro, 1961.

Pilot Project—India, 1962.

Films Division

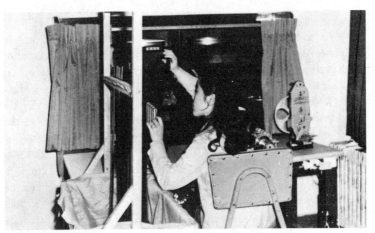

". . . expression of nationhood. . . ." Editor in Seoul, Korea.

National Film Production Center

of Niger, where his interests had shifted rapidly from road-building to the life of Africa. After the war he had become one of its leading chroniclers. His early films—such as *Hippopotamus Hunt* (*Chasse à l'Hippopotame*, 1946), *Cliff Cemetery* (*Cimétière dans la Falaise*, 1951), *The Rain Makers* (*Les Hommes Qui Font la Pluie*, 1951)— were traditional, narrated reports, but he gradually became an innovative influence. Based at the Musée de l'Homme in Paris, he gave anthropological film making much impetus in Europe. A similar role was played by the leaders—including Gotthard Wolf—of the Institut für den Wissenschaftlichen Film in Germany, which established an anthropological archive in Göttingen. A parallel role was played in United States by Gregory Bateson and Margaret Mead, whose *Trance and Dance in Bali* and *Childhood Rivalry in Bali and New Guinea* appeared in 1952, though based on prewar field work. Another figure of influence was Paul Fejos, a Hungarian-born film director who had given up a Hollywood career (*The Last Moment, Broadway, The King of Jazz*) and turned to anthropology, and who after the war became head of the Wenner-Gren Foundation, with a policy of aiding anthropological field work, including film-making.[6]

Among the most celebrated products of the new anthropological surge were *The Hunters* (1958), by John Marshall, tracing a giraffe hunt in the Kalahari desert—a product of his years of work among the Bushmen—and *Dead Birds* (1963), by Robert Gardner (who had helped to complete *The Hunters*)—a film about ritual warfare among tribes of New Guinea, made under Harvard University auspices. Still another was the epic-sized *Netsilik Eskimos* film series, a project begun in 1963 and continuing for a number of years—the work of anthropologist Asen Balicki of the University of Montreal in association with various film makers, notably Robert Young. The films were made under the auspices of Educational Services of Newton, Mass.

A somewhat parallel activity, burgeoning in countries around the world, was the documentation of all kinds of wildlife. Some of this work reached theater and television screens through Walt Disney, in such films as *Seal Island* (1948), *Beaver Valley* (1950), and *The Living Desert* (1953). However, Disney was criticized by naturalists for "anthropomorphizing" animal life; through his editing and his use of music, he often seemed intent on portraying animals as burlesque humans. On a more rigorously authentic level, likewise chronicling a strange world, was the work of Jacques-Yves Cousteau. As a

Dead Birds, 1963.

Contemporary Films—McGraw-Hill

National Film Board of Canada

Netsilik Eskimos series, 1963–67.

naval officer he had experimented in undersea photography; after the war he achieved global success with *The Silent World* (*Le Monde du Silence*, 1956), *World Without Sun* (*Le Monde Sans Soleil*, 1964), and later television series.

The camera seemed determined, during these same years, to plunge into unexplored worlds. X-ray cinematography had been developed before the war—with special brilliance in the short German film *X-rays* (*Röntgenstrahlen*, 1937), by Martin Rikli. This had shown diverse human and animal movements via X-ray photography, repeating Muybridge achievements in a new dimension. The postwar years carried the process much further; camera lenses, miniaturized, began to delve within the human body, into lungs, stomach, intestines, vagina—photographing from within the actions of breathing, digesting, peristalsis, coitus. Cameras also became capable of incredible magnifications, and of photographing high speed actions at thousands of frames per second. Pushing outward as well as inward, the camera even began to chronicle explorations in outer space.

In range of possibilities, size of audiences, number of projects, the film chronicler made staggering advances during the two postwar decades. In statistical terms, the expansion was awe-inspiring. As the television screen began to rivet the attention of men everywhere, its potentialities as a window on the world seemed limitless. They seemed to augur a golden age for documentary.

Yet documentarists—especially those concerned with current history—were not inclined to feel that a golden age was in the making. They had, instead, a sense of corrupting influences at work, and growing. Most troublesome seemed those which had not readily been seen as dangers, but had been welcomed as benefactions. Among these was the corporate sponsor.

He had been a part of documentary history for some time. He was sometimes seen as a reincarnation of the half-legendary patron of other times, credited with enabling artists to pursue their work untrammeled. Modern industry, as sponsor, was not usually such a phenomenon. It was generally concerned with promotion—of sales, policies, institutions, views. This became a dangerous force only as its influence began to saturate a medium and to exclude other forces. This was the problem that began to face the documentary film.

Promoter

To the rise of the documentary, industrial sponsors had contributed intermittently, but with distinction. The fur merchant Revillon Frères had made possible the first documentary masterwork, Flaherty's *Nanook of the North*. The auto manufacturer Citroën had sponsored the Poirier film *The Black Cruise* and its sequel *The Yellow Cruise*. In launching the documentary film movement in Britain, Grierson had persuaded a number of industrial companies to follow in this path.

Prominent among them was Shell. A 1933 memorandum by Grierson led the following year to formation of a Shell film unit, at first headed by Edgar Anstey. Later Arthur Elton became the leading force in Shell film activity, which soon acquired global reach because of the company's international ramifications. By the end of the 1930's Shell film units were in action at a number of affiliates, and the company was establishing film libraries on every continent. Shell films were being translated into Dutch, French, German, Italian, Portuguese, Spanish. Interrupted by World War II, the film activity proliferated after the war with production in Australia, Egypt, Hong Kong, India, the Netherlands, South Africa, the United States, and Venezuela.[1]

Early in their history, Shell sought to dissociate the film activities from traditional advertising. Policies excluded "internal reference" to any Shell product or to the company. The company was to be credited at the opening, and its symbol would appear at the end of each film; no further mention was to be made.

Many subjects were, however, related to Shell interests, and long-range promotional value could be inferred. Aviation and automobiles were favored topics. The films *Airport* (1935), *Powered Flight* (1951), and *History of the Helicopter* (1951) exemplified this. Documentaries on automobile races, such as *Grand Prix* (1949) and *21st Monte Carlo Rally* (1951), became standard Shell projects; they unquestionably served as stimulus to auto zealots and were popular among sport groups. Some projects, among them a series on *How an Airplane Flies* (1947), were designed for class instruction.

Many films touched on broad cultural concerns while stimulating interest in travel. John Meyer's *The Back of Beyond* (1954), a fea-

A Village in Travancore, 1957.

Martial Dances of Malabar, 1957.

Paul Zils and Fali Bilimoria, India.

Zils collection

ture-length documentary sponsored by Shell of Australia, had as its central figure the man who carried mail along the Birdsville Track —a 300-mile trail through sandy wastes of central Australia. The formula provided fascinating glimpses of the few precarious settlements along the route, and the ruins of others. Similarly the Burmah-Shell film unit in India, under James Beveridge of Canada, explored aspects of Indian life in *A Village in Travancore* (1957), by Fali Bilimoria, and *Martial Dances of Malabar* (1957), brilliantly executed by UFA fugitive Paul Zils. In the same tradition, the Southeast Asia Shell film unit produced an absorbing study of Hong Kong in *The Boat People* (1961).

Science films of painstaking craftsmanship became a specialty. Shell's interest in insecticides was reflected in such films as *Atomization* (1949), involving cinematography at the rate of 3000 frames per second, and a spectacular film on the war between man and insect, *The Rival World* (in Dutch, *Onze Grootste Vijand,* or *Our*

Greatest Enemy, 1955), made by Bert Haanstra of the Netherlands and shot in Egypt, Iraq, Kenya, Sudan, Tanganyika, Uganda. Its close-ups of insects provide a grotesque portrait gallery. The film also offers a perilous airplane ride through a locust swarm, in which we see countless locusts smashing to death against the airplane windshield. As in many documentaries, the sound for this sequence—impossible to record amid the roar of the propeller plane—was synthesized later. Made by dropping peas on a plastic sheet placed on the strings of a grand piano, the effect was considered highly authentic.

The Shell film units earned a wide reputation. Their aim, as explained by their able guiding spirit, Arthur Elton, was to present Shell as a company with "a lively sense of international responsibility, and a leader in the field of science and technology."

The postwar years brought a huge expansion in film sponsorship by large corporations, especially multi-national corporations—which were increasing in number and size. Enhancement of company "image" was the objective most often cited, but other motives clearly played a part.

The most celebrated sponsored film of the era was unquestionably *Louisiana Story* (1948), financed by Standard Oil of New Jersey. As the last film made by Robert Flaherty, and an unusual example of industrial sponsorship, it deserves a close look.[2]

In January 1946, after preliminary discussions, Flaherty received from Standard Oil a check for $175,000 to make a film having some relation to oil exploration. Later advances brought the total to $258,000. The terms of the agreement surprised many people. Flaherty was to have a free hand, and he would own the film, including all distribution rights. Standard Oil did not even ask to be identified as sponsor.

Accompanied by Frances Flaherty, he went traveling to observe oil operations: plains dotted with derricks; boom towns; ghost towns. Then they came to the beautiful bayou country of Louisiana, where oil explorations were in progress. They stopped one day for lunch at the edge of a bayou, and saw an oil derrick approaching over the marsh grass—a haunting sight.

The region was a paradise, sparsely inhabited by Cajuns—descendants of Acadian immigrants from Canada. Flaherty was captivated by the people, who had clung to their old customs and beliefs,

Louisiana Story, 1948.

and by the lush, mysterious environment in which they lived. He knew he had found his setting, and wrote to Standard Oil to describe the opening of the film as he envisaged it: "We are spellbound by the mystery of the wilderness." It would be seen through the eyes of a Cajun boy.

It seemed to Frances Flaherty that Flaherty was reliving his own childhood with his father, exploring the Canadian wilderness.

In each of his feature documentaries—*Nanook of the North, Moana, Man of Aran*—Flaherty had portrayed a way of life doomed by intrusion of the industrial world. In each case he had kept the intruder, the enemy, out of the film. But this time the intruding force would be part of the film: it was sponsoring the film.

Toward this force Flaherty had ambivalent feelings. If it was the enemy, it was also himself, his father, his sponsor. The pattern of *Louisiana Story* became a strategy for resolving this conflict. In the film, oil exploration produces a blow-out that spews fantastic jets of mud and oil into the air. But the drillers—friendly, modest, magnificent in action—surmount the crisis, cap the well, and eventually leave

Shooting *Louisiana Story.*
Below, at right, Frances Flaherty. Behind camera, "Rickie" Leacock.
Museum of Modern Art

the paradise as they found it. The crew and the Cajun boy have meanwhile become firm friends.*

Flaherty thus imposed, on the documentary substance of *Louisiana Story,* a fable-like framework related to his own experience and conflicts. The over-all effect was a magical one. The photography by Flaherty and a young assistant, Richard Leacock, the editing by Helen van Dongen, the score by Virgil Thomson, rich in Cajun themes, combine to make *Louisiana Story* a film of lasting fascination.

Its value to Standard Oil was not as elusive as some have thought. Corporate image was not the issue; anonymous sponsorship could hardly have affected this. Another problem loomed for the company: resistance to oil explorations, to the invasion of unspoiled lands and seas. Standard Oil could expect that Flaherty would make precisely the kind of film he had always made, and of which *Louisiana Story* became another example: an expression of his love for the unspoiled wilderness and its life. By focusing on this—and de-emphasizing oil— the film had the message: have no fear, the wilderness is safe. This

---

* The blow-out was not filmed at the setting depicted in the film; it took place sixty miles away. The film makers sped to the scene to utilize it as their climax.

became in subsequent years—despite oil slicks in bayou, stream, and sea, or perhaps because of them—the recurring theme of countless oil-sponsored films and television commercials. They exemplified a political trend in business-sponsored films.

The Flaherty name gave the message force. The company name might have been counterproductive. Thus the anonymous sponsorship was not merely generosity.

During the first decade after World War II, production of industry-sponsored films—mostly short—rose in the United States to some 4000 films per year. Some were for intra-company use as training films, or as records of research. Many others went into theaters, schools, clubs, churches, to influence the climate of ideas. Offered free to these organizations, the films were propelled on their way by a business device of increasing significance. The distributor who arranged the "free" booking received payment from the sponsor—usually $7.50 to $15 per theatrical booking, $2.50 to $3.50 for each school, club, or church booking. The collection of such rewards—modest-sounding in themselves—was turning into a farflung industry, and the mechanism was spreading to Europe and parts of Asia. Substantial sums were involved. Many a sponsor, having spent $50,000 on the production of a short film, spent an additional $300,000 subsidizing its distribution over a period of years. While major studios were phasing out production of short films and newsreels, films distributed under business-subsidized arrangements were rapidly filling the vacuum. By the mid-1950's they were the main source of short films in American theaters and were pushing into many theaters elsewhere. Glossy and brisk, they generally promoted the more abundant life via travel, sports, fashions, beauty contests; their sponsors, not always identified, included airlines, auto manufacturers, oil companies, lumber companies, textile manufacturers, liquor merchants. A 1956 brochure of Modern Talking Picture Service, specialists in business-subsidized distribution, reported that its films were being used by more than 19,000 theaters and drive-ins, as well as by 53,000 schools and colleges, 36,000 churches, 26,000 clubs and youth groups. Individual films—such as *Green Harvest,* sponsored by Weyerhaeuser—received as many as 80,000 bookings. Curious associations developed. Old Crow Bourbon specialized in sponsoring skiing films. The film-goer might not notice its name, but would see brilliant skiing in breath-taking surroundings, culminating in joyful social

Robert Flaherty, 1949.

Photograph by Suchitzky—from Museum of Modern Art

gatherings at which beautiful people drank bourbon. Bourbon makers thus became apostles of radiant health, as oil and lumber companies were apostles of the unspoiled wilderness.[3]

In American television the purchase of time had become the controlling mechanism, but business-subsidized films were used to fill unsold time. According to Modern Talking Picture Service, 99 per cent of United States television stations were using the films in 1956, filling an average of three to four hours per week.

Films sponsored by non-profit agencies—distributed via sale or rental of prints—seldom achieved comparable distribution. Business-subsidized material was rapidly saturating channels of communication.

All this reflected changes in the role of the corporation in society—changes that were making long-held economic theories obsolete. Instead of producing to meet demand, large corporations manipulated demand to meet production. Production was an autonomy; all else had to be adjusted to its needs. Its protection demanded control—or neutralization—of communication media and agencies supervising them. It also demanded control of supply sources. In the postwar years, as multi-national corporations—largely under American control—expanded abroad at an unprecedented rate, the drive to control markets, resources, and media went with them.[4]

The beginnings of the cold war were related to this development. Starting shortly after World War II, this confrontation between capitalist and socialist powers involved struggles for markets and resources, but proclaimed itself in ideological terms. On both sides it brought a stiffening of controls over mass media—with drastic impact on documentary content and style.

In socialist countries the controls were not new. The Soviet Union had generally regarded them as essential for rechanneling social drives toward new goals, and countering intrusions felt to be hostile to socialism. Thus the stiffening process was a matter of degree.

In the United States, where tradition sanctioned a much wider freedom of expression, the trend to authoritarianism brought bitter upheavals. One began in the U.S. House of Representatives in 1947, when a committee on "un-American activities," promising dramatic revelations, launched a probe of "communism in the film industry." It produced many diatribes, virtually no revelations. However, a number of prominent screen writers went to prison for refusing, on constitutional grounds, to testify about political beliefs or associations. Various industry leaders first applauded their stand, then found it prudent to launch "anti-communist" films and draw up blacklists of uncooperative artists.[5]

Another upheaval began early in 1950 in the U.S. Senate, and was led by Senator Joseph R. McCarthy. His attack was on another segment of the mass-media world: remnants of the Office of War Information that had been incorporated into the State Department and were continuing to produce films, broadcasts, and other items for audiences abroad. Charging that they were riddled with "communists and spies," he brought another wave of "loyalty" investigations and purges.[6]

At the same time a group of former FBI agents, calling themselves American Business Consultants, began advising broadcasting executives and sponsors about "communist" infiltrators in television and radio. In June 1950 they jolted the industry with a 205-page book titled *Red Channels,* listing 151 prominent writers, directors, and others alleged to be subversive. This led to another purge and a rapidly growing blacklist. Many artists became unemployed, or went abroad, or sought other occupations.[7]

In all these purges, such terms as *communists, subversives, fellow-travelers, pinks, dupes, undesirables* were used interchangeably. "They" were essentially blacklisted for having backed causes: loyalist Spain, racial equality, American-Soviet friendship, recognition of communist China. Involvement with any of a long list of organizations—attendance at a meeting was sufficient—was considered "guilt." The list included Film and Photo League, Frontier Films, *Hollywood Quarterly, New Theatre.*

Thus the purge—which came to be known as McCarthyism—fell on many whose work had been prominently used during the war by the War Department, the State Department, and the Office of War Information. Their footage was in the much-honored *Why We Fight* films. The wartime truce between leftist and rightist forces was ending explosively, coincident with rupture of the wartime alliance. The formative years of American television coincided with these purge years, and were unquestionably shaped by them.

The pervasiveness of the purge makes all the more remarkable the achievement of one documentary series, *See It Now.* Started in 1951 by Edward R. Murrow and Fred Friendly over the CBS television network, it was sponsored by Alcoa. The company felt its image had been tarnished by an anti-monopoly case, and this seemed good reason to entrust its first television venture to Edward R. Murrow. His quietly eloquent wartime radio broadcasts from England had won him a devoted following and made him a symbol of integrity.[8]

Murrow's wartime stature had also gained him special standing at CBS. He had become a network vice president and member of its board of directors. His status gave him autonomy on *See It Now,* regardless of where the series might fit on an organization chart. It also made him immune from sponsor interference, at a time when most sponsors exercised detailed control over series they sponsored.

Though he had this freedom, Murrrow scarcely ruffled the waters during the first two years of *See It Now.* He and his young associate, Fred Friendly, were new to television, as they were to film. They were beguiled by the wonders of the new medium, and played with technical experiments. For almost two years *See It Now* made no comment on purges or blacklists. Some admirers feared that Murrow had been swept along by McCarthyism. But he was more disturbed than he seemed.

Late in 1953 *Sée It Now* launched a series of documentaries on McCarthyism and its influence. All were narrated by Murrow and supported by actuality footage. The first, *The Case Against Milo Radulovich, A0589839* (1953), concerned the dismissal of an Air Force lieutenant as a "security risk," mainly on anonymous charges that his sister and father read dangerous literature. The second, *Argument at Indianapolis* (1953), documented efforts of a civil liberties group to hold a meeting in Indianapolis and of self-styled patriots to prevent the meeting. A third, *Report on Senator McCarthy* (1954), was a compilation of film footage of McCarthy—an anthology of his various charges. Their wildness, contradictions, bumptiousness, and repeated—but undelivered—promises of "documentation" gave the compilation potent anti-McCarthy impact. Murrow added only brief comments of his own.

MURROW: . . . The actions of the junior Senator from Wisconsin have caused alarm and dismay amongst our allies abroad and given considerable comfort to our enemies, and whose fault is that? Not really his. He didn't create this situation of fear; he merely exploited it, and rather successfully. Cassius was right: "The fault, dear Brutus, is not in our stars but in ourselves. . . ."

Good night, and good luck.

Edward R. Murrow, narrating *See It Now*, 1954.

Wide World

Senator Joseph R. McCarthy, with aide Roy M. Cohn, 1954.

The film infuriated the Senator, who demanded CBS time to reply—an awkward demand, since he would be largely answering himself. CBS granted the request.

At Fox Movietone Studios, Senator McCarthy filmed a vitriolic reply statement, but it failed to recoup his momentum. He himself became a subject of investigation and was finally censured in the Senate by a decisive vote. His influence declined; he died suddenly in 1957.

Many assumed that the eclipse of McCarthy was the end of McCarthyism, but this was hardly the case. Blacklists remained in force. The impact on Murrow himself was ironic. He had played a major role in toppling McCarthy. He had also helped to make television an indispensable medium—to viewer and sponsor alike. New sponsors came by dozens but, wishing to avoid controversy, chose safer vehicles than *See It Now*—mostly quiz programs or adventure drama. By 1958 thirty weekly western series were scheduled in evening time, dominating all networks. Crime and spy series comprised another thirty. Reflecting the purge era, some took a patriotic stance, claiming to be "based on" case histories of the Federal Bureau of Investigation, the Central Intelligence Agency, or police departments. Amid this avalanche, there was soon no room for *See It Now*. For a time it was shown intermittently; then moved to a Sunday afternoon period; finally, in 1958, dropped. Alcoa had continued to sponsor the series until 1955, although under strong pressure from McCarthy supporters; then it too had looked for safer vehicles.

McCarthyism, without McCarthy, was winning. This was true also at the international film and television service of the State Department, which in 1953 had been incorporated into a new U.S. Information Agency. The purge demanded by McCarthy had in fact been carried out by Secretary of State John Foster Dulles; it represented a major American shift.[9]

In the early postwar years, a schism had divided the service. Its announced peacetime purpose—to fight the "war of ideas"—scarcely constituted a clear guideline. *For* what, *against* what, was it to fight? Some staff members saw the United States as the natural champion of those looking for independence from colonial rule. The inspiration these peoples derived from American experience seemed, to many in Washington, an asset to American prestige; they felt the link should be stressed in U.S. broadcasts and films.

But others preferred to see the United States as champion of private enterprise in a global crusade against communism, even though it meant friendliness with military dictatorships. They were more interested in stability and commerce than in independence movements. Many industrial leaders shared this view. The huge production level of wartime could be maintained, even expanded, if based on world markets. This was the imperative that demanded support, and won the day. Reassured by a vast chain of American military bases, and by readiness of the Eisenhower administration to protect overseas investments—via CIA interventions, if necessary—corporations expanded globally. To them, developments such as a communist China, and its friendship with independence movements in Indonesia and Indochina, spelled possible disaster; American support for such movements was readily seen as "communist." The purge of media, at home and abroad, reflected this view.

Thus American television, as it evolved by the late 1950's, was in considerable part a product of cold war and blacklists. Divisions over China played an especially crucial role. Although it was not generally known at the time, *Red Channels* and the organization behind it, American Business Consultants, were financed by the importer Alfred Kohlberg, who was a leader of the "China lobby" dedicated to blocking recognition of the People's Republic of China; he was also a leading supporter of Senator Joseph R. McCarthy.[10]

The television pattern shaped by such pressures was meanwhile spreading to scores of other countries. Here the same American western, crime, and spy series appeared in numerous languages, watched over by branches of the same advertising agencies, and often sponsored by branches or affiliates of the same corporations.

In this pattern, at home and abroad, documentaries continued to play a part. But they were usually tamed documentaries, with content and style reflecting their evolution. Abroad they included free offerings of the U.S. Information Agency—which, in turn, included business-subsidized documentaries, in a series titled *Industry on Parade,* organized with the cooperation of the National Association of Manufacturers. In United States television, the independence enjoyed by Edward R. Murrow was a thing of the past. From 1959 on, authority over documentaries was firmly centered in network news departments. Policies proclaimed that year barred the work of outside producers if any "opinion-influencing" content was involved. In structure, the documentaries were authoritarian. Narration by a newsman, omniscient in tone, was the cohesive factor. It proclaimed objectivity. It quoted dissent, but regularly paired it with official refutation. Through mazes of controversy, newsmen walked a tightrope labeled truth. The phrase "on the other hand . . . on the other hand . . . on the other hand . . ." became a documentary refrain. Closely watched by top executives, documentaries became institutional, depersonalized. In dealing with remote eruptions—Cuba, Congo, Indonesia, Indochina—they tended to rely heavily on official statements. Broadcasters, licensed to serve "the public interest," considered documentaries obligatory, but were not happy about them. They represented a large investment, which was often lost. For financial security, most documentaries were designed to be suitable backdrops for advertising, but topics chosen to this end—*i.e.,* not likely to stir up public relations crises—tended to lose audiences. Such topics as *Ireland: the Tear and the Smile* (1961) and *Fire Rescue* (1962) exemplified the play-it-safe trend. Occasionally a peripheral subject produced bold investigative reporting, as in *Biography of a Bookie Joint* (1961), made with hidden cameras by CBS documentarist Jay McMullen. But almost any vigorous probing, on any subject, seemed to generate protest, and crises in executive nervousness. A revealing CBS documentary on migrant labor produced by David Lowe, *Harvest of Shame* (1960), resulted in congressional storms and in government efforts to forestall exhibition abroad—efforts in which even Edward R. Murrow, who had narrated the film shortly before leaving CBS, was persuaded to participate.* International factors came into play more tellingly in the case of NBC's *Angola: Journey to a War* (1961), for which documentarist Robert Young had made his way from the Congo through 300 miles of jungle to record Portuguese efforts to quell an African uprising. It was a venturesome film project, but NBC eliminated evidence that the Portuguese used American-made napalm bombs; the executive producer, Irving Gitlin, told Young this material could not be included because the Russians would "use it against us." Such moments made a documentarist ponder his role: was he a chronicler of current history, or a promoter?[11]

---

* Murrow was appointed by President Kennedy in 1961 to head the U.S. Information Agency. For a time his presence seemed to revitalize the agency, but he soon fell ill with lung cancer. He died in 1965.

In 1961 President Eisenhower, in the final statement of his presidency, warned against the growing role of the "military–industrial complex." The phrase, supplied by a speechwriter, came oddly from a leader who had presided over the growth. But its ascendancy had apparently made Eisenhower uneasy.

On both sides of the cold war, television schedules showed the military-industrial stamp. It tended to have a polarizing effect throughout the world; nations, as well as people, were pressed to "stand up and be counted." Amid the pressure, documentarists grew restive.

From the late 1950's on, the history of documentary involved the rise of several genres of dissent. Impelled by ideological considerations, and by dislike for a "brainwashing" documentary style, documentarists found opportunity in new technical developments. These assumed increasing importance during the 1960's.

The dissenters appeared in many places. At the American networks they continued as a restless force, still moved by the Murrow tradition, and often in conflict with sales and management personnel. Dissent also continued, against odds, at the U.S. Information Agency. It also powered, in many countries, hosts of new film makers, seeking expression through various outlets. For many of them, a sense that their own cultures were being overwhelmed by sponsor-power was a motivating factor. Through the fabric of establishment communication, several threads became visible.

5

SHARP FOCUS

crescendo poco a poco

Yanki No!, 1960.

Drew Associates

Observer

In London in 1956 people were talking about Free Cinema. That was the title of showings organized at the National Film Theatre by Karel Reisz, Lindsay Anderson, and others—young critics and film makers intent on prodding film into new paths. The title had the ring of a manifesto.

Actually it was a convenient label for a potpourri of items that even included public-relations films, such as the touching *Thursday's Children* (1954), made by Lindsay Anderson and Guy Brenton for a school for deaf children, and Anderson's *Every Day Except Christmas* (1957), made under Ford Company auspices. But the films that caused a stir—they included British films, and others from abroad—were documentaries of a very different sort, all having certain traits in common.[1]

One was their stance. The film makers were *observers*, rejecting the role of promoter. New, light equipment made possible an intimacy of observation new to documentary, and this involved sound as well as image. These film makers were as intent on listening as on watching. It was as though the tape recorder had opened a new world to them, and they were fascinated by its sounds and speech rhythms. They often poked into places society was inclined to ignore or keep hidden. Leaving conclusions to viewers, the films were ambiguous. When they seemed iconoclastic, it was not because of superimposed commentaries, but because there were new sights, sounds, and juxtapositions from which viewers—or at least some of them—drew disturbing inferences. The ambiguity was exhilarating to some film goers, infuriating to others.

Free Cinema selections of this sort included films by the organizers, such as *O Dreamland* (1953), by Lindsay Anderson, a phantasmagoria of popular culture glimpsed through people and exhibits at an amusement park, and *Momma Don't Allow* (1956), by Karel Reisz and Tony Richardson, a candid study of a jazz club and its members. From the United States came Lionel Rogosin's *On the Bowery* (1956), which followed the ups and downs of an alcoholic through New York bars, flophouses, and shelters. From Poland there were several films including *Paragraph Zero* (*Paragraf Zero,* 1956),

On the Bowery, 1956.

Rogosin collection

On the Bowery, 1956.

by Wlodzimierz Borowik, about the life of prostitutes, and *House of Old Women (Dom Starych Kobiet, 1957)* by Jan Lomnicki, a close-up of women living out their final days in isolation. From France came *Blood of the Beasts (Le Sang des Bêtes, 1949)*, a meticulous look at a slaughterhouse set in mistily peaceful Parisian surroundings, directed by Georges Franju, who was generally associated with fiction films, but whose documentaries were especially admired by the Free Cinema group. He also made *Hôtel des Invalides* (1952), a film about a veterans' home and military museum, in which we meet the human wrecks of warfare, and follow schoolchildren on a guided tour of weaponry exhibits. The Franju documentaries, with their disturbing metaphoric overtones, seemed to have the precise beauty of nightmares.[2]

The Free Cinema showings lasted just three seasons, and its leaders moved into fiction films—Richardson with *The Entertainer* (1959) and *A Taste of Honey* (1961), Reisz with *Saturday Night and Sunday Morning* (1960), Anderson with *This Sporting Life* (1963), all reflecting the influence of the Free Cinema ideas. But other film makers carried on, in documentary, the intimate-observer role. In England it flourished especially in the BBC-TV documentaries of Denis Mitchell.

Mitchell, a veteran of radio work with tape recordings, had acquired an obsessive interest in popular speech and the values and tensions implicit in it. His documentaries, both for radio and television, were full of memorable—at times bizarre—portraits of people, usually representing submerged groups. Mitchell seemed to relish their muddled thinking, sometimes involving zigzags beyond the ken of script writers. In the film *In Prison* (1957), about life in Strangeways Prison in Manchester, a woman prisoner tells us:

WOMAN PRISONER: I mean, I've known women that's gone out of here and have met men out of here and are quite happy together and have never come back. I myself know a man—a gentleman—who was in here and was doing three years. And I went to live with him and he was a good man—only for one thing: he was too fond of the women.

In 1960 Mitchell took his special talents to Chicago where, with the cooperation of its Channel 7, he produced the BBC-TV documentary *Chicago: First Impressions of a Great American City.* Here was a "city symphony" of a new sort—with speech. Mitchell was assisted by the Chicagoan Studs Terkel, who had similar enthusiasms. The 1961 première telecast in England was highly acclaimed, but Chicagoans who saw it there expressed such rage that the film was kept off the Chicago air for six years. Controlling "these monstrosities," said Mayor Richard Daley of Chicago, was always a problem. He had not seen the film but said: "Maybe I ought to go right over and punch the producer on the nose." Among critics who did see a Chicago preview, one called it (Chicago *American*) "dishonest, distorted, and disgusting," while another (Chicago *Tribune*) described it as "by turns, tender, brutal, lyric, evil, ironic, and imaginative . . . a highly impressive documentary . . . an extraordinarily adult and exciting documentary." A Channel 7 spokesman concluded that there was "absolutely no chance" of telecasting it in Chicago.[3]

That the cool stance of the observer-documentarist could produce such diverse and emphatic reactions tells something about the genre. Mitchell was not a pamphleteer, though he was interested in social problems. He did not formulate these as problems, but instead tried —as Karel Reisz put it—"to convey their feel in terms of people." Reisz continued:

If in doing this he uses "untypical" characters, it is because he tries to find those who are most vulnerable to the social pressures he is describing. The outsider who has most to fear from the majority community can provide us with deeper insights into the workings of that majority community than those who are safely inside it.[4]

In the new focus on speech—talking people—documentarists were moving into an area they had long neglected, and which appeared to have surprising, even revolutionary impact. Since the advent of sound —throughout the 1930's and 1940's—documentarists had seldom featured talking people, except in brief, static scenes. Synchronized sound had involved too much cumbersome equipment for use in spontaneous, unpredictable encounters that might require movement. So they had kept the camera on people *doing* something—something other than talking. Talk, on the sound track, had usually been an after-the-fact supplement.

The non-talking people had tended to be puppets, manipulated in the editing. Their silent gestures and looks always had various potential meanings, which context or the sound track could modulate. But talking human beings with their own, spontaneous talk were not puppets, as experiments were demonstrating. In a sense they began to take control away from the director. It was to these people—including people whom the audience had not counted as part of their world —that viewers were reacting.

Among American documentarists, maneuverable 16mm equipment rapidly displaced 35mm during the 1950's. Use of the tripod, once regarded as essential, was in decline. Yet mobility was hampered by several remaining problems. The documentarist, for optimum quality and editing flexibility, preferred to record image and sound separately.* But to maintain synchronization, camera and tape recorder had to be connected by a cable. This meant that a synchronized-sound shooting team was, at best, an awkward four-legged creature. For full maneuverability the cord had to be abolished. Some alternative synchronization method was needed.

In addition, the system that obliged talking people to hover near microphones, which were fastened by cable to recording equipment (in turn, fastened to the camera), had to be abolished.

During the late 1950's, groups in various places were striving for these goals. One such group was formed in 1958 at Time, Inc., in New York, by Robert Drew. He persuaded the organization to finance experiments that would carry the candid photography tradition of *Life* magazine forward into film, with mobile, synchronized-sound shooting. His enthusiasm had been ignited by a cameraman whose work he had long admired, and who became a leader in the experiments—Richard Leacock.[5]

"Ricky" Leacock was born in 1921 in the Canary Islands, where he had a carefree childhood on his father's banana plantation, until he was shipped to England for schooling. The routine there was grim, but on Sunday the school scheduled edifying events, and one Sunday it was a showing of the Russian film *Turksib*. This was, to Leacock, a momentous experience. He acquired a camera and began experiments. During a summer vacation back home, at thirteen, he made a *Turksib*-like documentary about banana-growing, *Canary Island Bananas* (1935). In the fall his film won him new standing at school. In the school were two daughters of Robert Flaherty, and when the great man came for a visit, young Leacock was summoned to the

---

* An alternative procedure, standard in newsreel work, was the use of "single-system" cameras, which record image and sound on one strip. Some documentarists used them, but mainly as a supplement.

principal's office, presented as a prize exhibit, and taken along for a spin in a rented auto. Flaherty did not quite know how to deal with the prodigy. "He probably didn't know whether to offer me a chocolate or a drink of Scotch." But before leaving he said that they would some day make a movie together. Years later, after World War II—and action as a U.S. Signal Corps combat photographer in India, Ceylon, Burma, China—Leacock dropped in on Flaherty in New York. Flaherty was delighted. "I'm going down to Louisiana to make a film, and I'd like you to come with me." Thus Leacock became a cameraman on *Louisiana Story*, and learned something he never forgot. One day they were to shoot a tree-climbing sequence, with the Cajun boy and his pet raccoon. But on the way Flaherty saw a beautiful spider web, and they spent the whole day filming it. Such Flaherty behavior was considered very undisciplined in the film world, but Leacock came to regard it as "the most difficult discipline"—never to stop looking, never to stop responding to the world around one. This became a key to Leacock's film-making—along with the quest for synchronized sound.[6]

This quest seemed increasingly urgent in the years that followed, as he made documentaries for the U.S. Information Agency and television networks, and acquired a growing aversion to voice-over narration. "It is when I am not being *told* something, and I start to find out for myself, this is when it gets exciting for me. . . . The minute I sense I'm being *told* the answer, I tend to start rejecting it."[7]

At Time, Inc., the Drew unit began a series of experiments—some disastrous, some fruitful. They tested endless variations of standard equipment, to increase maneuverability. In a crucial breakthrough, they developed a wireless synchronizing system, based on the use of tuning forks—later replaced by another, based on crystal-controlled motors. They acquired wireless microphones, utilizing miniature transmitters. At times, nothing worked. But by 1960 things looked promising. In technical terms, the work reached a peak in 1961 in the film *Eddie,* about the racing-car driver Eddie Sachs, in which camera, recorder, and microphone became independently mobile elements.

Meanwhile the social values of these developments were indicated by *Primary* (1960), a film that, in spite of technical snags, emerged as a scintillating and illuminating document. Drew and Leacock had persuaded two United States Senators, John F. Kennedy and Hubert

Richard Leacock.

Photograph by Bruce Harding

Humphrey, to allow themselves to be photographed and recorded throughout their campaigning in Wisconsin for the Democratic presidential nomination. Drew stressed the historic value such a record might have. The film makers promised never to ask or suggest an action. They only wanted continued access—at speeches, meetings, strategy sessions, interviews, telethons, motorcades. Both candidates agreed, and the result was astonishing. No previous film had so caught the euphoria, the sweat, the maneuvering of a political campaign.

Primary was telecast by a scattering of stations including a few owned by Time, Inc., but was rejected by all networks—in conformity to their policy against documentaries made by others. But the work of the Drew unit impressed the ABC network, with the result that it made a contract with Time, Inc., by which the Drew group became, in effect, an ABC unit. Thus a series of Drew synchronized-sound documentaries became network programs, including *Yanki No!* (1960), a vivid and ominous picture of Latin-American unrest and the rise of Castro; *Crisis: Behind a Presidential Commitment* (1963), on a confrontation between the Kennedy administration and Governor George C. Wallace of Alabama over admission of blacks to the University of Alabama; and *The Chair* (1963), which showed the attorney Louis Nizer and others in a crisis over a commutation appeal, involving a man sentenced to the electric chair. Most of the Drew documentaries were sponsored—several, by Bell & Howell.

The ABC-TV network thus contributed to the pioneering of a genre. But the special glories of the genre were its unpredictability and its ambiguity, qualities that scarcely made for comfortable relations with sponsors. Inevitably resistance developed—from network and sponsor. This was clearly shown by a celebrated film shot in Aberdeen, South Dakota.

The Fischer family of Aberdeen had produced quintuplets, all healthy, and the news circled the world. The market town of Aberdeen found itself famous, and dreamed of processions of tourists. Chamber of Commerce meetings discussed promotion plans. Souvenirs were planned and manufactured. There were solemn speeches about protecting the privacy of the Fischer family, but meanwhile there were great plans for press conferences, banquets, parades, reviewing stands. From afar the family was showered with corporate gifts—baby foods, shoes by the hundreds, clothing, dishwasher, new

Yanki No!, 1960.

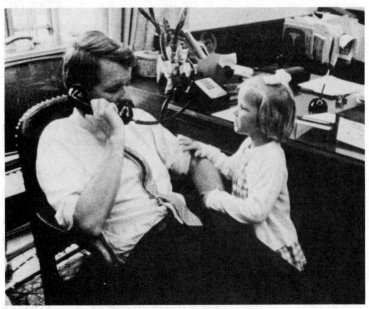

Crisis, 1963.

refrigerator, new toilet. Reporters and photographers swarmed over the premises. Leacock, assisted by Joyce Chopra, was among them, painfully conscious that they were part of the problem afflicting the Fischers. As unobtrusively as they could, they filmed and recorded the family's half-paralyzed reactions, the press at work, Chamber of Commerce, souvenir industry, banquet. "Never in history," said the Mayor, had a city official presided over more momentous events or had more awesome responsibilities. The film showed a feverish microcosm of enterprise. Amid the hubbub the quietly suffering Mrs. Fischer, trying to be cooperative, is an unforgettable figure. Her laconic bits of dialogue are miracles of simple eloquence. The film, titled *Happy Mother's Day* (1963), won awards at the Venice and Leipzig film festivals, was shown on European television, and widely discussed in European film journals. But it never went on American television.

The ABC network, using the same footage, eliminated all shots that might suggest an overeagerness to cash in. The Chamber of Commerce meeting was eliminated. The Mayor was saved from his more fatuous remarks by judicious cuts. Some of the most touching glimpses of Mrs. Fischer were cut. Pronouncements in defense of the privacy of the Fischers were retained; anything that might cast doubt on their wholeheartedness was eliminated. To fill the gaps, narration by a newsman—sometimes on camera—was added. He was seen against Aberdeen backgrounds, providing statistics on the community and its business, interviewing officials, hospital personnel, clergy. The film appeared to be an assurance that when quintuplets are born in an American town, everyone rallies round to make sure things go happily. Titled *The Fischer Quintuplets,* the program was sponsored by Beechnut baby foods.

The remarkable group assembled by Drew was beginning to scatter, but virtually all its members carried on in the technique they had helped to develop. Donn A. Pennebaker, whose engineering background had made him a key figure in the early experiments, joined with Leacock in *Don't Look Back* (1966), a profile of singer and songwriter Bob Dylan; *Monterey Pop* (1968); and other projects. Albert Maysles, who preferred to call the technique *direct cinema*— a term also adopted by others—teamed with his brother David Maysles to make *Showman* (1962), *What's Happening! The Beatles in the U.S.A.* (1964), *Meet Marlon Brando* (1965), *Salesman* (1969),

Gimme Shelter (1970), and other works. In most of these the film makers, stung by their mismatch with commercial television, looked to the theater for a market. Most of the films dealt with people leading highly public lives, and some were little more than studies of performers and audiences in action. These yielded some spectacular sequences, and won audiences, but suggested a limitation in the technique. However, with *Salesman* the Maysles moved into a very different world, and gave direct cinema an unexpected dimension.[8]

Albert Maysles was the cameraman, David, the younger, the sound recorder. Albert had taught psychology at Boston University before turning to film-making; David had Hollywood experience as assistant to the producer of *Bus Stop* and *The Prince and the Showgirl*—Marilyn Monroe films. They had grown up in the Boston area, where their father was a civil servant working in the post office—a life leading to retirement on a modest pension. But the atmosphere of the 1920's, when Albert was born, deprecated such marginal security. The idea was to share the American dream. For many this meant salesmanship, as a road to affluence. Both the Maysles had done selling: Fuller brushes, Avon calling, encyclopedias. They felt they had moved beyond this part of their lives, but its memory clung to them, as a symbol of an important element in the American experience. They became determined to make it the theme of a direct cinema documentary.

The main characters of *Salesman* were four door-to-door Bible salesmen. The principal focus came to center on one—Paul. With approval of the company they represented, the Maysles brothers accompanied them on their selling efforts. The salesmen obtained names of possible customers at community churches. At the time of the home calls, the Maysles sometimes started filming as the salesman knocked. They would shoot and record the opening talk at the front door. Then the salesman would introduce the Maysles, and one of them would explain: "We're doing a human interest story about this gentleman and his three colleagues. And we'd like to film his presentation." (The word "sell" was not used.) Usually the reply would be: "Oh, a human interest story. OK, come in." Very few people declined to be filmed.

Once the Maysles were inside, there was seldom an obstacle to continued filming. Since the salesman was really performing, it was easy for the Maysles to become relatively invisible. Afterwards they would ask the customer to sign a release. Only one refused.

Salesman, 1969.

Maysles Films

The result was such scenes as the following. Paul is seen in a small living room, talking to a young housewife. Her four-year-old daughter looks on.*

PAUL: The best seller in the world is the Bible. For one reason. It's the greatest piece of literature of all time. (*He leafs through the book.*) It's really tremendous, isn't it? Here are the Shepherds and the Three Kings. The flight into Egypt. The childhood of Jesus. Mary returns to Naz. . . . Mary finds Jesus in the temple. So you can see how this would be an inspiration in the home. (*Talking to the child.*) You like that, honey? What's your name?

WOMAN: Christine.

PAUL: Well, she's as bright, she's pretty like her mother. Huh? (*Pats the girl's head.*) Christine. You know what my name is? Paul . . . Paul, you know? Paul.

WOMAN: You have a cousin named Paul, don't you, Chris?

PAUL: You can see how complete it is. The Bible runs as little as forty-nine ninety-five. And we have three plans on it. Cash, (*Child yawns.*) C. O. D., and also they have a little Catholic Honor Plan. Which plan would be the best for you, the A, B or C?

WOMAN: I'm really not interested in . . .

PAUL: Yeah . . .

WOMAN: I speak it over with my husband.

PAUL: Yeah . . . yeah . . . yeah . . . you wouldn't want to give him a surprise? Does he have a birthday coming up? It would be a lovely gift.

WOMAN: That's true.

PAUL: We place a tremendous . . . (*Stroking the book lovingly.*) the Bible is still the best seller in the world, so . . . (*The child, bored, starts plunking at the piano.*)

WOMAN: I just couldn't afford it now. We've been swamped with medical bills. (*Piano continues.*)

(PAUL, *a beaten expression across his face, stares abstractly at the floor.*)

The Maysles also filmed get-togethers of the four salesmen at motels, comparing notes, playing poker, phoning their wives and girl-friends; also, a sales conference at which "the world's greatest salesman of the world's best seller" assures them their task is a holy one and that

---

* This dialogue is, of course, a transcript of spontaneous talk. Nothing was staged or repeated. The complete transcript is in *Salesman,* published by New American Library, © The Bible Salesman Co. 1969.

they are doing their "Father's business." The sales manager tells them: "If a guy's not a success, he's got nobody to blame but hisself." The men believe it.

The film elicited complex reactions. Many viewers are at first horrified at the Bible-hustling, but in the end feel sympathy for Paul, the least successful of the salesmen. He feels he is slipping, and reproaches himself for "thinking negatively." He too is a victim. Many viewers tend to develop a feeling of identity with him—as did the Maysles.

Although American commercial television was seldom hospitable to the ambivalence of direct cinema, noncommercial television was another matter. In the United States "public" television became a principal source of support for one of the most subtle and masterful exponents of the genre, Fred Wiseman.

A lawyer turned producer, he concentrated—after a brief fiction experiment—on films about institutions. He foreswore narrative explanations and comments. He selected institutions through which society propagates itself, or which cushion—and therefore reflect—its strains and tensions. All his films became studies of the exercise of power in American society—not at high levels, but at the community level. Together they constitute a revealing panorama of American life—especially fascinating because of interrelationships between the films.[9]

The films included *Titicut Follies* (1967), filmed in a Massachusetts institution for the criminally insane; *High School* (1968), in a Philadelphia high school; *Law and Order* (1969), in a Kansas City police station; *Hospital* (1970), in a New York center serving poor patients; *Basic Training* (1971), in the Fort Knox army training camp; *Essene* (1972), in an episcopal monastery in Michigan; *Juvenile Court* (1973), in a Memphis courthouse.

Each film has echoes of others. In *Basic Training* we sometimes feel we are in school. Counselor, chaplain, disciplinary officers cope with the misfits while the drill sergeants, like football coaches, pummel the others into shape. At the end there is a "graduation" for the survivors, and a group picture is taken. The school in *High School* sometimes resembles a training camp. A boy is told to accept his punishment "to establish you are a man and that you can take orders." The principal reads aloud a letter from an alumnus in Viet-

Frederick Wiseman.

WNET

nam, who expresses his love for the school and what it taught him. He is about to take part in a landing in hostile territory but doesn't want people to worry. "I am not worth it. I am only a body doing a job." The principal adds: "When you get a letter like this, it means you are successful."

All the films give glimpses of tenderness, brutality, apathy, dedication, pompousness, integrity. In most we see busy action in a factory atmosphere: a product is being processed. We see the rejects in each of the films, especially in *Police Court,* and even more in *Titicut Follies.* The title of this film refers to a musical show put on by the insane to entertain the staff. It may call to mind a musical sequence in *Basic Training:* the trainees marching and chanting, "Mr. Nixon drop the bomb, I don't want to go to Nam!" They are the ones making good, and are led by the drill sergeant.

Significantly Fred Wiseman, the controlling artist in these films, manned the tape recorder himself, while signaling his cameramen with photographic instructions. The division suggests the importance the speech elements had achieved. Footage shot usually totaled some thirty hours for each hour used. Wiseman watched over every detail of the editing process.

Titicut Follies, the first of the films, won the Best Documentary award at the Mannheim film festival, and several other awards, but its distribution was blocked by legal action of the State of Massachusetts, despite prior approvals at various levels. Wiseman did not encounter such problems with later films, even though he did *not* ask for legal releases. He took the position that if an institution receives tax support, citizens have a right to know what happens in it, and reportorial access is a constitutional right. If, at the time of filming, anyone objected to being photographed, Wiseman discarded the material; this rarely occurred.

At later stages, no one was allowed veto rights. It sometimes happened that a participant, on seeing a completed film, was pleased with his action in it but later—after noting reactions of others—became troubled. This happened especially with administrators and teachers, and suggests an important point. Through these films, people were enabled to see themselves as others saw them—although more than one screening might be needed to achieve this.

As an educational force, the films were, above all, destroyers of stereotypes. Issues were always shown to be more complicated—and

Lonely Boy, 1961.
National Film Board of Canada

Allan King Associates

Warrendale, 1967.

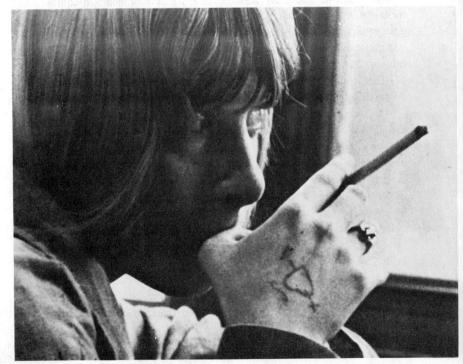

Everyman, 1963.

more fascinating—than dogma was inclined to make them.

Direct cinema had been made possible by developments in equipment—facilitating mobile synchronized-sound shooting on location. The equipment had helped documentarists open new worlds, involving spontaneous communication. At first they had focused on the famous, but the spotlight had shifted to the lowly, filmed at junctures of stress. Such material, while dramatically compelling, could also be revealing, reflecting stresses of society on the individual.

As the equipment spread, the same documentary trend appeared throughout the world. It had an early start in Canada, as exemplified by *Lonely Boy* (1961), by Wolf Koenig and Ralph Kroitor, focusing on a teen-age idol and his following, and reached memorable heights a few years later in *Warrendale* (1967), by Allan King, filmed at a home for disturbed children. In this film the sudden death of a much-loved cook, and its impact on the troubled young, provided an extraordinary and deeply moving climactic sequence. In Sweden, Jan Troell, schoolteacher turned documentarist, proved a brilliant exponent of the genre with *Portrait of Osa* (*Porträtt av Åsa,* 1965), a close-up of the complex life of a four-year-old. In Holland, Bert Haanstra varied the genre by working from concealed camera positions—a procedure adopted by few other observer-documentarists.

He had explored this method with beguiling results in *Zoo* (1962), looking at human beings from the point of view of caged animals; combining the technique with synchronized sound, he provided a rich panorama of Dutch life in *Everyman* (*Alleman,* 1963), winner of a top award at the Berlin festival.* In Japan, Kon Ichikawa filmed the 1964 Olympic games with innumerable cameras and recorders, but the oustanding feature of his *Tokyo Olympiad* was not its rich spectacle, nor its competitive drama, but its wondrously minute observation of individuals—as in the preparatory rituals of a runner at the starting line, shown in extreme close-up. Also in Japan, Nagisa Oshima provided Nippon TV with powerful direct-cinema works including *Forgotten Imperial Army* (*Wasurerareta Kogun,* 1963), portraying a ragged group of maimed Korean veterans conscripted long ago to fight for the Japanese Emperor, and still living in Tokyo. Oshima shows us their destitution and their plight: Japan says Korea should pension and support them; Korea, that they were wounded in service of Japan. Still they hold annual reunions, and hobble in their own straggly, defiant parade. In India, direct cinema found an avid recruit in the young film maker S. Sukhdev; his *India 67* (1967) and its shortened version, *An Indian Day* (1972), tapped wells of popular humor seldom noted in Indian documentaries.

The observer-documentary genre strongly influenced the French director Louis Malle. He gave up film directing to become a cultural attaché in India; confronted with the pageant of India, he became an obsessed documentarist with *Phantom India* (1968). A six-hour film, product of half a year of spontaneous filming and recording, it was later broken into shorter films, especially for television use. Of these, *Calcutta* was most widely shown. Malle felt the need for stretches of explanatory narration; between these the viewer was left to his own devices. Far from drawing conclusions, Malle's comments expressed his inability to reach any, and virtually invited viewers to share his helplessness over the contradictions in his vast canvas. It indeed presented a staggering pageant, filmed intimately, with love and horror, full of tantalizing fragments. For all its sympathy, it was not a public-relations version of Indian life. Like so many films of the genre, it stirred indignation in officialdom, and brought forth misguided efforts to suppress it.[10] A somewhat similar project, Michel-

---

* Released in English under the unfortunate title *The Human Dutch.*

Tokyo Olympiad—released 1965.

Toho

Tokyo Olympiad—photo finish.

angelo Antonioni's *China*—made for Italian television—provoked a similar reaction in China.

The documentarist's conquest of synchronized sound decisively influenced makers of ethnographic films. Until the 1960's, most such films tended to be illustrated lectures. The sound track was scholarly pronouncement; pictures supplied illustrative support. When the field footage began to talk and assumed human dimensions, it raised problems: the commentary was in the way. Besides, in the presence of so much evidence, it seemed less adequate. It now seemed preferable that the material, with all its ambiguities, be offered as a basis for discussion. Commentary began to be seen as a limiting rather than a liberating factor. With full sound, but without official guidance, filmed material seemed to offer a far greater diversity of vistas to probe and assess.[11]

Such works as *Tidikawa and Friends* (1971), made among the Bedamini of New Guinea by Jef and Su Doring; *Last of the Cuiva* (1971), made by Brian Moser in eastern Colombia; *Kula* (1971), made by Yasuko Ichioka among the Trobriand islanders of the Western Pacific; and *To Live With Herds* (1973), made in northern Uganda by David MacDougall, gave audiences—whether the language was understood or not—a sense of immersion in the societies they portrayed. They made some use of narration, but modestly—for essential information, not interpretation.

Synchronized sound affected editing style. The silent-film editing tradition, under which footage was fragmented and then reassembled, creating "film time," began to lose its feasibility and value. With speech, "real time" reasserted itself. Along with this came the feeling that ethnographic film should in any case respect "the structural integrity of events," as anthropologist Roger Sandall put it.[12] This resulted sometimes in long films depicting long rituals, as in Sandall's *Gunabibi* (1971), made in Australia; sometimes in short episodic films such as *Dedeheiwa Weeds His Garden* (1971) and *Dedeheiwa Washes His Children* (1971), and numerous others of the same sort made by Napoleon Chagnon and Timothy Asch among the Yanomamo Indians of southern Venezuela. Some of these fascinating real-time sequences were curiously reminiscent of the very beginnings of film history. Lumière aspired to catch life *sur le vif*. With sound, the phrase was beginning to have a new, heightened meaning.

One of the problems hanging over observer-documentarists was

An Indian Day, 1972.

Films Division

Filming *Kula* among the Trobriand islanders: director Yasuko Ichioka, producer Junichi Ushiyama. Released 1971.

Nippon AV

the extent to which the presence of the camera influenced events before it. Some practitioners—Leacock, Malle—worried about this. Others—Maysles, Wiseman—tended to minimize it. Some film makers, notably Jean Rouch, held still another view. Rouch maintained that the presence of the camera made people act in ways truer to their nature than might otherwise be the case. Thus he acknowledged the impact of the camera but, instead of considering it a liability, looked on it as a valuable catalytic agent, a revealer of inner truth. This idea propelled documentarists into still another genre.

Catalyst

Jean Rouch, liberal friend of black Africans, was disturbed that many of them disliked his early films. His concentration on weird religious practices—as in *The Manic Priests* (*Les Maîtres Fous,* 1955), in which we see possessed Hauka adepts, their mouths foaming, slaughter and eat a dog—seemed to his African critics to exemplify a colonialist predilection, by which white men buttressed assumptions of superiority. The critics asked whether weird practices were not available to film makers elsewhere—in Europe and America, for example.* As for the scholarly voice-over explanations, punctiliously researched, was Rouch really so confident of their significance?

Rouch, stung by the criticisms, began to try new approaches. While working on a fiction film to be titled *Jaguar,* he showed the footage to a black African, while recording his impromptu comments. Their wit and penetration so delighted him that he used the material in his sound track, and repeated the experiment in *I, a Black* (*Moi, un Noir,* 1958), a documentary on rootless, destitute, semi-employed workers of Abidjan, on the Ivory Coast. This time Rouch went further: he got his main characters not only to lead him through their daily lives, but also to improvise their fantasy life for the camera. In Abidjan, places of business had names like Chicago, Hollywood, Pigalle; the workers called each other Edward G. Robinson, Eddie Constantine, Dorothy Lamour, Tarzan. Rouch felt they survived the near-catastrophe of their lives in part through a high-spirited fantasy

---

* The film *Mondo Cane* (1961), global compilation of strange practices, by the Italian director Gualtiero Jacopetti, provided some documentation on this point.

life, and he managed to tap this in several scenes. The result was an infectious film in which one seldom senses a director; the characters are bursting with "themselves." Rouch began to ask himself more and more: how can one instigate moments of revelation?[1]

These ideas crystalized in *Chronicle of a Summer* (*Chronique d'un Été,* 1961), co-produced with Edgar Morin, and photographed by Michel Brault, a veteran of synchronous-sound experiments in Canada. *Chronicle of a Summer* continued those experiments, but moved them into a new world of provoked action.[2]

On Parisian boulevards, in view of the camera, people were stopped with a microphone and asked: "Tell us, are you happy?" A curious question but, in the France of 1960, a meaningful one. The Algerian war that had sickened and split the nation—and had aggravated crises in economics, race relations, education—seemed at last to be drawing to a close, a withdrawal from old concepts of *gloire*. It was a moment with many personal meanings. Some Parisians brushed the question aside; others stopped to consider. In some, the mere consideration brought on an emotional crisis, even tears. Thus Rouch was embarking on a kind of hometown anthropology, a study of "this strange tribe living in Paris." Unlike observer-documentarists, Rouch and Morin were on-camera participants in the venture, and evolved procedures that seemed to serve as "psychoanalytic stimulants," enabling people to talk about things they had previously been unable to discuss. The film participants were eventually invited to see the footage in a screening room and to discuss it, and the discussion was filmed, and became part of the film, as did a discussion between Rouch and Morin on their deductions from the film experience. It all seemed to have aspects of psychodrama.

In homage to Vertov, the film makers called their technique *cinéma vérité*—translated from *kino-pravda,* film-truth. It indeed had echoes of Vertov, particularly of *The Man With the Movie Camera,* in that it was a compendium of experiments in the pursuit of truth. Some people promptly applied the term *cinéma vérité* to what others called direct cinema—the cinema of the observer-documentarist. But the new approach was in fact a world away from direct cinema, although both had stemmed from synchronous-sound developments.

The direct cinema documentarist took his camera to a situation of tension and waited hopefully for a crisis; the Rouch version of *cinéma vérité* tried to precipitate one. The direct cinema artist aspired to invisibility; the Rouch *cinéma vérité* artist was often an avowed participant. The direct cinema artist played the role of uninvolved bystander; the *cinéma vérité* artist espoused that of provocateur.

Direct cinema found its truth in events available to the camera. *Cinéma vérité* was committed to a paradox: that artificial circumstances could bring hidden truth to the surface.

Chronicle of a Summer was a difficult film, and received limited distribution. But its rationale was widely discussed in film journals and ignited countless similar projects. Echoes of it may be found in *The Lovely May* (*Le Joli Mai,* 1963), by Chris Marker—also a study of Paris, but made just after the end of the Algerian war, and reflecting the optimism of the hour. Marker (originally named Christian François Bouche-Villeneuve) was an ex-journalist who—like Rouch—had done much of his early film work abroad, having filmed the Finnish Olympic games in 1952 and later won attention with *Sunday in Peking* (*Dimanche à Pékin,* 1955), *Letter from Siberia* (*Lettre de Sibérie,* 1957), and *Cuba Si!* (1961). In his portrait of Paris, *Le Joli Mai,* he focused not on a limited group, as Rouch had done, but on a broad social and political spectrum. Portions of the film are in traditional voice-over style, with commentary that is in turn witty, ironic, lyrical, statistical. But this is punctuated by numerous interviews in brisk, probing, catalyst-film fashion. "Was the month of May important to you?" "Did anything happen to you during May?" "What does money mean to you?" "Do you feel we live in a democracy?" The kaleidoscope of material suggests a "city symphony" adapted to the new catalyst genre.[3]

Rouch-style projects erupted far and wide. The Russian director Grigori Chukrai, who had made the enormously successful fiction film *Ballad of a Soldier* (*Ballada o Soldate,* 1959), had been asked by his studio to make a film on the battle of Stalingrad, in which he himself had fought and been wounded. He felt the subject was "too important" for fiction; on the other hand, he found the archival footage equally inadequate. The Rouch experiment suggested an approach. Chukrai took his cameras to the Place de Stalingrad in Paris; there passersby were confronted with a microphone and the question: "Excuse me—could you tell me—what is this Stalingrad? Why is it called Place de Stalingrad?" Again, some brushed the query aside, others pondered it; most could not dredge up an answer. One thought it had a connection with Napoleon. A few knew precise dates and details. Similar interviews were filmed in other countries. In the final film, *Memory* (*Pamat,* 1969), such sequences are alternated with Stalingrad war footage so that viewers are again and again whisked from the oblivious 1960's back to the drama of the 1940's. Some of the war sequences are accompanied not by battle sounds but by Bach-like music, giving them an unearthly requiem feeling, and lending special poignancy to the transitions. The combination of old and new material yielded a classic among war films.[4]

The film maker as catalyst began to tackle diverse projects. In Japan a broad tragedy was unfolding in the coastal town of Minamata. Strong men began to twitch and drool; women gave birth to strange-shaped creatures, some of whom survived. The "Minamata disease" was traced to mercury effluents from a factory; these, eaten by fish, had found their way into the food chain. The factory disclaimed responsibility; so did government authorities. Many sufferers hid themselves and their misshapen offspring, sensing a pariah status; stores were afraid to serve them lest they lose business. Thus efforts to organize the afflicted developed slowly. The film maker Noriaki Tsuchimoto began to visit victims and, via film and tape, draw out their stories. A feature-length film took shape. The making of the film tended to unify and fortify the group. They raised funds, developed strategy. Each of several dozen victims bought a share of company stock, with the purpose of attending a company meeting and confronting the board of directors. The strategy and the film reached their climax simultaneously at this meeting, in one of the most dramatic of filmed confrontations. In an auditorium, the twisted, twitching victims; facing them, in a line across the stage—in seemingly identical business suits—the company directors. The president begins to read a public-relations statement. The victims, under the impression the directors have agreed to hear *their* statement, begin to shout: "Let the Minamata victims speak! Let them speak!" The president keeps reading, impassively. The victims begin to clamber onto the stage; security guards push them back, but the protesters are too numerous. A woman reaches the president, clutches his lapels, shouts her desperate accumulation of grievances. He stands rigid, looking straight before him, as she shakes the lapels. The other directors, following his example, stand rigid as monuments; the stage is filled with the screaming victims. The film—*Minamata* (1971)—won the Japa-

effluents . . .   shapes . . .

confrontation.

nese film critics' award, an unusual honor for a documentary. It was shown many times on the periphery of the 1972 Stockholm environment conference, much to the annoyance of Japanese officials; it was not an official entry.[5]

Anthropologists found special reasons to be interested in film as catalyst. In field studies it had always been they who held the cameras, deciding what to shoot and how to edit it—until it occurred to Sol Worth and John Adair, in studying the Navajo, to find out what filming and editing decisions the Navajo themselves would make if they had unhampered control. The researchers taught Indians to use cameras and editing equipment and encouraged them to make films about their lives. No specific content was suggested. Similar experiments were done with black ghetto teenagers in Philadelphia. The results were often difficult to interpret, but tantalizing in their revelations, and the technique was rapidly adopted elsewhere. It became an important element in Challenge for Change—an activity launched by the National Film Board of Canada.[6]

Challenge for Change, begun in 1967, was a response to the upheavals that visited many parts of the world in the mid-1960's. It aimed to "promote citizen participation in the solution of social problems"—among which minority dissatisfactions were considered especially crucial. An early decision was to train and equip Indian film crews so that the Indians themselves might document their problems.

One such crew represented Mohawk Indians near Cornwall, Ont., where a bridge joins Canada and the United States. The Indians had long complained that a 1794 treaty guaranteeing them duty-free passage was being violated; their protests had apparently gone unnoticed in Ottawa. The Indian film group, under their leader Mike Mitchell, now planned a demonstration, and a film to give it impact. The demonstrators would block the international bridge, halting the traffic, as a means to publicize their case. Demonstration and film were planned together.

The executive in charge of Challenge for Change was George C. Stoney, best known for his brilliant film *All My Babies* (1953), made for the training of Georgia midwives. Though a United States citizen, he was recruited for Challenge for Change because of his impressive films on social problems, often involving minority groups. Stoney strongly supported the work of the Indian film units; when he learned of the Mohawks' demonstration plans, he sent additional cameramen and recordists to help cover the events. The following confrontation between police and Indians on a snowy highway in eight-degree weather—including some fascinating parleying, and culminating in the arrest of the Indian leaders—became the electrifying film *You Are on Indian Land* (1969).

The events were undoubtedly more than the founders of Challenge for Change had bargained for, and brought criticism on Stoney for his involvement in the Cornwall upheaval. Old timers at the National Film Board wondered if this was *really* the time to risk the long-range welfare of the organization on a less than world-shaking issue. But Stoney felt it essential to settle whether "a program entitled Challenge for Change is to be more than a public relations gimmick to make the Establishment seem more in tune with the times. . . ." The film did appear to settle the question. The footage won the Indians an Ottawa hearing. And *You Are on Indian Land,* though a source of discomfort to the Canadian government, was put into distribution by its National Film Board. The film meanwhile brought a new unity to the Indians.[7]

You Are on Indian Land, 1969.

National Film Board of Canada

Challenge for Change moved into a new phase of catalytic production with *VTR St. Jacques* (1969). VTR—videotape recording—became a crucial factor in Challenge for Change and similar programs because of ease of operation, instant playback capability, and easily portable equipment. Residents of St. Jacques, a depressed section of Montreal, were invited to tell their problems to VTR recorders—manned by volunteers from St. Jacques itself. A community meeting discussed the accumulated taped testimony, and this discussion was taped, and in turn viewed and discussed. As members of the community saw themselves and others in discussion, subtle shifts of opinion took place. The tapes thus stimulated and improved intra-community communication, as well as serving as a bridge to officialdom outside the community.[8]

Among early triumphs of the catalyst-documentary, one of the most remarkable was *The Sorrow and the Pity* (*Le Chagrin et la Pitié,* 1970), by Marcel Ophüls.[9]

Ophüls, son of fiction-film director Max Ophüls, was born in Germany in 1927 and moved with his family to France at the time Hitler came to power. In 1940 the family fled to the United States, where Marcel attended Hollywood High School and Occidental College. In 1950 he returned to France and became active in French film and television—for ORTF, L'Office de Radiodiffusion-Télévision Française. His documentary on events leading to World War II, *Munich, or the Hundred-Year Peace* (*Munich, ou la Paix pour Cent Ans,* 1967), was broadcast by ORTF with much success, but was then withdrawn from circulation and suppressed; it had apparently touched sensitive nerves in high places. Ophüls was fired the following year after his involvement in a strike of film directors against ORTF. But the work begun with the Munich film—originally projected as the first part of a trilogy—had achieved momentum: the second part, dealing with the war years, won a combination of West German and Swiss backing. Completed as *The Sorrow and the Pity,* it was rejected by French television but went on to smashing successes on television in several other countries, and in theaters in France and elsewhere.

The subject: wartime France under Nazi control. The method: interviews with survivors, alternating with archive footage. The results were unexpected and explosive, largely because of skillful work by Ophüls as interviewer and provocateur. The war years were veiled in myth—the heroic saga of the resistance, as built up over a quarter of a century. With patient prodding and questioning, Ophüls reached a more complex reality behind it, a mixture of courage, cowardice, venality, dedication. Like the psychoanalytic process, his quest was simultaneously resisted and welcomed by interviewees. Some agreed to be interviewed, then delayed, finally went ahead. Former Premier Pierre Mendès-France agreed to a half-hour interview, then talked seven hours. To audiences, the revelations brought feelings of horror and release. Precisely because of these tensions, the probe had the impact of high drama.

A Gaullist official, explaining why he had rejected the film for French television, was quoted: "Myths are important in the life of a people. Certain myths must not be destroyed." But the 1960's were a myth-destroying period.

Film as catalyst was finding diverse applications. While at one extreme it could probe festering social sores, at another it could tackle playfully sadistic projects like the American television series *Candid Camera,* produced by Allen Funt. Via concealed cameras and microphones, it tested such curious questions as: how would people in a laundromat act if a lady came in with her husband on a leash, and tied him up while she attended to her wash? (Result: most pretended not to notice.) Or: how would a man act if, mailing a letter, he heard a voice from inside the mailbox saying, "Hey, help me get out of here, will you? I'm stuck! Please help me!" (Result: most people hesitated, then pretended they had heard nothing.) Funt successfully applied his approach to the skinflick field with *What Do You Say to a Naked Lady?* (1970). It tested variations of the question: how would a man waiting for an elevator in an office building act if a naked lady, encumbered only by an attaché case, stepped off an elevator, came up to him, and asked him how to get to room 602?[10]

Catalyst cinema—*cinéma vérité*—influenced the evolution of film technique in ways ranging from beneficial to disastrous. It gave status to the interview, a device that had been shunned by most documentarists. Documentaries began to be crammed with interviews. When used for purely informational purposes, the results were generally drab and pedestrian. Their effectiveness in such films as *The Sorrow and the Pity* was closely related to tensions surrounding the question, the interview, the situation.

Skillfully used, the *cinéma vérité* interview became a valuable tool for biographical documentary—as suggested by such films as *Bethune*

(1964), made by Donald Brittain and John Kemeny for the National Film Board of Canada, and the American film *I. F. Stone's Weekly* (1973), an engaging study of a dissident journalist by Jerry Bruck, Jr.

Cinéma vérité, like direct cinema, often focused on the great and powerful, but also helped the lowly become articulate participants in society. Voice-over narrators of previous decades had almost always been elitist spokesmen. Thus the new genre had a certain democratizing effect—or a disruptive one, depending on the point of view.

Since the technique often involved the precipitating of crises—usually, but not necessarily, of a personal sort—it raised ethical and social issues not easily resolved.

The effectiveness of *cinéma vérité,* as of direct cinema, was somewhat limited by its heavy reliance on "talking heads"—often using vernacular speech. This raised difficult translation problems, and tended to give these techniques a national rather than international role. This problem had its tragic aspects. In the silent film era, great documentaries like *Nanook of the North* easily traveled world-wide. Now the travels were no longer easy. Voice-over documentaries, presenting a more manageable translation problem than talking-head documentaries, were perhaps more likely to remain a factor in international communication.

Cinéma vérité, like direct cinema, could have strong controversial impact. It achieved it by inquiry, rather than by protest. In both these genres, documentarists were trying to throw light on dark places, while avoiding editorializing. But in an era of rising tensions, other documentarists were overtly critical. Impelled by world crises, they seemed to increase in number, and every continent saw its eruptions of guerrilla documentary.

Guerrilla

In countries of eastern Europe there was talk about "black films." The term apparently originated in Poland in the mid-1950's, the time of de-Stalinization, when there was a "springtime thaw" in socialist areas. In the liberalized atmosphere fostered by Khrushchev, films with a critical point of view seemed to be tolerated. The novelty of the phenomenon called for a new term, and "black film" was the result. It carried—at least at first—no unfavorable connotations. The term simply recognized a kind of film different from the rosy-hued booster-films that had predominated.[1]

Students at the state film school at Łódź made a number of black films. Others came from established leaders of the industry. The films criticized administrative shortcomings, not socialism.

A typical black film was *Warsaw 56* (*Warszawa 56*, 1956), made by Jerzy Bossak, one of the creators of Poland's postwar film industry, and Jarosław Brzozowski. It spotlighted a war-inherited housing situation that remained in a crisis stage. Narrated by a woman, it begins, "This is my city, my home, Warsaw." These words, on a prideful note, introduce postwar rebuilding achievements, including the Palace of Culture donated by the Soviet Union—built in the ornate style favored by Stalin. Then she says, "This too is my city. . . . This is my home." Now we look at ruins, precarious shells of prewar apartment houses, and focus on one—fully inhabited—in which a whole wall was sheared away by a bomb so that its inhabitants resemble cliff dwellers. "In 1956 we live in the shadow of 1945 . . . only the gunfire is missing." In an upper-floor apartment we see a toddler; the mother has tied it with a rope anchored to a bed, because on one side their room ends in a precipice. The film dramatizes terrors faced by the cliff dwellers—not far from the "Stalin-style" Palace of Culture. In like fashion, other films of the period protested other unfinished business. *Where the Devil Says Goodnight* (*Gdzie Diabel Mówi Dobranoc*, 1956), by Kazimierz Karabasz and Władysław Ślesicki, focused on an even more deprived segment of urban life.

The black-film eruption, with the same terminology, spread to Hungary, Czechoslovakia, Yugoslavia—not without opposition. Khrushchev apparently grew fearful that liberalization was getting out of hand and introducing capitalist subversions. In 1957 troops were sent into Hungary, ending the springtime thaw there, and slowing it also in Poland—at least temporarily. Film makers soon found that through historic fiction, ostensibly placed in the Stalin period, they could still attack current problems. Even in documentary, subtle strategies evolved. The Hungarian director András Kovács, inspired by the work of Jean Rouch, produced a long *cinéma vérité* documentary titled *Difficult People* (*Nehéz Emberek*, 1964), in which he interviews scientists about inventions that have *not* seen the light of day. Pursuing the trail of aborted invention, he uncovers fantastic obstacle

Polish film school, Łódź: faculty interviews student from Ghana. Extreme right, Jerzy Toeplitz; at his right, Jerzy Bossak—both members of prewar Start society.

Bossak collection

Goldberger collection

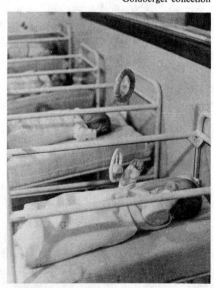

Children Without Love, 1964.

courses of bureaucratic red tape, lack of initiative, and dread of responsibility, as well as professional jealousy and malevolence. In the words of István Nemeskürty, Hungarian film historian, the "cruel logic of the director's quiz-like questions" develop into a devastating revelation of a kind of Parkinson's Law in action.[2]

In Czechoslovakia, where the black film had a similar—somewhat later—evolution, its role may be suggested by the documentary *Children Without Love* (*Děti Bez Lásky,* 1964), by Kurt Goldberger. In the postwar years there had been a huge development in crèches, day nurseries where even young infants could be deposited by working mothers, at minimal cost. The government wanted to offer strong incentives for women, including mothers, to go into industry, and the crèches effectively served this purpose. The validity of the large—often well-equipped—day nurseries was at first unquestioned. But by the 1960's a large population of institution-raised children was growing into early adulthood. Kurt Goldberger, studying the rise of juvenile delinquency and filming interviews with delinquents, was struck by the number who were products of early institutional care. He became convinced that they had been "understimulated intellectually and emotionally" in early childhood. This became the theme of *Children Without Love,* a forty-five-minute film made in consultation with psychiatrists. Goldberger had a substantial reputation in scientific films, and his film was sent to the Leipzig film festival, and also went into theaters, where it was found to have unexpected impact. As its implications became clear, the film came under sharp attack from elements in the Czechoslovak government. But it also won support, and before long government officials tended to associate themselves with the film and its views. It apparently contributed to a policy shift. Under new legislation, the government paid the working mother to stay home with her child for a substantial time after its birth.[3]

The Czechoslovakian thaw ended in 1968 with the arrival of Warsaw Pact troops and tanks. Again the spirit of protest could not be totally silenced. One student, Jan Palach, protested the military occupation by burning himself to death. Huge crowds made his act symbolic by silently attending his funeral. The documentary *The Funeral of Jan Palach* (1969) placed these events on the screen without comment. Thousands watched it in silence. It was black film at its most subtle and eloquent.

In Yugoslavia black films distinguished themselves by geniality and wit. Hard-hitting and at the same time good-natured, the black film became a special source of pride to the Yugoslav film industry.[4]

It began to develop about 1963, when film makers found censors more permissive than they had been. A light tone was struck with enormous success by Dušan Makavejev in his film *Parade* (*Parada,* 1963). Assigned to cover the semisacred May Day parade, he concentrated on preparations for it. The jockeying for position, the primping of officials, the disputes over protocol, became a hilarious direct-cinema kaleidoscope. The film satirized bureaucracy and the apparatus behind public spectacle rather than the event itself, but the May Day parade was never the same thereafter. Having seen itself in action in *Parada,* bureaucracy veered toward simpler rituals.

Makavejev saw cinema as a "guerrilla operation . . . against everything that is fixed, defined, established, dogmatic, eternal"—which meant, for him, Stalinism and the Pentagon alike. He saw the guerrilla film maker as having an infinite diversity of techniques and weapons at his disposal, including *joie de vivre.* After making several documentaries he moved into fiction, usually putting his stories in historic context via documentary sequences, and always showing irrepressible humor. His work was described by the critic David Robinson as *"joie de vivre* at the barricades."[5]

The combination of gaiety and purpose was carried on by other documentarists in such works as *The Rubber Stamp* (*Pečat,* 1965), by Branko Čelović, a mock-serious history of the rubber stamp from primitive days (when mankind somehow had to get along without them) to the present. In glittering montage we see the government seal of approval stamped onto everything from marriages to beef carcasses, and learn the triumphant news that "today, everyone has his own stamp"—a fingerprint on file at government bureaus. In high-spirited fashion, the film gives a disturbing sense of the reach of government into all aspects of life.

Kolt 15 Gap (1970), by Jovan Jovanović, had a similar antic spirit. Its narrator, often on camera, begins by proclaiming himself a fanatic marxist. More energetic application of marxism, he says, is all the country needs. He sometimes carries this theme in zany directions: women, he says, should be nationalized, and the new Belgrade hotel should have 500 women. But he is also deadly serious. Lunging in arm-waving fashion from place to place—like a socially aroused Groucho Marx—he identifies inequalities, injustices, failures—all, he

One More Day, 1971.

says, needing *more* marxism. He says he himself has worked at scores of jobs for fifteen years and has often been unemployed, and eaten scrapings from the plates of the more prosperous, but he is still a devout marxist. To show how devout, he reminds us of the marxist prediction that under socialism the state would wither away. For him, says the hero, it already has. (The title is an acronym that refers to his fifteen years of eating scrapings.)

Black films of more serious tone included *Little Pioneers* (*Pioniri Maleni,* 1968), intimate close-up of young slum groups living on pickpocketing and prostitution, by Želimir Žilnik—who describes his work as "self-critical realism"; *Special Trains* (*Specijalni Vlakovi,* 1971), by Krsto Papić, on Yugoslavia's unemployment problem and the reluctant emigration of labor to factory jobs in West Germany; *One More Day* (*Dan Više,* 1971), by Vlatko Gilić, poignant study of a mud-bath spa where the desperate go for miracle cures.

Such films were produced by studios organized as cooperatives. Each of Yugoslavia's republics and autonomous districts had at least one studio. Part of its funds—generally less than half—came from a state subsidy; the remainder was earned via revenue from theaters and television, at home and abroad. Foreign distribution was promoted through film festivals, where Yugoslavian short films often won top honors.

Yugoslav views toward black films were interestingly reflected in a film about black films—*Intersection* (*Cvor*, 1969), by Krsto Papić. A film maker arrives at a railway station—a new, handsome one—and starts to interview travelers about their problems, which seem numerous and overwhelming. A station official arrives to protest. Why doesn't the documentarist make a film about the beautiful station? He proceeds to point out its glass and marble wonders. People are tired of misery and poverty, he argues. It is the beautiful that should be filmed. The documentarist is skeptical. The film leaves their debate unresolved.

But the station official was not alone. Black films flourished in Yugoslavia for about a decade, but 1973 brought a wave of criticism from government officials against several who had led the trend, including Makavejev. The springtime thaw showed signs of abating—at least temporarily.

The ups and downs suggest important points. The essential role played by criticism has been widely recognized. Policies cannot well be evaluated without it. The need for organized self-criticism has been established doctrine in the socialist countries, including the Soviet Union. But disputes over allowable limits have been persistent, and seem inevitable. Criticism via the film medium, especially on television, has been least welcome to officials because of its power and reach. Embarrassments and challenges to officialdom have, sooner or later, invited retaliation and attempts at repression. Yet critical films have clearly contributed to public enlightenment and social sanity. Returning springtime thaws and winter frosts seem equally inevitable.

All this has been no less true in capitalist countries, though the struggles have been more complex—in that they have involved not only governments but also corporations, some holding enormous international power. The vicissitudes of dissident films and of efforts to suppress, smother, deflect, and neutralize them have been dramatically illustrated in the case of the Vietnam war—a war fought not only with bombs and booby traps but also with documentaries—by governments, corporations, and others throughout the world.

Documentary film first called attention to Vietnam and other areas of Indochina at the dawn of film history, when Lumière cinematographers filmed *Coolies at Saigon* (1897), *Elephant Processions at Phnom Penh* (1901), and other scenes, including a brick factory at Hanoi. The following decades brought explorer-documentarists to Indochina, most notably the group that made *The Yellow Cruise (La Croisière Jaune,* 1934), sponsored by Citroën. Starting from Lebanon, they sought Marco Polo's eastward route through China. At Shanghai they came on beginnings of bloody Chinese-Japanese warfare and were glad—in the words of the narrator—to reach the "peace and security" of Hanoi, where the French Governor General received them ceremoniously. During the 1930's the French made many documentaries that, like films of Britain's Empire Marketing Board, were intended to strengthen the bonds of empire. They included such titles as *Peaceful Shadows of Indochina (Harmonieux Ombrages d'Indochine)* and *Perfumed Hills of the Tonkin Plains (Collines Parfumées des Plateaux Moïs).*[6] They were seen by French audiences, few others.

After World War II, as the Vietnamese under Ho Chi Minh fought for independence, Russians became conscious of their struggle through film reports and writings of Roman Karmen, culminating in his feature *Vietnam*—released in 1955 but begun early in 1954, when the French still controlled all Indochinese cities. Karmen was astonished at the life he found among Ho Chi Minh forces in the jungles. "Publishing houses, factories, scientific institutes, universities, art exhibitions—this jungle life, it was astonishing, absolutely astonishing, because at the same time there was such bloodshed."[7]

Few Americans had at this time seen any film on Vietnam, or knew such a place existed, although the United States was airlifting supplies to the French, and its Secretary of State John Foster Dulles was offering them atom bombs—which the French declined.[8] The French debacle at Dienbienphu led to a 1954 Geneva agreement, calling for an internationally supervised election, which the United States pledged to support. But American intelligence reported that 80 per cent of the Vietnamese, north and south, would vote for Ho Chi Minh, and the Eisenhower administration considered this good reason to avoid the election and, via massive aid, build an independent South Vietnam.[9] The Kennedy administration continued this policy, and enlarged on it. The American efforts—like those of the French—met powerful partisan resistance.

During these years Americans saw vivid documentaries on do-

Vietnam—feature documentary released 1955 by Central Documentary Film Studio, Moscow.

Karmen collection

French prisoners, Dienbienphu, 1954—from Soviet feature *Vietnam*.
Staatliches Filmarchiv der DDR

Karmen collection

Filming the Soviet feature *Vietnam:* the French
yield Hanoi.

mestic civil-rights struggles, none on Vietnam. American television networks had no bureaus there. Correspondents flew in occasionally from Tokyo or Jakharta on special assignment. No television documentaries told of CIA and "adviser" operations in Vietnam or in adjoining Laos.

Nor did newsreels. During the 1950's America's main surviving newsreels—*Fox Movietone News* and the MGM-Hearst *News of the Day*—had become government-subsidized under a highly secret arrangement with the code name "Kingfish." They were still ostensibly private, but foreign editions carried items prepared by the U.S. government. For the newsreels, survival depended on this secret government relationship.[10]

The first documentary on Vietnam seen by many Americans was *Why Vietnam?* (1965), made to aid the huge war escalation—including attacks on the north—determined upon in 1964 by the Johnson administration. Produced by the Department of Defense, the film was used to indoctrinate Vietnam-bound draftees, and was also loaned to schools. It followed the formula and rhetoric of the famous *Why We Fight* films. But it distorted history in ways that made historians fume, once they became aware of the film. Henry Steele Commager, reviewing it almost two years after its production, found it "not history . . . not even journalism . . . as scholarship it is absurd. . . . When Communists sponsor such propaganda, we call it 'brainwashing.'" Revelations later published in *The Pentagon Papers* showed the film to be even more deceptive than it had previously appeared to be.

Why Vietnam? begins with footage of Hitler and the Nazis. Just as Americans had to go to Europe to crush Hitler, says the film, it is now necessary that they go to Vietnam and crush Vietnamese "aggressors." Vietnam had become "our front door."

To pin down the "aggressor" charge, the film pretended that the Geneva conference had created an independent South Vietnam. As Commager pointed out, the conference had done no such thing. It had stipulated that Vietnam was *one* country; division into two administrative areas was to be temporary, until the agreed-on election. Commager saw the United States as "chiefly responsible for putting off the election."[11]

To bolster the word "aggression" further, the film showed a pile of weapons captured from South Vietnamese partisans, or "Vietcong"—weapons with "unmistakable" Chinese markings, said the narrator, underscored by ominous "Chinese" music. The weapons in the demonstration may well have been Chinese; during an 18-month period before the escalation decision (June 1962 through January 1964) 179 weapons from communist countries—the Soviet Union, Czechoslovakia, China—were captured from Vietcong partisans. What the film did not say (the Pentagon released the information long afterward) was that American weapons by the *thousands* had also been captured from Vietcong. The Vietcong were at this time fighting almost wholly with American weapons which American "advisers" or Vietnamese units equipped by them had lost or sold or smuggled to the Vietcong. After escalation, the foreign help rose sharply.[12]

As the escalation began and a *de facto*—though undeclared—war came into being, network documentaries on Vietnam appeared at regular intervals. Most adhered to government rationales. For several years network policy seemed determined to shield the public against doubts about the war. "Prime time"—the large-audience hours—was a fortress not to be pierced.

The policy caused restiveness and disaffection among network staffs, but pressures for conformity were massive. Any statement casting doubt on the government version of events was likely to bring a furious telephone call from President Johnson himself—directed to network executive or commentator.

For networks and their sponsors it was a prosperous period. Schedules were virtually sold out. Many major sponsors were also war contractors. To avoid rocking the military boat was made to seem both patriotic and, from a business point of view, good sense.

The sponsor and his business were even in evidence on the battlefield. Film maker Marvin Farkas, based in Hong Kong—who sometimes covered Far Eastern events for American networks—was engaged by Lockheed to make a film in Vietnam, documenting the performance of the Lockheed C-130 on airlift duty in combat. The company contract with the Pentagon apparently called for proof of performance in action. Thus the 1967–68 siege of Khe San found Farkas bottled up there with Marines, sharing their perils but fulfilling a far more lucrative contract. Cessna engaged him for a similar assignment, to document its A-37 jet bomber in action; eleven bombing runs got Farkas the footage he needed.[13]

The claim was often made that television was bringing the war "into the home." This was true. News telecasts provided daily vignettes—sometimes splendidly produced—of American soldiers pushing through swamps, or the wounded being brought in on stretchers. Unquestionably these nourished hopes for an end to the conflict. But they also made war a customary daily item and, by the one-sided focus, supported it. Even fund appeals for USO and Red Cross, stressing services to men "fighting for you," promoted the war. Christmas programs like those of Bob Hope entertaining troops in Vietnam were powerful promoters of the war. What was missing from the television picture was a real sense of the duplicities that had been used to launch the war, the horrors it was inflicting on the people of Vietnam, and its corrupting influence on America itself.

These missing ingredients were amply available in documentaries from other lands, friendly and unfriendly. Kept from the eyes of most Americans, they were giving much of the world a picture of the war very different from what Americans saw.

Films from the Vietcong partisans began early. Among the first was *Nguyen Hun Tho Speaks to the American People* (*Chu Tich Nguyen Hun Tho Noi Chuyen Voi Nhan Dan My,* 1965), a straightforward statement by the partisan leader, intercut with illustrative footage. It was seen by few Americans. As a film it was a modest achievement, but subsequent Vietcong films grew rapidly in skill and ambition. Especially effective was *The Way to the Front* (*Duong Ra Phia Truoc,* 1969), the saga of a young group carrying supplies a huge distance via stream and forest trail to a partisan unit, with periodic crises precipitated by prowling planes. The determination to get the supplies through, colored by infectious camaraderie and good humor, would have given Americans a very different picture of the Vietcong than that provided by Secretary of State Dean Rusk, who described "the enemy" as living in a reign of terror, fighting at the behest of tyrannical madmen.

Among North Vietnamese films, *Some Evidence* (*Vai Toibac Cua de Quoc My,* 1969) presented a relentlessly detailed demonstration of the effects of American pellet bombs, incendiary bombs, napalm, phosphorus, and other weapons—on people, animals, crops, buildings. Filmed autopsies were used to show effects on people and animals. Statistics summarized damage to villages, schools, churches, hospitals.

Such films were shown in communist countries—and in others. In Stockholm a Film Centrum, specializing in films on social issues, established a special collection of Vietcong and North Vietnamese films, making them widely available for rental. An American distributor agreed to distribute some of these in the United States, but the company he represented, American Documentary Films, was instantly warned by the U.S. Treasury Department that the films would not be allowed into the United States.[14] A few did enter clandestinely, and circulated among campus groups—along with films from *Newsreel,* an anti-war film group based in New York. Most Vietnam films were seized by customs officials.

Meanwhile films about Vietnam erupted in a chain explosion throughout the world. The fertile young chief of the Cuban newsreel, Santiago Alvarez, who had attracted international attention with *Now!* (1965), an exuberant manifesto on minority rights—using a Lena Horne song as sound track—followed with several films on Indochina: *Hanoi, Tuesday the 13th (Hanoi, Martes Trece,* 1967), a close-up of one day of war; *Laos, the Forgotten War (La Guerra Olvidada,* 1967), portrait of life in caves under American saturation bombing; and *79 Springtimes (79 Primaveras,* 1969), a paean to Ho Chi Minh. East Germany contributed *Pilots in Pyjamas (Piloten in Pyjama),* four unusual *cinéma vérité* films based on long interviews with American airmen in the "Hanoi Hilton" prison camp during the summer of 1967. The films were the work of Walter Heynowski and Gerhard Scheumann, who specialized in skillfully probing interview films. It interested them that the pilots viewed their bombing activities simply as "the job" they had been assigned to do. One of the films was called *The Job (Der Job).* American Documentary Films attempted to import both the Cuban and East German films; both attempts ended in seizures by U.S. customs. However, NBC-TV was allowed to import *Pilots in Pyjamas* but used only fragments in newscasts, with a superimposed warning that it was "communist" material.

Many countries friendly to the United States engaged in documenting the war—sometimes with explosive results. Junichi Ushiyama, prolific Japanese producer who had developed several successful documentary series for Nippon TV, spent a month with a South Vietnamese Marine battalion assigned to search-and-destroy missions. The result was three films titled *With a South Vietnamese Marine Battalion (Minami Betonamu Kaiheidaitai Senki,* 1965), among the earliest Vietnam films to document atrocities. We follow the Marine group as it moves cautiously from village to village, looking for Viet-

In France:. *The Seventeenth Parallel,* 1967.

In Japan: *With a South Vietnamese Marine Battalion,* 1965.

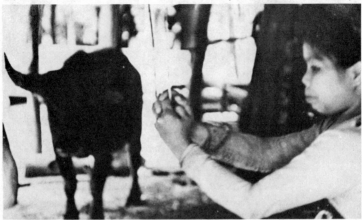

In Poland: *Fire*, 1968.

In Canada: *Sad Song of Yellow Skin*, 1970.

Staatliches Filmarchiv der DDR

Pilots in Pyjamas, 1967: East German television crew makes four half-hour films in the "Hanoi Hilton."

American airman adjusts mike for interview.

Interviewers Walter Heynowski and Gerhard Scheumann with cameramen.

cong "suspects." In most villages, only silent women and children are found. When a man is found, he is subjected to an "interrogation" that usually leaves him dead. In one case, an officer ends the questioning by hacking off the man's head. This episode climaxed the second film, and resulted in termination of the series—at the request of the Japanese government.

In Britain Granada-TV, in its *World in Action* documentary series, turned repeatedly to topics relating to Vietnam, notably in *The Demonstration* (1968), study of a huge anti-war demonstration outside the American embassy in London, and police efforts to cope with it—a Cannes festival award winner, but ignored in the United States; and *The Back-seat Generals* (1970), an investigation of the CIA war in Laos. Among numerous Canadian documentaries on Vietnam, the National Film Board contributed the very moving *Sad Song of Yellow Skin* (1970), by Michael Rubbo, picturing the disruption of Vietnamese life more vividly than anything seen on American television. In France the veteran Joris Ivens, having established his base in Paris, released the feature-length *17th Parallel* (*17e Parallèle,* 1967), a *cinéma vérité* portrait of the North Vietnamese at war, and *The People and Their Guns* (*Le Peuple et ses Fusils,* 1970), on the war in Laos—banned by France as a concession to American sensibilities, but distributed elsewhere. Syria contributed *Napalm* (1970), by Nabil Maleh, a searing little film in the form of an American-style television commercial, advertising napalm as though it were a beauty aid or patent medicine, extolling its thorough and rapid action. It was a film-festival favorite. So was Poland's *Fire* (*Ogien,* 1969), one of several Vietnam films directed by Andrzej Brzozowski. There were scores of others including composite projects like *Far From Vietnam* (*Loin de Vietnam,* 1967), by leading French film makers, and *Arts Vietnam* (1969), a joint protest by Australian artists.

Almost all these films were known to American television networks, and available to them. Except for a few fragments on news programs, the networks seldom deviated from their policy of showing only their own documentaries. A standard rationale was that they could not assess the authenticity of material produced by others. This was plausible: they could not always assess the authenticity of their own. More to the point, a different policy would have plunged them into fierce controversy, and brought charges of "aiding the enemy." Such perils were neatly sidestepped by the adopted policy. But it also meant that the networks were abetting a national adventure in self-delusion concerning the war—its origins, purposes, effects, legality, morality, and international acceptance.

Yet within network staffs, awareness and uneasiness grew. Occasionally the concern showed itself—as in the 1967 CBS documentary *Morley Safer's Vietnam,* in which Safer presented without comment his interview with American airmen back from a successful "mission." He asked how it felt to "make a kill like that," and they answered:

CAPTAIN: I feel real good when we do it. It's kind of a feeling of accomplishment. It's the only way you're going to win, I guess, is to kill 'em.

PILOT: I just feel it's just another target. You know, like in the states you shot at dummies, over here you shoot at Vietnamese. Vietnamese Cong.

ANOTHER: (*Off, interrupting*): Cong. You shoot at Cong. You don't shoot at Vietnamese.

PILOT: (*laughing*): All right. You shoot at Cong. Anyway, when you come out on the run and then you see them, and they come into your sights, it's just like a wooden dummy or something there, you just thumb off a couple pair of rockets. Like they weren't people at all.[15]

The next year brought a more important breakthrough. It came not on a commercial network but on public television, which had too long been a still backwater of the television scene. Operating on minuscule budgets, it had seldom captured more than one per cent of available viewers. But in the late 1960's it began to stir into life—partly with material rejected or ignored by sponsored television.

The State Department had forbidden Americans, including reporters and film makers, to travel to North Vietnam—or to China, North Korea, Cuba, Albania. Passports of offenders had been revoked. The ban was explained as necessary for the "protection" of American citizens, but had unquestionably served to insulate the American public against unfavorable news and views. The networks tacitly accepted the ban. Some Americans challenged it on constitutional grounds, and several cases were in litigation. Meanwhile one film maker, Felix Greene, went to North Vietnam and made a film. Though a long-time United States resident, he was a British citizen; he had at one time been a BBC representative in the United States. In the early 1960's he had been to China and made the documentary *China!* (1963). Though its distribution had been harassed by federal authorities, the film had won showings in art theaters and film societies and had given Americans a glimpse of a forbidden land. In 1967, when he proposed to go to North Vietnam, CBS offered him film, an advance, and laboratory services in exchange for an option on the completed film. The following year Greene returned with *Inside North Vietnam* (1968). At this point CBS lost courage and decided to show only brief fragments on its newscasts—as NBC had done with *Pilots in Pyjamas*. But public television agreed to broadcast a forty-nine-minute segment, followed by discussion.

The decision brought weird eruptions. Thirty-three Congressmen, none of whom had seen the film, signed a letter demanding cancelation of the booking. One told an executive he would never vote for a television appropriation if *Inside North Vietnam* were broadcast. But the telecast proceeded. The film gave Americans a glimpse of matters already familiar to audiences in other parts of the world; the impact may well have been strengthened by the blackout that preceded it. Cleveland Amory, writing in *The Saturday Review,* found the film "so moving it will make you first ashamed, then angry, and finally utterly determined to make everybody you know see it."

What audiences saw was a people whose lives were disrupted in fantastic ways, and marked by ceaseless work, but strangely joyful, proud, and dignified. To Amory the film was important because it showed "what kind of people we are fighting—and why their record against us is bound to go down in history alongside Thermopylae, Stalingrad—or, for that matter, Valley Forge."[16]

War protests subsided briefly after the election of President Nixon, his withdrawal of ground troops, and his references to a plan to end the war. But as its outlines became clear—it involved intensified bombing and expansion of the war into Cambodia—the guerrilla film attacks resumed. The film *Interview with My Lai Veterans* (1971), by Joseph Strick—stark confirmation of incredible horrors—was shown in theaters and won an Oscar. About the same time, protest found one of its most important expressions in *The Selling of the Pentagon* (1971), a CBS News documentary written and produced by Peter Davis.

It was broadcast in prime time. It breached the fortress. Considering its relentless forthrightness, this was historic. The film did not attack the war as such, but exposed the multitudinous ways in which the Department of Defense had promoted it. The Department's cosiness with industry and key Congressmen was well illustrated. The film showed how, with its huge public-relations funds—exceeding the combined news budgets of all networks—the Pentagon had spread the gospel of militarism. Its salesmanship directed toward children was disturbingly exhibited. The film included excerpts from various Pentagon films. It showed how the Pentagon public relations apparatus had on occasion hoodwinked and misled news media, including television.

Roger Mudd, newsman-narrator of the film, summed up:

MUDD: Defending the country not just with arms but also with ideology, Pentagon propaganda insists on America's role as the cop on every beat in the world. Not only the public but the press as well has been beguiled, including at times, ourselves at CBS News. This propaganda barrage is the creation of a runaway bureaucracy that frustrates attempts to control it.[17]

The film was met with hosannahs and outrage. A telephone caller during the telecast denounced Mudd as an "agent of a foreign power." Vice President Agnew called the program "disreputable." The Pentagon and others attacked details of treatment; none of these attacks struck at the substance of the film. CBS-TV rebroadcast the film within a few weeks; the second broadcast reached a larger audience than the first.

In the course of the hubbub the Pentagon withdrew some of its war-promotion films from circulation.

Denunciations leveled at *The Selling of the Pentagon* had depicted it as radical and irresponsible. During the following months, revelations published in *The Pentagon Papers* and emerging from the Watergate hearings made *The Selling of the Pentagon* seem restrained. The film had identified a cancer that was unquestionably threatening the democratic tradition. While critical, it was essentially a conservative document, defending traditional values. And it made clear once more the potential importance of criticism—especially, the importance of black film. Much of what *The Selling of the Pentagon* revealed had been discussed in print, without wide impact. Prime-time documentation had ringing reverberations.

The global film struggles over Vietnam hold numerous implications. They suggest the many ways in which an establishment can silence, muffle, discourage, deflect, isolate expressions it does not favor. The film maker, in his dependence on distribution systems, is often a helpless entity.

Yet the situation changes. The multiplication of distribution systems permits one system to bring pressure on others. In the United States the pressure of protest films, foreign and domestic, eventually had its impact—via campus, film society, citizen group, public television—on prime time.

The spirit of protest generated by Vietnam meanwhile spilled into other fields, creating a guerrilla-film era. In Sweden, when demonstrators protested a scheduled Davis Cup match with Rhodesia, because of Rhodesia's racial policies, young film makers under Bo Widerberg documented the event in electrifying fashion in *The White Game* (*Den Vita Sporten,* 1968). Curiously the protest—almost by way of habit—became also a protest over "imperialism" and Vietnam.

In Japan, guerrilla film activity reached high intensity during the war. The use made of Japan as a conduit for Vietnam war supplies generated strong anti-government feelings and many "protest films"—the Japanese equivalent of black films. These were seldom seen in theaters or on television, but reached a substantial audience via 16mm in clubs, unions, and other groups. Ironically, wide distribution of 16mm projectors ("Natco" projectors) by the American occupation after World War II, for reindoctrination purposes, had laid the basis for this rise of a 16mm system. It now saw such films as the powerful *Sanrizuka* series—three feature-length films. The heavy air traffic through Japan—swollen by the war—had prompted a 1966 decision to build a new international airport for Tokyo. The area chosen, Sanrizuka, was occupied by farmers who were determined to block seizure of their lands. For four years the film maker Shinsuke Ogawa documented their struggle, which reached its climax in the third film, *The Peasants of the Second Fortress* (*Daini Toride no Hitobito,* 1971). Here we see resistance turning into a pitched battle with riot police as farm women chain themselves to improvised stockades, and students join the struggle for anti-government, anti-war motives. Ogawa, patiently recording the growth of resistance into an Armageddon, achieved an extraordinary social document, and one of the most potent of protest films.

The film of dissent even made an appearance in India where, through most of the years since independence, the Ministry of Information and Broadcasting had held a tight monopoly over documentary production. The film maker Khwaja Ahmad Abbas—who was also a widely read newspaper columnist—made a film in the tra-

Svenska Filminstitutet

The White Game, 1968. Student demonstration against a scheduled Davis Cup match with Rhodesia–to protest racial policies–turns into a demonstration against "imperialism" and the Vietnam war.

PROTEST ERA: TOKYO AIRPORT
The Peasants of the Second Fortress, 1971.

Tricontinental

Film crew at fortress built to block airport project.

Farm women chain themselves to fortress stockade.

Students join battle against riot police.

dition of the Polish black film *Warsaw 56*. Titled *A Tale of Four Cities* (*Char Shehar Ek Kahani*, 1968), it paid tribute to what India had achieved in its major cities, but finally focused on unfinished business, including Bombay slums and prostitution. He surprised the board of censors by refusing an "adults only" certificate, insisting his film was relevant for young people. The case was therefore referred to the Ministry of Information and Broadcasting, which offered to approve the film if Abbas would—

shorten the scene of women in the red light district,

deleting specially the shot showing the closing of the window by the lady, the suggestive shots of bare knees,

and the passing of the currency notes.

Abbas refused, and replied:

I think, once for all, the courts and even the Supreme Court will have to decide the issue, of whether a documentary of social protest can be banned or distorted under the cover of clauses which were originally intended to eliminate obscenity and pornography. That is where I propose to take the issue, besides the court of informed public opinion. This is not a threat. It is a promise.

He brought suit, carrying his case to the Supreme Court. A year later, the Justices apparently advised the Ministry that it was about to lose the case. In open court, as a decision was awaited, the government announced that it had changed its mind, and would approve *A Tale of Four Cities* without restrictions. It was an astounding moment in Indian film annals.[18]

In most periods of documentary history, production has been controlled by groups in power. In some instances, groups newly achieving power have found it valuable in consolidating their position; this was the case with work of Vertov in Russia, of Riefenstahl in Germany, and of Lorentz in the United States. In the 1930's, documentary began in a small way to serve non-government groups as a medium of dissent. This development was snuffed out by World War II, but began again in the postwar era, stimulated by social ferment and upheaval, and at the same time facilitated by various technical breakthroughs. Lighter, cheaper equipment constantly tended to democratize a medium once reserved for the few.

In the 1970's the base of documentary activity was dramatically broadened by the rise of *video*—a term that began to be applied to the use of videotape as a new medium of expression. Videotape had arrived on the scene in a different role: when videotape recorders first appeared in the 1950's, at prices ranging upward from $40,000, their function was to make copies of television programs for preservation, rebroadcast, promotion, or syndication. The bulky recorders used large reels of videotape of 2-inch width. Networks and stations were the main buyers. Simpler equipment and falling prices gradually enabled some educational institutions and individuals to buy them—likewise, at first for copy purposes. Then the advent of compact video cameras and editing equipment, easy to operate and moderate in cost, brought videotape into a new arena. These cameras—including *porta-paks* using ½-inch tape—apparently enabled almost anyone to make brilliant images. These required no laboratory processing—the images could be evaluated instantly. In most cases no special lighting was needed. Unlike film, tape could be reused; low in cost, tape for the small video cameras could be expended almost as freely as a novelist uses paper. A single individual could now be a production unit. Videotape, no longer serving merely a copying function, became a canvas for independent work—video.

During the 1970's these advantages suddenly encouraged all sorts of people—alone or in schools, churches, businesses, and community groups—to plunge into video production. Working in every conceivable genre, for every conceivable communication purpose, they inevitably included guerrilla film makers. New distribution systems—cable, public-access channel, public-service satellite—provided further incentive.

An early video experimenter was the National Film Board of Canada. In *VTR St. Jacques,* a 1969 production of its Challenge for Change program, it had foreshadowed the social-action possibilities of video. George Stoney, the American who had for a time headed the program, moved to New York University in the early 1970's and founded its Alternate Media Center, concentrating on video. He saw video as a means by which citizen groups could exert effective pressure via the public-access channels included in many cable systems.[19] The speeches and panels generally seen on these channels seemed to him to doom them to minuscule audiences. Stoney encouraged students to take portapaks into the field to document crises and disputes in housing, health, pollution, unemployment. Tapes of this sort, sometimes dramatic and challenging, soon found a place on the public-access channels of various cable systems.

But they were not, for a time, welcomed for broadcast use. Broadcasters were intent on color programming, and the first portapaks made only black-and-white images. Sony introduced an experimental ½-inch color portapak in 1973, which promised eventually to resolve this issue, but there were further obstacles. Images from the small cameras, while beautiful to the eye, tended during broadcast to reveal elements of instability such as jitter and white flashes or "glitches." A New York engineer, John J. Godfrey, working at the experimental program laboratory of the public television system, developed an obsessive determination to overcome this problem. Excited by the extraordinary aliveness he saw in many video documentaries, he realized that the compactness and portability of the equipment had been essential elements in producing such work. He gradually devised a procedure for upgrading small-format video work to "broadcast quality" via a series of post-production dubbings.[20] Opening a new chapter in television documentary, all this gave renewed impetus to video experimentation. Much of it came from independents organized in cooperatives—with such names as Global Village, Optic Nerve, The Kitchen, TVTV (Top Value Television). Most did their documentary production on ½-inch or ¾-inch tape.

The technology kept evolving. At first, picture and sound had to be handled separately; in the 1980's video cameras with built-in microphones became available. Sound recordists poking intimidating microphones at interviewees were no longer a necessary intrusion. And the action of video cameras became virtually inaudible.

All this continued to excite independents. Much of their work had a guerrilla aspect. Their tapes were not merely programs but links in a chain of social action. This tended to create, in administrative circles, some wariness of the video upsurge. Some observers saw the documentary entering an era of broad participation and wider, freer use. Others suggested that techniques of surveillance and control would multiply as rapidly as media technology.

The rise of the video fever and its eventual impact on establishment media may be suggested by the saga of New York's Downtown Community Television Center (DCTV) founded in 1972 by Jon Alpert and Keiko Tsuno in an antique baroque-styled firehouse at the edge of New York's Chinatown. Alpert, after studies at New York Univer-

Early video: A group from New York's Downtown Community TV Center
taping *Chinatown: Immigrants in America,* a 1976 public television broadcast.
Corky Lee

sity, drove a taxi in this multi-ethnic area and became involved in
efforts to reform the taxi union. Keiko Tsuno—who became Mrs.
Alpert—introduced him to video. She had come from Tokyo for art
studies, and her earnings as waitress in a New York Japanese restau-
rant financed the purchase of a Sony portapak. Together they made
a tape about the taxi union and the problems of taxi drivers. The
tape tended to serve as an organizing tool. The excitement it caused
among taxi drivers propelled Alpert and Tsuno further into video. At
the firehouse they launched free training in video. During a four-
week course students had free use of equipment and were sent into
Chinatown and other nearby areas to document conditions, conflicts,
cultures. At first the tapes were only shown on street corners and in
neighborhood meeting places. But demand for the courses became
overwhelming. Initially financed by earnings of Alpert and Tsuno,
the work attracted grants from the New York State Council on the
Arts and other agencies. During its first seven years DCTV gave free
training to no less than 7000 people, with instructions in English,
Chinese, and Spanish. Some of the graduates went on to spearhead
other video centers. The tapes that emerged from DCTV, in some

fifteen languages, were welcomed by stations in various parts of the world, earning fees that helped in a small way to support the center. At home the support of the public television system, made possible by the technical work of John J. Godfrey, became an important factor. Godfrey eventually joined DCTV.

Meanwhile, productions by Alpert and Tsuno spread the fame of the enterprise. Among the most powerful was *Health Care: Your Money or Your Life* (1977), a devastating close-up of a city hospital hard pressed by a staggering case load and at the same time by equipment shortages and a budget squeeze. The tape reflected a warm relationship between the video group and hospital personnel, yet the impact of the tape was dismaying. Implicitly, it was a protest against draconian governmental budget-cutting. One sequence concerned an aging radiation machine in the cancer center that was thought to destroy so much healthy tissue that one staff member referred to it as "The Killer." In one overwhelming sequence a heart-attack patient dies on camera, apparently because out-of-order equipment and a lack of supplies delayed his emergency operation. The program became, not without protest, a public television network program.[21]

Alpert, wandering with his equipment, apparently had an uncanny ability to get people to react to him as a person, not a media visitation. His encounters, whether in private session or jostling crowd, produced colloquies that seemed oblivious to the fact that he was shooting and recording. He proved able to carry these abilities into foreign settings, even where linguistic confusion was involved. Participation in Sunday afternoon baseball games with members of the Cuban mission to the United Nations led to Alpert and Tsuno becoming the first Americans in a dozen years to be invited to Cuba to make a documentary. Using the new Sony ½-inch color portapak they produced *Cuba: The People* (1974), the first ½-inch color video work to find its way onto television. It was described by UPI as "the best look at Cuba since Castro toppled the Batista regime." It led to an Alpert-Tsuno visit to Vietnam as the first American television journalists admitted there after the fall of Saigon. The result was the revealing and deeply moving *Vietnam: Picking Up the Pieces* (1977), shot in ¾-inch color. In its final sequence, showing a visit to an orphanage filled with children of American servicemen, a girl bursts into tears on seeing Alpert. He reminds her of her father, who died when she was four.

Both the Cuba program and the Vietnam program were shown on the public television system, to resounding critical applause. And they resulted in a further breakthrough. They helped propel the commercial networks toward use of the small, light formats. NBC, losing ground to its rivals ABC and CBS and now even to PBS, sought to enlist Alpert in its news operations. He declined a staff role but was glad to undertake documentary ventures for NBC's *Today* series on a project by project basis. Thus, fees from the mighty RCA-NBC began to contribute to the support of the bustling cooperative in the disused firehouse at the edge of Chinatown. For network viewers Alpert began to provide memorable sequences videotaped in Cambodia, Nicaragua, Iran, Afghanistan, as well as in United States crisis spots.

His work tended to bring viewers something different from the more ritualized network staff productions. In Iran, during the 1980 hostage crisis, network crews seemed to be anchored to the front of the American embassy, showing endless shots of the occupying "students" shouting threats and anti-American slogans. Meanwhile, Alpert with his portapak was strolling, accompanied only by a sound recordist and a translator, through marketplaces and back streets, surrounded by curious Iranians—some hostile, others ready to protect him—eliciting enlightening shots and comments, often fascinating in their contradictions. Alpert relished ambiguities of the sort avoided by network newsmen, who preferred to appear knowledgeable, and able to explain things. He showed that Iranians, for all their revolutionary turmoil, were eager for American pop music and blue jeans. They were still assembling American automobiles. He visited a popular "American" spot, the Mafia Pizza Parlor.

During the early Reagan years the U.S. government became increasingly involved in military and other aid to authoritarian regimes seeking to repress reform movements, which in some cases had precipitated civil war. Video documentaries on these movements, by video practitioners in the Alpert mold, became occasional television features. Officialdom became increasingly restive about independent video reports that undercut its claims and rationales.

In much of the world, documentary was indeed taking a growing role in political disputes and involving an increasing spectrum of participants. Film had already become an activity of revolutionary undergrounds in many countries. In Argentina, during 1966–68,

Jon Alpert and Keiko Tsuno, venturers in video.

© 1982 Maureen Lambray

Fernando Ezequiel Solanas made *The Hour of the Furnaces* (*La Hora de los Hornos*), three films designed to serve as an underground organizing instrument. They comprised a harsh, revolutionary political manifesto. Underground film makers in South Africa were responsible for the footage in *End of the Dialogue* (*Phela-Ndaba,* 1971), smuggled to the outside world with vivid revelations about apartheid. A Uruguayan underground, with direction from the Swedish film maker Jan Lindquist, proclaimed itself to the world in the startling film *Tupamoros* (1973), which showed an interview with a kidnapped diplomat in a "people's prison." The advent of video seemed to assure continuing works of this sort. They represented a new direction for documentary—especially explosive examples of an explosive era.

6

LONG SHOT

largo

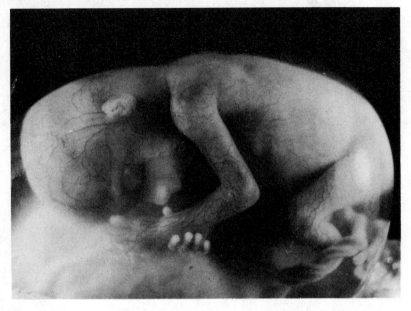

BBC-TV's *Everyday Miracle: Birth,* 1981.

Discoverer

We have traced throughout a century, from the first screen projections of Muybridge, Marey, and others, the evolution of the documentary. We have seen the documentarist rise and fall in status, sometimes working in obscurity, sometimes at the center of the world's stage.

We have noted his varied roles: explorer, reporter, painter, and so on. We have emphasized that these roles were not mutually exclusive. The documentarist has always been more than one of these. Yet different historic moments have brought different functions to the fore, tending to create different sub-genres. New technologies effected similar shifts.

As the documentary approached its second century, all this continued. Each of the roles remained in action, but each underwent change. During the 1970's and 1980's the communication media were in a constant state of upheaval, as a result of numerous technical breakthroughs. The documentarist discovered important new opportunities in the new technologies.

In earliest years of the documentary we saw the explorer-documentarist lead the way, providing glimpses of the exotic and faraway. The new technologies vastly expanded his role. He could take cameras into undersea worlds of astounding beauty, and also into other worlds. He could show, from regions of the moon and beyond, distant shots of our own earth, a green oasis in endless nothingness. His cameras, remotely controlled, went on to peer into the hostile atmospheres of other planets. Such ventures stirred increasing concern for spaceship earth and its blessings, seemingly so unique and perhaps more fragile than was thought. Addressing this concern was one of television's most awesome achievements, the BBC-TV series *Life on Earth* (1979), in which David Attenborough crisscrossed the globe, pinpointing the rise and decline of innumerable species.

In the role of reporter, the documentarist likewise achieved growing virtuosity. Via satellite, his reports on the activities and disputes of nations became a continuing television feature in all parts of the world. Video increased his mobility, while electronic video editing speeded the processing of the news. A by-product of video, the instant replay—developed spectacularly for sports programming—proved valuable also in other reporting, as of riots, assassinations, blast-offs, battles. Combined with slow motion, this technique could provide minute and sometimes eerie analysis of rapid, violent action.

When concentrating on spectacle, the documentarist generally escaped dissension. But when reporting matters touching on public policy, he often found himself at odds with administration officials, or attacked by television sponsors or trade associations. Charges of bias and distortion, especially by government spokesmen, appeared to have become an inescapable part of journalistic documentary.

But sometimes government policy shifts validated, in retrospect, what had been condemned. For a quarter of a century communist China had been, in the eyes of American administrations, the villain of international affairs. American journalists were forbidden to go there. Violators of the ban were stripped of their passports. American distribution of the film *China!,* a favorable portrayal by the British film journalist Felix Greene, had been subjected to official harassment. Then, in 1972, a sudden shift, as planeloads of American journalists and television gear were flown to Peking to portray lavish ceremonials of friendship between Nixon and the Mao regime. The love feast atmosphere set the stage for other journeys to and from China, often undertaken for documentary-film purposes. In *The Other Half of the Sky* (1975), made by Shirley MacLaine and Claudia Weill, a group of American women made the China journey, forming bonds of friendship with Chinese women. In *From Mao to Mozart* (1980), the most revealing and heartwarming of such films, it was the violinist-conductor Isaac Stern who was on tour, engaging in Chinese-American musical collaboration that both sides would have considered subversive a few years earlier. The sudden shifts of attitude implicit in such films must have made some viewers skeptical of government policy statements—or of documentaries, or of both.

As growing numbers of independents, representing a growing diversity of vantage points, engaged in journalistic reports, friction over documentaries was inevitably on the increase. It was in evidence when American public television showed *Waiting for Fidel* (1974), a generally friendly report on Cuba by the Australian Michael Rubbo, made for the National Film Board of Canada; *Compañero* (1975), a British film about the murder of Chilean folksinger Victor Jara, an ardent supporter of Allende, quietly and movingly narrated by his

British widow; *From the Ashes: Nicaragua Today* (1981), by Helena Sollberg Ladd, on the Sandanista movement that overthrew the Somoza dictatorship; *El Salvador: Another Vietnam* (1981), an Oscar nominee produced by Glenn Silber and Tete Vasconcellos; and *Blood and Sand: War in the Sahara* (1982), in which the enterprising American Sharon Sopher provided a unique close-up of the Polasario independence movement, under sharp attack by the King of Morocco with help from U.S. military advisers and weaponry. All these films gave impressions at variance with administration pronouncements. Official displeasure, even when conveyed only after the event, inevitably created increasing tensions in the documentary field, and a tightening of broadcast policies. Some people wondered whether such documentaries might be an endangered species.

While some documentarists were intent on reporting world quarrels, others—as in earlier periods of documentary history—continued to function as painters, concerned more with pictorial values than narrative content. In the tradition of Hans Richter and Man Ray, they often used documentary images but abstracted them into fascinating action patterns. In this work the documentarist not only embraced video but linked it with the computer. Ed Emshwiller, photographing dancers, added his own pictorial choreography to create fugues of interweaving motion. Woody and Steina Vasulka, starting with common images, such as trees or traveling automobiles, constructed computerized video works that were like the "theme and variations" of the composer. This processing seemed to stimulate a heightened awareness of the familiar; it fostered what Vertov had called "the maturing eye." In 1974, video works became an ongoing exhibit at New York's Museum of Modern Art. The most successful of the video painters, the Korea-born Nam June Paik, was represented by showings at numerous museums, often marked by antic humor. At the first National Video Festival of the American Film Institute, a 1981 event at the John F. Kennedy Center in Washington, D.C., he exhibited a "video installation" entitled *Kennedy/Olympic* (1981), in which interlacing shots of Olympic athletes were seen through goldfish bowls, so that the movements of taped humans and live fish intertwined in surprising and evocative patterns. At New York's Whitney Museum of American Art collaborators Stan Vanderbeek and Joan Brigham created the video installation *Steam Screens* (1979), in which computer-generated images were projected onto steam, so that the steam added its own swirling movements to the projected images. It was an adaptation of a magic lantern technique of nineteenth-century magicians, involving projections onto smoke.

While such work was winning a vogue among museum-goers, many documentarists continued to focus on current issues, often—in the Grierson tradition—in works of frank advocacy. Atomic power and atomic weapons were among the most agitated issues of the day, and evoked works by numerous advocate-documentarists.

Until the 1970's, films on these topics had been made mainly by the U.S. government and its major contractors, and had disseminated sunny optimism. Nuclear power had been described as safe, bountiful, and so cheap that metering might become unnecessary. As for nuclear weapons—scarcely a problem. Films made during the 1950's for schoolchildren showed that all you had to do in case an atomic bomb fell nearby was close your eyes and duck. "Duck and cover!" was the slogan used to inculcate this wisdom. Disneyesque turtles, retracting charming pop-eyed heads against danger, provided demonstration. In other scenes, children dived under school desks in brisk, cheerful drills.

Assessments of a different sort appeared in print but almost never on film or television—for compelling reasons. The quest for visual material led producers to the Atomic Energy Commission, which at the time occupied a monopolistic position. It had charge of the "peaceful atom" and also the less publicized job of providing the military with fissionable material and weaponry. The "peaceful" and military programs were more closely related than was generally realized. The AEC barred cameramen, other than those from the Signal Corps, from all atomic installations. But it arranged for the Signal Corps cameramen to shoot, during the 1950's, a collection of stock footage on nuclear matters, which private producers could have "with AEC permission." Producers were asked to submit scripts to show how the footage would be used.[1]

Through this authority over access, along with script review, the AEC was able for many years to control what went into documentaries about the atom and its uses in peace or war. A pervasive public ignorance was maintained. The earliest Japanese footage of the Hiroshima and Nagasaki havoc remained impounded by the Pentagon throughout the 1950's and most of the following decade. Audiences occasionally saw awesome telescopic shots of mushroom clouds—which an army chaplain in one film described as "a wonderful sight to behold"[2]—but they saw almost nothing about effects on life and habitat. Most people seemed, for the moment, content not to know more.

The AEC's monopoly position was ended by Congress in 1974. Sharp contention had for some time been stirring in publications such as *The Bulletin of the Atomic Scientists*. And documentarists, spurred by such publications, had begun tackling films of anti-nuclear thrust. A short Columbia University compilation of Japanese Hiroshima and Nagasaki footage appeared in 1970 under the title *Hiroshima-Nagasaki, August 1945* and was shown on public television.[3] In 1975 the public television series *Nova* showed *The Plutonium Connection*, produced by John Angier. It presented the case of a twenty-year-old student, who, using information available in libraries, had designed a plutonium bomb. A physicist, examining the design, concluded that the bomb would go off with a force of 1000 tons of TNT. The program cast doubt on the wisdom of government plans for promotion of the "breeder" reactor, which was designed to produce extraordinary quantities of plutonium for nuclear power generation at home and abroad. The possible use of this by terrorist groups suggested a security nightmare. Confidence in government assurances was further undermined by the 1977 *Nova* broadcast of *Incident at Brown's Ferry*, by Robert Richter, about an Alabama nuclear power accident stemming from deficiencies in both design and staff training.

The nuclear industry, represented by the Atomic Industrial Forum, complained bitterly over these telecasts, and even more so over *Danger: Radioactive Waste*, a 1977 NBC documentary produced and written by Joan Konner. Virtually the first film to deal with the nuclear waste impasse, it provided glimpses of the Hanford atomic graveyard or "industrial park"—575 square miles in Washington state near the Columbia River, operated under government contract by Atlantic Richfield, where 55 million gallons of high-level waste from the military program lay buried and quantities of obsolete radioactive equipment was also stored, all in ways considered unsatisfactory, temporary, potentially dangerous, waiting for a solution. The nation had created, said the documentary, a "radioactive monster with no cage to keep it in." The Atomic Industrial Forum launched a letter-writing attack on the network and the film makers, but films of similar impact nevertheless continued, and came from many sources. The ferment was no longer to be stilled or quashed.

From California television Station KTEH-TV, San Jose, came *The Day After Trinity: Robert J. Oppenheimer and the Atomic Bomb* (1980), by John Else, causing wide comment and winning a Columbia University-Dupont Award. *Prophecy* (1982), a postscript on the Hiroshima survivors by Japan's Susumu Hani, had an international distribution that included a New York showing coinciding with United Nations hearings on atomic weapons. From the Netherlands came the unusual *My God, What Have We Done? (Mijn God, Wat Hebben We Gedaan?,* 1981), by Roelof Kiers. Learning that the U.S. Air Force's 509th Composite Group, the group that had prepared and carried out the Hiroshima and Nagasaki missions, held reunions every three years, Kiers arranged for a Netherlands television film crew to cover one. At a Smithsonian storage depot outside Washington the reunion participants climbed in and out of the *Enola Gay,* took snapshots of each other waving from the plane, and reminisced. Interviewed, all denied troubled thoughts about having inaugurated the nuclear era, although some participants had apparently had periods of emotional depression. The program suggested the impossibility of absorbing an event of this sort into one's life experience. The group could come to terms with it only by treating it as no more than a college reunion—the old gang reassembling. The program left viewers baffled by their behavior, yet sympathetic, for their behavior seemed only a metaphor for that of society as a whole—which had likewise, over the years, shown a preference for evading the issue.

The Reagan regime was bringing concern over these matters to a peak with references to first-strike nuclear attack as a necessary American option, and to statements envisioning "protracted" nuclear war. Anger and agitation over such statements became worldwide. Films assessing the issues included a notable five-part CBS documentary, *The Defense of the United States* (1981), produced by the Englishman Howard Stringer—shown widely in Europe after American network telecasts. While it gave the American military full opportunity to state its rationales, it also left the unmistakable impression that the medical problems posed by the government scenarios would be insoluble. An organization called Physicians for Social Re-

No Place To Hide, 1982.

sponsibility was giving the widest possible circulation to this same view. Working in collaboration with the Council for a Livable World, it distributed a documentary titled *The Last Epidemic* (1981), a compilation of archive material and taped statements by physicians.

Amid the succession of such works came two which, to the surprise of many people, involved a quizzical touch. One was *No Place To Hide* (1982), a short film for television by Tom Johnson and Lance Bird; the other was *The Atomic Café* (1982), made for theatrical distribution by a group calling itself the Archives Project, which included Kevin Rafferty, Jayne Loader, Pierce Rafferty. The producers of both these films had found their inspiration in archive research. Both had unearthed the reassuring government films of earlier years and made compilations of them. These now seemed not only ludicrous but extraordinarily cynical. Scarcely believing, crowds flocked to theaters to see *The Atomic Café*. *No Place To Hide* won a place on a public television series titled *Matters of Life and Death.* Both films received foreign distribution. The government films had, in the long run, backfired.

The same was true of an American government production of 1982, which might be seen as in the tradition of the bugle-call film. This was *Let Poland Be Poland,* a cold-war bugle call. Highly rhetorical, it treated history in the same sweeping fashion as the *Why We Fight* films and other World War II bugle-call films. Such films had been especially successful in the controlled situations of war, in which audiences were largely captive, seldom exposed to contrary views. But *Let Poland Be Poland,* produced by the U.S. International Communication Agency,[4] was disseminated under very different circumstances. Sent by satellite throughout the world, for broadcasting systems of other nations to receive and rebroadcast, it seemed to many of them so oblivious to their own views and experiences that some—after taping and previewing—decided to ignore the offering, or to schedule it in a less than favorable time slot. Many systems carried only excerpts. Critical reactions showed little enthusiasm, although the work had been offered as a major initiative and included statements by numerous prime ministers.

The documentarist as prosecutor, active after World War II in efforts to bring war criminals to justice, was another continuing phenomenon, but for different purposes. Here too, new technology came into play. In 1981 the American FBI, using concealed video cameras and an agent pretending to be an oil-rich Arab seeking investment opportunities, recorded several Congressmen accepting substantial bundles of cash from a suitcase, in return for a pledge to push legislation of interest to the alleged Arab and his company, Abdul Enterprises. The tapes, which became known as *The Abscam Tapes*—for the "Abdul scam"—were used for prosecution purposes and made available to television. The sequence of events caused various disputes. One concerned the issue of entrapment; another, the issue of whether television exposure might fatally prejudice future jurors in these and other "scam" cases. But such procedures were apparently finding widening use, in the United States and elsewhere. In Britain in 1977 a woman suspected of homicidal intent toward her mother, aged eighty-seven, was videotaped by police during a hospital visit, for which hidden equipment was brought into play. As seen on the tape, she urged her mother to kill herself: "It isn't cowardly,

Mum, for goodness sake. . . . If you had a dog in this state you would take it to the vet, wouldn't you?" The daughter was seen to slip her mother a dose of some fifteen barbiturate tablets, urging her to take them with "a big drink of whiskey—that's always fatal, Mum." Then the daughter walked out. The videotape was used to convict her—apparently the first time British courts had admitted such evidence. The tape was then released to television.[5]

As in earlier decades, poet-documentarists continued to deal with very different themes, and to offer odes on the beautiful and tragic, the permanent and passing. Again new technologies played a role, proving especially valuable in celebrating the wonders of nature. In the case of *The Incredible Machine* (1977), a National Geographic film, ultraminiaturized equipment made possible photography from inside many parts of the human body. In the BBC-TV's *Everyday Miracle: Birth* (1981) similar photographic wizardry was combined with ultrasound recording to provide an interior audiovisual record of life before birth. Both these films evoked reverent wonder. In the case of *To Fly* (1976), a Francis Thompson production introduced at the Smithsonian Air and Space Museum, the screen was enlarged to huge dimensions, with unprecedented height, to convey all the sensations of flight. Much of the photography was done from cameras mounted outside planes, so that no glimpse of plane window or wing appeared at the edge of the screen and the viewer had the sensation of flying through vast space, across a whole continent, without benefit of equipment.

In more personal projects the poet-documentarist was finding inspiration in the capabilities of video. One such project was *The Love Tapes* (1980), which many critics visited with skepticism and left with admiration. Its producer, Wendy Clarke, had set up a booth in which volunteers were invited to videotape for three minutes, to music of their choosing, their feelings about love. In the booth, face to face with their own image, they could see and replay what they had done, and remake it as often as they wished. It was an exceptional example of video as a tool for self-examination and self-assesment— which seem to spur a remaking of the public self, and perhaps of the self. For some it seemed a disturbing experience; for many, a kind of therapy. *The Love Tapes,* after showings in the PBS *Non-Fiction Television* series, became a popular museum exhibit.

Another video poem, also with a therapy aspect, was *Smothering*

Smothering Dreams, 1980.

Debra Schweitzer

Dreams (1980). It was by Dan Reeves, a Vietnam veteran who had been a member of a unit caught in a jungle ambush, in which virtually all around him had been killed. The subsequent years of nightmare were, to some extent, exorcized by a re-enactment of the event; under his direction, numerous friends assisted with film and video cameras. In its intimacy with the action, it seemed to many the most graphic portrayal of jungle war they had ever seen. This action was threaded with images from childhood, fragments of the messages of home and school and mass media that had impelled him, an eager volunteer, to seek combat service in Vietnam. The tape, a dazzling sequence of montages, emerged as a cry of protest against a society increasingly organized for hostility and violence.

Still another moving video poem was *The Last Dance (El Ultimo Baile,* 1981), by Regge Life, made in Venezuela. Here the narrative voice represented the body of a man in a coffin who, after a long and lusty life, is carried by pallbearers down a trail to his village grave, jouncing on their shoulders in his "last dance."

The issue of violence was implicit in many films, in numerous ways.

In *Birth Without Violence* (1974) we watch a baby enter the world into the gentle hands of the French physician Dr. Frederick Leboyer, who felt that the shock of birth—a trauma in itself—was being systematically magnified by conditions under which babies were born in hospitals, under glaring lights, manipulated by tools, surrounded by a crowd of bustling medical technicians. In *Birth Without Violence* we see Dr. Leboyer substituting gentleness, low lights, soft music, quiet talk. A warm bath, with support from the doctor's hands, begins the child's career on earth in a way that minimizes the transition from the womb. Watching the child's face, we sense we see a response to this wooing of the newborn. Dr. Leboyer's implication: with violence we create troubled—and perhaps violent—men and women.

A tradition that had grown impressively after World War II, that of the documentarist as historic chronicler, was likewise continuing to evolve as documentary approached its second century. In a number of widely admired television series, noted scholars guided viewers through centuries of history, not sitting at a studio desk but appearing suddenly in places scattered throughout the world—at ruins, museums, archaeological digs, battlefields, ancient marketplaces, castles, homes. Shard, bone, cave relic, tool, statue, painting, musical instrument, manuscript, gravestone inscription, all were enlisted to bring to vivid life, via the threading commentary of the traveling host, the panorama of ages past. The genre established itself with the BBC-TV's *Civilization* (1970), featuring Kenneth Clark as roving savant, and directed by Michael Gill. The form reached a special brilliance in the BBC-TV's *The Ascent of Man* (1974), with Jacob Bronowski, in which Adrian Malone became associated with the medium, resulting in a Gill-Malone partnership.[6] Bronowski's intense, searching commentary, never hinting at prepared text, was extraordinarily compelling. Other widely distributed examples of the genre included *America* (1972), with Alistair Cooke, and *Cosmos* (1980), with Carl Sagan, in which special-effects techniques were invoked.

Other chronicler-documentarists tended to find their chief inspiration in film archives. Since World War II such collections had proliferated as new countries established archives, often stressing their own roots and traditions. Archives grew rapidly with the addition of videotape and, later, videodisc. They swelled further as film companies and private collectors donated their holdings. Material from such collections, used in combination with interviews, sometimes

Carl Sagan in *Cosmos,* 1980.

Films, Inc.

threw doubt on accepted versions of past events—as had been the case with Marcel Ophuls's 1970 film *The Sorrow and the Pity.* The combination continued to play a revisionist role in such projects as *World at War* (1973), a detailed re-examination of World War II by Thames Television. An especially stirring contribution to revisionist history was William Miles's film *Men of Bronze* (1977), the fruit of long research concerning a New York unit of black American soldiers trained for action in World War I. Rejected by General Pershing, who wished only white soldiers under his command, they were accepted by the French army, which was hard pressed for trained men. In French uniform they were at once thrown into a crisis action, and half of them died. Miles ended his film with a postwar shot of remnants of the brigade parading up Fifth Avenue and into Harlem, a sequence with both triumphant and tragic overtones. Among old men playing chess and checkers in a park at the edge of Harlem, William Miles found survivors of these long-ago events, and one of them became his riveting film narrator. Miles followed with a television series titled *I Remember Harlem* (1981), another absorbing chronicle with a revisionist edge.

Two feature-length films of this genre threw new light on labor history, while focusing on the role of women. Both used newly unearthed archival film plus reminiscence elicited through interview, featuring women workers of long ago, remembering past struggles—sometimes with anger, sometimes through a joyful mist. They were *With Babies and Banners* (1977), about the role of women in a massive automobile strike of the Depression era, made by Lorraine Gray, Lyn Goldfarb, and Anne Bohlen; and *The Life and Times of Rosie the Riveter* (1980), by Connie Field, about the countless women who joined factory assembly lines during World War II.

It had long been clear that the documentary could be a powerful biographical tool, using the same combination of techniques. Notable among such biographical documentaries were several by Perry Miller Adato, including especially *Gertrude Stein: When This You See, Remember Me* (1971) and *Georgia O'Keeffe* (1977). Other biographical documentaries of special interest were *Eadweard Muybridge, Zoopraxographer* (1976), by Thom Anderson; *Paul Robeson: Tribute to an Artist* (1980), directed by Saul Turell and narrated by Sidney Poitier; and *Wasn't That a Time!* (1982), an exuberant celebration of the career of the singing group The Weavers, produced by George Stoney and directed by Jim Brown. The field of biography appeared to offer documentarists an inexhaustible resource.

The field was, however, confused by floods of scripted, acted biographical "docudramas"—works belonging to the world of historical fiction rather than documentary. Ranging from scrupulous portraiture to unrestrained mythmaking, they had their own resources for revisionism.

As documentary approached its second century, its most prolific sub-genre—especially in countries with commercial television systems—appeared to be the promotion documentary. For the service of sponsors, tens of thousands of commercials were being produced annually, along with thousands of longer films on business and industry. Many were documentary in form. Commercials, most often of 30-second or 60-second length, were no longer merely instruments of product merchandising. A commercial was likely to sell not only a product but a way of life, a view of the world, a philosophy. Commercials had become the main instrument for military recruitment, political campaigning, image-glossing by companies and by cities, regions, and countries. Commercials were deeply involved in ideological conflict.

Georgia O'Keeffe, 1977.

Films, Inc.

While scorned by many, or dismissed as passing ephemera, commercials were increasingly winning attention from social historians and gaining a place in film and video archives. It seemed likely that these capsule creations, regardless of technique, would eventually be seen as documents highly expressive of their times and would—justifiably—find their way into documentary compilations, just as the U.S. government's nuclear-reassurance films became historic nuggets.

A system of awards for commercials, known as the Clio Awards, had been established in New York in 1960. Named after Clio, the muse of history, the awards were in numerous subject categories, and the system was expanded to include commercials from all continents, in many languages. Each year the Clio-winning commercials were assembled onto compilation reels by the Clio organization. Over the years, the accumulating compilation reels began indeed to seem like a panorama of social history.

Another documentary sub-genre, that of the observer-documentarist eschewing intervention in events before his camera and generally avoiding spoken commentary, remained widely in evidence. Among its latter-day classics was *How Yukong Moved the Mountains* (1976), a series of twelve films about China by Joris Ivens and Marceline Loridan. The China Film Bureau, honoring the achievement with an unusual exhibition formula, opened the films simultaneously at different Peking theaters. By going from one theater to another one could see the entire series in a matter of days. Presenting a sweeping view of a new China, the China of Mao, they represented for Ivens a gratifying return to places where, under less happy circumstances, he and John Ferno had made *The Four Hundred Million.* Ivens had been an active force through much of documentary film history and had worked his way through almost all its phases of technique and theory. Returning to China after a lapse of decades, he found in the Museum of the Revolution the camera he had used in 1938 for *The Four Hundred Million,* which he had left in China.

Another impressive film of 1976, Barbara Kopple's *Harlan County, U.S.A.,* was likewise dominated by the observer or "direct cinema" approach, although it also drew on archival material. Over a period of years Kopple had patiently photographed and recorded, with startling intimacy, the often bloody struggles of a Kentucky coal-mining area, involving miners, mine owners, strikebreakers and others. Achieving a powerful emotional impact, the film won wide theatrical showings and the Academy Award for best documentary.

The observer-documentarist found fruitful new opportunities in the video medium. In the United States Julie Gustafson and John Reilly, following four pregnancies from diagnosis to delivery, produced an absorbing and valuable document in *Giving Birth* (1976). The four cases represented four different procedures, ranging from the most elaborate hospital delivery, with all possible equipment and no husband present, to a home delivery attended by a midwife, with the husband participating. At a time when expectant parents were making divergent choices of this sort, *Giving Birth* gave ample food for thought. The unobtrusiveness of video production was facilitating projects of new and unusual scope.

Another impressive observer-documentary of the period was *The Campaign* (1982), an episode in the *Middletown* series produced by Peter Davis, maker of *The Selling of the Pentagon*. Following the contesting candidates in a midwestern mayoralty election, *The Campaign* was reminiscent of *Primary,* the Drew-Leacock film of 1960 that had done so much to establish the observer-documentary style. It also reflected important technical improvements of the intervening decades.

The documentarist as catalyst, setting into motion events to be recorded, was a continuing phenomenon. In earlier years we saw the anthropologist Jean Rouch use this approach to study the response of people to unexpected questions or situations. His rationale: an artificial stimulus may bring out truths not readily brought to the surface. The television series *Candid Camera,* confronting people with bizarre situations photographed by unseen cameras, was using a similar procedure for titillation rather than anthropological study. Though some documentarists have felt they should shun a catalytic role, they have inevitably influenced many events by their presence. And whenever arranging an interview for the purpose of obtaining a filmed statement, they are deliberately acting as catalysts, creating an event that would not otherwise exist. In this sense, the producer as catalyst is constantly with us. The "Presidential Debates" periodically featured on American television have become notable examples of the technique, in that they have been created entirely for camera purposes, and would not otherwise have happened. The purpose:

close-up observation of candidates in situations of extreme pressure, intensified by worldwide satellite transmission.

Virtually every kind of documentary, from that of the explorer to that of the guerrilla, has been influenced by new technical developments—video, satellite, computer, miniaturization, recording improvements. Documentarists have found new opportunities in all of them, expanding the scope and resources of their medium.

Meanwhile, the essential task of the documentary has remained unchanged. It is, as Vertov defined it, to capture "fragments of actuality" and combine them meaningfully. It remains, as Grierson defined it, "the creative treatment of actuality." Such formulations stress two functions: (1) recording—of images and sounds—and (2) interpretation.

The interpretive role has kept the documentarist under fire. In contentious times especially, he has been under frequent attack. To be sure, some documentarists deny any interpretive element in their work, and claim to be "objective." This may be strategic, but is surely meaningless. The documentarist makes endless choices. He selects topics, people, vistas, angles, lenses, juxtapositions, sounds, words. Each selection is an expression of his point of view, whether he is aware of it or not, whether he acknowledges it or not. The documentarist who lays claim to objectivity is merely asserting his conviction that his choices have a special validity and deserve everyone's acceptance.

Even behind the first step of selection, the choice of topic, there is a motive or set of motives. Someone feels there is something about the topic that needs clarification, and that if one can document aspects of it—the whole truth is a legal fiction—the work will yield something useful in comprehension, agreement, or action. Still, the cry for objectivity is used to lambaste the documentarist. He is constantly accused of "propaganda."

There is irony in this. When a film maker has been unfair with his audience, and has so foolishly rigged his presentation that he raises our hackles, so that we feel compelled to declare our independence, our determination not to be brainwashed, then we are inclined to invoke the word "propaganda." The irony is that we invoke this word just when a film has failed as propaganda. While the choices please us, we do not invoke it.

But of course a propagandistic role *is* involved. One can hardly imagine a documentary, or a film, or any other kind of work, that is *not* propaganda—in the sense of trying to convey some view of the world, narrow or broad, in a way that will get an audience to share it. This is simply to say that communication is not without a purpose.

While documentary has this aspect of propaganda—a word of honorable lineage—documentary should be seen as a very difficult medium for propaganda, precisely because it confronts its subject matter openly. It announces its topic. It alerts our critical facilities. A more potent and pervasive propaganda medium is popular fiction, precisely because it is received as something else—"entertainment," a word associated with relaxation. As used by Hollywood and television, entertainment has always been assumed to be something free of "messages." The word lulls our critical faculties. But behind entertainment are always unspoken premises, which we are maneuvered into accepting.

Spy and outer-space dramas throughout much of the world are based on the premise that "we" are surrounded, on earth and throughout the universe, by enemies capable of diabolical villainy, who must be countered in kind before they wreak their havoc on us. Police dramas are based on the premise that social problems are solved by the violent defeat of villains by heroes. Dramas about superheroes and superheroines assume an ultimate ability to solve all technical problems: Superman can swallow a pill that makes him immune to atomic wapons. For such drama to work, one must subliminally accept the premises. The unspoken premises are never confronted—they don't have to be. That is the propaganda power of popular fiction.

Thus the assumptions and myths of a society are so constantly recycled in its formula fiction that its audience ceases to notice the assumptions. They become part of our mental circuitry. Other people's fiction we can recognize as propaganda—and they, ours. One's own is "entertainment."

A reason for its seductiveness is that it pictures a world that makes sense, in cause and effect. It is internally consistent, in contrast to the world shown in many documentaries—a world that is full of contradictions and loose ends, and that seldom makes sense. Is it any wonder that many people lean toward the substitute world of fiction, a world that nowadays, via television, begins to seduce us in cradle or playpen? From earliest years of consciousness it begins to form patterns in our minds about the world that awaits us, patterns that may for years determine what ideas and information will stick in our minds, and what will not. If it fits the pattern, it will stick.

All this suggests the difficulty of the role facing the documentarist. His work, at its best, is likely to run counter to endlessly recycled mythologies. A politician who lives by mythologies may well look on the documentarist as a subversive influence. And indeed, his work may well be considered a kind of subversion—an essential one. And a difficult one.

Though sometimes surrounded by animosities, the documentarist nevertheless persists, survives, and multiplies. He also rejoices in his difficult mission—that of presenting evidence that may change ideas.

The multiplication of documentarists that has been made possible by new technologies, and the broadening range of their activities, must be considered long-range blessings to society, so long as we hold to the democratic tenet that in many voices there is safety.

The true documentarist has a passion for what he *finds* in images and sounds—which always seems to him more meaningful than anything he can *invent*. He may serve as catalyst, not as inventor. Unlike the fiction artist, he is dedicated to *not* inventing. It is in selecting and arranging his findings that he expresses himself; these choices are, in effect, his comments. And whether he adopts the stance of observer, or chronicler, or whatever, he cannot escape his subjectivity. He presents his version of the world.

In denying himself invented action, the documentarist adopts a difficult limitation. Some artists turn from documentary to fiction because they feel it lets them get closer to the truth, their truth. Some, it would appear, turn to documentary because it can make deception more plausible.

Its plausibility, its authority, is the special quality of the documentary—its attraction to those who use it, regardless of motive—the source of its power to enlighten or deceive.

SOURCE NOTES

Prophet (pp. 3–30)

1. For the prehistory of cinema see Ceram, *Archaeology of the Cinema;* also Jacques Deslandes , *Histoire Comparée du Cinéma,* v. 1; Macgowan, *Behind the Screen.*
2. Ramsaye, in *A Million and One Nights,* is intent on ridiculing Muybridge, while concentrating all honors on Edison. Muybridge's odd adopted name (he was born Edward James Muggeridge) may have encouraged this, but his achievements were formidable. For discussion and a Muybridge bibliography, see *Film Comment,* Fall 1969; also Hendricks, *The Edison Motion Picture Myth;* MacDonnell, *Eadweard Muybridge.*
3. Macgowan, *Behind the Screen,* p. 276; Sadoul, *Histoire du Cinéma,* p. 17.
4. Sadoul, *Louis Lumière,* is a good introduction to the Lumière saga; but see Jacques Deslandes , *Histoire Comparée du Cinéma,* v. 2, for additional material, and corrections of Sadoul errors. Mesguich, *Tours de Manivelle,* is an absorbing memoir by a widely traveling Lumière *opérateur.* English-language material on Lumière is scant, but the impact of his shows is reflected in film histories of various countries, as noted below.
5. See the chronology and filmography in Sadoul, *Louis Lumière.*
6. Robinson, *The History of World Cinema,* p. 23.
7. As told to Jay Leyda by Doublier. Leyda, *Kino,* p. 19.
8. Baxter, *The Australian Cinema,* pp. 2–3; Barnouw and Krishnaswamy, *Indian Film,* pp. 2–5. Sestier's *Melbourne Races* survives in the Australian compilation film, *The Pictures That Moved* (1968).
9. Mesguich, *Tours de Manivelle,* p. 10.
10. "Half a Century in Exhibition Line: Shri Abdullally Recalls Bioscope Days," *Indian Talkie,* pp. 121–22.
11. Smith, *Two Reels and a Crank,* p. 148.

12. Ibid. p. 102; Dickson, *The Biograph in Battle,* p. xiii.
13. Ramsaye, *A Million and One Nights,* pp. 520–21.
14. The Ponting material reached the screen again in 1930 in the film *Ninety Degrees South.* Low, *The History of the British Film 1906–1914,* p. 156.

Explorer (pp. 33–51)

1. The quotation—one of several accounts of this episode—is from an autobiographical document in *The Flaherty Papers,* Box 59. *The Flaherty Papers* are the main source for this section, along with Calder-Marshall, *The Innocent Eye,* and other sources as noted.
2. All diary quotations are from *The Flaherty Papers.*
3. The letters are dated April 14 and March 6, 1915. *The Flaherty Papers,* Box 15.
4. Griffith, *The World of Robert Flaherty,* p. 38.
5. Flaherty, Robert J., "Life Among the Eskimos," *World's Work,* October 1922.
6. *Theatre Arts,* May 1951.
7. New York *Times,* June 12, 1922.
8. Sherwood (ed.), *The Best Moving Pictures of 1922–23.*
9. From the autobiographical document, *The Flaherty Papers,* Box 59.
10. See de Brigard, *Anthropological Cinema.*
11. *Film Culture,* Spring 1972.

Reporter (pp. 51–71)

1. The section is based largely on Drobaschenko, *Dsiga Wertow* (German edition); Sadoul, *Dziga Vertov.* Other sources as noted. There is scant English-language material on Vertov.
2. Leyda, *Kino,* pp. 138–39. Leyda worked for a time with Vertov.
3. See *ibid.* p. 163, for a list of features playing in Moscow's "NEP-nourished" theaters late in 1922.
4. *Sovietskoye Kino,* November-December 1934; quoted by Leyda, *Kino,* pp. 161–62.
5. Interview, Mikhail Kaufman.
6. Sitney (ed.), *Film Culture Reader,* p. 362.
7. Note ebullient comment by French documentarist Chris Marker: "Let us now praise Dziga Vertov, for if I had to choose the Ten Best Documentaries of All Time, I'd call it preposterous, but if there's ONE to choose: *A SIXTH OF THE WORLD.*" Quoted, Klaue *et al.* (eds.), *Sowjetischer Dokumentarfilm,* p. 70.
8. Leyda, *Kino,* p. 176. The lecture, translated by S. Brody, appeared in *Filmfront,* 1935.
9. *Film Comment,* Spring 1972, offers an illuminating discussion by David Bordwell on disputes surrounding Vertov.
10. See Leyda, *Films Beget Films,* pp. 22–28, for Shub's contribution to the evolution of the compilation film.

Painter (pp. 71–81)

1. Richter, "The Film as an Original Art Form," *Film Culture,* January 1955.
2. Manvell and Fraenkel, *The German Cinema,* pp. 45–47.
3. See Klaue (ed.), *Alberto Cavalcanti,* for several discussions of *Rien Que Les Heures.*
4. Interview, Boris Kaufman. Gomes, *Jean Vigo,* pp. 55–80.
5. Interview, Henri Storck. Maelstaf, *Henri Storck,* pp. 5–23. The Vigo-Storck letters were published in *Centrofilm,* February-March, 1961.
6. Ivens, *The Camera and I,* pp. 13–46.

Advocate (pp. 85–139)

1. For the early Grierson years, see Jack C. Ellis, "The Young Grierson in America, 1924–1927," *Cinema Journal,* Fall 1968.
2. Quotations are from Hardy (ed.), *Grierson on Documentary,* except as otherwise noted.
3. Interview, Edgar Anstey.
4. Material on the EMB and GPO units is based on Rotha, *Documentary Film,* and reminiscences by Grierson co-workers in *Sight and Sound,* Summer 1972, and in *The Journal of the Society of Film and Television Arts* (II, 4–5), 1972—reminiscences gathered as Grierson memorials. A similarly illuminating document in cinema form is the film *Grierson* (1973), produced by James Beveridge for the National Film Board of Canada; it includes historic Grierson footage and interviews with co-workers in Europe, America, Asia, and Australia.
5. *Sight and Sound,* Summer 1972.
6. *Take One,* January-February 1970.
7. Interview, Basil Wright.
8. *Film News* (XIII, 3), 1953.
9. Rotha, *Documentary Film,* pp. 106–7.
10. *Ibid.,* 1951 preface by Grierson, p. 17.
11. Material on Goebbels is based on Hull, *Film in the Third Reich,* except as otherwise noted.
12. The account of Leni Riefenstahl's career is based largely on material assembled by Gordon Hitchens in *Film Culture,* Spring 1973, and, earlier, in *Film Comment,* Winter 1965. Other sources as noted.
13. Riefenstahl, *Hinter den Kulissen des Reichsparteitagfilms,* pp. 16–24.
14. *Ibid.* p. 15.
15. Interview, Leni Riefenstahl.
16. For Budd Schulberg comments, see "Nazi Pin-Up Girl," *Saturday Evening Post,* March 30, 1946.
17. The Jaworsky comments are in *Film Culture,* Spring 1972.
18. Fielding, *The American Newsreel,* p. 278.
19. See "Pioneers," an interview with Thomas Brandon, *Film Quarterly,* Fall 1973.

20. Quoted, Petric, *Soviet Revolutionary Films in America*, p. 443.

21. The Lorentz material is based on interview, Pare Lorentz; and Snyder, *Pare Lorentz and the Documentary Film*.

22. Elson, *Time, Inc.*, p. 237.

23. Fielding, *The American Newsreel*, p. 231.

24. Barsam, "This is America," *Cinema Journal*, Spring 1973.

25. Leyda, *Dianying*, pp. 150–51.

26. Interviews, Akira Iwasaki, Fumio Kamei, Taka Atsugi.

27. See the revealing 1940 Japanese newsreel compilation *History of the Newsreel* (*News Eiga Hattatsushi*), produced by *Asahi Shimbun*, with items from 1904 to 1940, reflecting the imperial-military dominance.

28. The following pages are based on Ivens, *The Camera and I*, pp. 49–183; additional sources as noted.

29. Interview, Henri Storck.

30. Interview, John Ferno.

Bugler (pp. 139–72)

1. The following is largely based on Hull, *Film in the Third Reich*, and Manvell and Fraenkel, *The German Cinema*.

2. For the script translations in this section the author is indebted to the Imperial War Museum, London.

3. Monograph on Humphrey Jennings, in Lovell and Hillier, *Studies in Documentary*, pp. 62–132.

4. Interview, Ib Monty; and Neergaard, *Documentary in Denmark*.

5. The following is based on Leyda, *Kino*, pp. 364–97; and interviews, Roman Gregoriev, Roman Karmen.

6. Capra, *The Name Above the Title*, is the main source of the following. Other sources: Leyda, *Films Beget Films*, pp. 49–72; Murphy, William Thomas, "The Method of *Why We Fight*," *Journal of Popular Film*, Summer 1972.

7. Lists of the sources are on file in the motion picture section of the National Archives. Signal Corps motion picture case files OF 1–7, NA.

8. National Archives.

9. Hughes (ed.), *Film Book 1*, pp. 28–29.

10. *Ibid*. pp. 30–33.

11. Leyda, *Films Beget Films*, p. 71.

12. Anderson and Richie, *The Japanese Film*, p. 158.

13. Interview, Paul Zils.

14. This section is based on *The Ivens Papers*, on file at the Nederlands Filmmuseum, Amsterdam; interview, Marion Michelle; and Ivens, *The Camera and I*, pp. 242–45.

Prosecutor (pp. 172–82)

1. Interview, Jerzy Bossak.

2. Interview, Stuart Schulberg.

3. Interviews, Pare Lorentz, Joseph Zigman.

4. *Filmdokumentaristen der DDR*, pp. 11–74.
5. Interviews, Akira Iwasaki, Fumio Kamei, Ryuchi Kano; Anderson and Richie, *The Japanese Film*, p. 182.
6. The full script, with description of images by Merle Worth, is in Hughes (ed.), *Film Book 2*, pp. 234–55.

Poet (pp. 185–98)

1. For the genesis of "neorealism" see Leprohon, *Le Cinéma Italien*, pp. 85–124, and Zavattini, *Sequences from a Cinematic Life*.
2. Interview, Arne Sucksdorff. Cowie, *Swedish Cinema*, pp. 82–89.
3. Interview, Henri Storck.
4. Interview, Bert Haanstra.

Chronicler (pp. 198–212)

1. Leyda, *Films Beget Films,* the classic work on compilation films, discusses the comedy usage, pp. 36–37.
2. See Barnouw and Krishnaswamy, *Indian Film*, pp. 117–18, for a list of British-banned newsreel sequences of the 1930's dealing with Gandhi.
3. Barnouw, "How a University's Film Branch Released Long-Secret A-Bomb Pic," *Variety*, January 5, 1972.
4. Interview, Colin Low.
5. See Myerson (ed.), *Memories of Underdevelopment*.
6. Interview, Jean Rouch; de Brigard, *Anthropological Cinema;* Haudiquet, *Paul Fejos*.

Promoter (pp. 213–28)

1. *The Shell Film Unit 1933–1954*. Also, Shell film catalogues.
2. Based on *The Flaherty Papers*, Columbia University, and comments by Frances Flaherty and Richard Leacock on the sound track of the *Louisiana Story Study Film*, Museum of Modern Art, New York.
3. *The Opportunity for Sponsored Films*, pp. 1–22.
4. See Galbraith, *Economics and the Public Purpose,* for a detailed analysis of this development. See Schiller, *The Mind Managers,* for its impact on communication media.
5. Cogley, *Report on Blacklisting, I: movies.*
6. Rovere, *Senator Joe McCarthy*. For the impact at the State Department, see Barnouw, *The Image Empire*, pp. 8–13.
7. Barnouw, *The Golden Web*, pp. 253–83, and *The Image Empire*, pp. 38–40.
8. See Friendly, *Due to Circumstances Beyond Our Control . . . ,* pp. 3–98, for the rise and fall of *See It Now.*
9. Barnouw, *The Image Empire*, pp. 85–117.
10. Miller, *The Judges and the Judged*, pp. 78–81. *The Reporter*, April 29, 1952.
11. Interview, Robert Young. For details on *Harvest of Shame,* see

Friendly, *Due to Circumstances Beyond Our Control* . . . , pp. 120–23.

Observer (pp. 231–53)

1. See the discussion of Free Cinema in Lovell and Hillier, *Studies in Documentary*, pp. 133–75.
2. For analysis of Franju's documentaries, see Durgnat, *Franju*, pp. 9–49, and discussion by Robin Wood in *Film Comment*, November–December 1973.
3. All quotations are from issues of Sept. 13, 1961. The Channel 7 (WBKB) statement, by Sterling Quinlan, was in the Chicago *Sun-Times*.
4. Discussion by Karel Reisz in *International Film Annual 1959–60*.
5. Based on interview, Robert Drew; the Richard Leacock interview by Bruce Harding in *Flaherty Oral History Collection;* and Levin, *Documentary Explorations*, pp. 195–221. Other sources as noted.
6. The cobweb incident is discussed by Leacock in comments on the sound track of the *Louisiana Story Study Film*, Museum of Modern Art, New York.
7. Interview by James Blue, *Film Comment*, Spring 1965. Republished in Jacobs (ed.), *The Documentary Tradition*, pp. 406–19.
8. Levin, *Documentary Explorations*, pp. 271–93; Rosenthal, *The New Documentary in Action*, pp. 76–91.
9. Levin, *Documentary Explorations*, pp. 313–28; Rosenthal, *The New Documentary in Action*, pp. 66–75; Denby, David, "Documenting America," *Atlantic Monthly*, March 1970; *Image*, October 1973.
10. See discussions of *Phantom India* by James Michener, *Newsweek*, June 12, 1972; and by Eusebio L. Rodrigues, of Goa, *Film Heritage*, Fall 1973.
11. The synchronized-sound reverberations in the ethnographic film field are reflected in Jay Ruby, "Toward an Anthropological Cinema," *Film Comment*, Spring 1971; de Brigard, *Anthropological Cinema;* and in numerous articles in the *PIEF Newsletter*.
12. *Sight and Sound*, Autumn 1972.

Catalyst (pp. 253–62)

1. Interview, Jean Rouch.
2. The evolution of Jean Rouch's ideas toward the catalyst role was discussed in absorbing detail in a two-hour video-taped interview with Rouch on Belgian television by André Delvaux, Jean Brismée, and others. It is in the archives of the Cinémathèque Royale de Belgique, Brussels. See also Levin, *Documentary Explorations*, pp. 131–45, and the discussion by Ellen Freyer in Jacobs (ed.), *The Documentary Tradition*, pp. 437–43.
3. Interview, Chris Marker. For an analysis of *Le Joli Mai*, see the discussion by Michael Kustow in *Sight and Sound*, Spring 1964.

4. Interview, Grigori Chukrai.
5. Interview, Noriaki Tsuchimoto. Also *The Asian,* March 5–11, 1972, and *Film,* Spring 1972. Japan's Supreme Court eventually ruled in favor of the sufferers, holding the factory responsible.
6. The genesis of the approach is discussed in Worth and Adair, *Through Navajo Eyes.*
7. George Stoney's review of events relating to *You Are on Indian Land* will be found in *Challenge for Change Newsletter,* Winter 1968–69. See also Patrick Watson, "Challenge for Change," *Artscanada,* April 1970.
8. The evolution of *VTR St. Jacques* is discussed in *Challenge for Change Newsletter,* Spring–Summer 1969.
9. A transcript and history of the film are in Ophüls, *The Sorrow and the Pity.*
10. See interview with Allen Funt, Rosenthal, *The New Documentary in Action,* pp. 251–63.

Guerrilla (pp. 262–93)

1. Interview, Jerzy Bossak. For historic background see Jerzy Toeplitz, "Cinema in Eastern Europe," *Cinema Journal,* Fall 1968. See also Klaue *et al.* (eds.), *Dokumentarfilm in Polen,* pp. 66–72.
2. Nemeskürty, *Word and Image,* p. 197.
3. Interview, Kurt Goldberger. Hibbin, *Eastern Europe,* p. 32. *Czechoslovak Short Film 1965–66,* pp. 8–9.
4. Interviews, Vicko Raspor, Vlatko Gilić, Krsto Škanata, Dušan Makavejev, Želimir Matko.
5. *Sight and Sound,* Autumn 1971.
6. *Catalogue Général des Films Français de Court Métrage,* pp. 358–60.
7. Interview, Roman Karmen.
8. Drummond and Coblentz, *Duel at the Brink,* pp. 121–22.
9. Eisenhower, *The White House Years: Mandate for Change 1953–1956,* p. 449.
10. Sorensen, *The Word War,* p. 65; *Variety,* May 7, 1969.
11. Commager, Henry Steele, "On the Way to 1984," *Saturday Review,* April 15, 1967.
12. Schlesinger, *The Bitter Heritage,* p. 35. A transcript of *Why Vietnam?* may be found in *Film Comment,* Fall 1966. See *Film Comment,* Spring 1969, for detailed discussion of U.S. films promoting the Vietnam war.
13. Interview, Marvin Farkas.
14. Interview, Jerry Stoll.
15. CBS-TV, April 4, 1967.
16. *Saturday Review,* February 3, 1968.
17. The script of *The Selling of the Pentagon* is in Barrett (ed.), *Survey of Broadcast Journalism 1970–1971,* pp. 151–71.
18. Interview, Khwaja Ahmad Abbas.

19. Public-access channels were for a time required of cable systems by the Federal Communications Commission, and were later included by many cities among franchise requirements.

20. A complex evolution was involved. Godfrey regarded the 1973 advent of the digital time-base corrector as especially crucial. Interviews, John J. Godfrey, George C. Stoney.

21. *Health Care: Your Money or Your Life* was shown at the first National Video Festival of the American Film Institute, held in Washington in June 1981. Copies of tapes shown at the festival have been preserved in the Library of Congress.

Discoverer (pp. 297–315)

1. *Information Sheet: Atomic Energy Commission Stock Film Footage.* Washington, D.C., U.S. Atomic Energy Commission, 1952.

2. The statement is included in the 1982 compilation film *The Atomic Café*.

3. For the history and eventual emergence of this footage see Barnouw, Erik, "The Hiroshima-Nagasaki Footage: A Report," *Historical Journal of Film, Radio and Television,* II, no. 1, March 1982.

4. Previously—and subsequently—known as the U.S. Information Agency.

5. *Washington Post,* August 26, 1977.

6. See Ledger, Marshall, "The Ascent of Adrian Malone," *New York Times,* March 15, 1981.

BIBLIOGRAPHY

Adair, John. See Worth, Sol, and—

Agel, Henri. Robert J. Flaherty. Paris, Seghers, 1965.

A.I.D. News: bulletin de l'Association Internationale des Documentaristes. Paris, irregularly, 1971–74.

American Film. Washington, American Film Institute, monthly, 1974—

Anderson, Joseph L., and Donald Richie. The Japanese Film: art and industry. With a foreword by Akira Kurosawa. Rutland (Vt.) and Tokyo, Tuttle, 1959.

Arlen, Michael J. Living Room War. New York, Viking, 1969.

Armes, Roy. French Film. London, Studio Vista, 1970.

Averson, Richard. See White, David Manning, and—

Aware publication. New York, 1954–56.

Babitsky, Paul, and John Rimberg. The Soviet Film Industry. New York, Praeger, 1955.

Bagdikian, Ben H. The Information Machines. New York, Harper, 1971.

Balázs, Béla. Theory of the Film: character and growth of a new art. Translated from the Hungarian by Edith Bone. New York, Dover, 1970.

Balcon, Michael, et al. Twenty Years of British Film 1925–1945. London, Falcon, 1947.

Balshofer, Fred J., and Arthur C. Miller. One Reel a Week. Berkeley, University of California Press, 1967.

Bardèche, Maurice, and Robert Brasillach. The History of Motion Pictures. Translated and edited by Iris Barry. New York, Norton, 1938.

Barnouw, Erik. The Golden Web: a history of broadcasting in the United States, v. II—1933–53. New York, Oxford University Press, 1968.

Barnouw, Erik. The Image Empire: a history of broadcasting in the

United States, v. III—from 1953. New York, Oxford University Press, 1970.

Barnouw, Erik. Tube of Plenty: the evolution of American television. Revised. New York, Oxford University Press, 1982.

Barnouw, Erik, and S. Krishnaswamy. Indian Film. 2nd ed. New York, Oxford University Press, 1980.

Barrett, Marvin (ed.). Survey of Broadcast Journalism 1968–69, 1969–70, 1970–71. New York, Grosset & Dunlap, 1969, 1970, 1971.

Barsam, Richard Meran. Nonfiction Film: a critical history. New York, Dutton, 1973.

Baxter, John. The Australian Cinema. Sydney, Pacific Books, 1970.

Bertina, B. J. See Prakke, Henk, and—

Billboard. Cincinnati, monthly, then weekly, 1894—

Bliss, Edward, Jr. (ed.). In Search of Light: the broadcasts of Edward R. Murrow 1938–1961. New York, Knopf, 1967.

Bluem, A. William. Documentary in American Television. New York, Hastings, 1965.

Blum, Daniel C. Pictorial History of TV. Philadelphia, Chilton, 1958.

Bogart, Leo. The Age of Television. New York, Ungar, 1958.

Boorstin, Daniel J. The Image: a guide to pseudo-events in America. New York, Harper, 1961.

Boost, C. Film. Amsterdam, Contact, undated (ca. 1958).

Boveri, Walter, et al. Morgarten Kann Nicht Stattfinden: Lazar Wechsler und der Schweizer film. Zurich, Europa Verlag, 1966.

Braddon, Russell. Roy Thomson of Fleet Street. London, Fontana, 1968.

Braden, Waldo W. See Pennybacker, John H., and—

Brasillach, Robert. See Bardèche, Maurice, and—

Broadcasting. Washington, semimonthly, then weekly, 1931—

Broadcasting and Government Regulation in a Free Society. Santa Barbara, Center for the Study of Democratic Institutions, 1959.

Broadcasting Yearbook. Washington, 1935, etc.

Brown, David, and W. Richard Bruner (eds.). How I Got That Story. New York, Dutton, 1967.

Brown, David, and W. Richard Bruner (eds.). I Can Tell It Now. New York, Dutton, 1964.

Brown, Les. Television: the business behind the box. New York, Harcourt Brace Jovanovich, 1971.

Brownlow, Kevin. The Parade's Gone By. New York, Knopf, 1968.

Brumsteede, Emile. Film. Amsterdam, Querido, 1958.

Bruner, W. Richard. See Brown, David, and—

Burden, Hamilton T. The Nuremberg Party Rallies 1923–39. New York, Praeger, 1967.

Cahiers du Cinéma. Paris, monthly, 1951—

Calder-Marshall, Arthur. The Innocent Eye: the life of Robert J. Flaherty. London, W. H. Allen, 1963.

Capra, Frank. The Name Above the Title: an autobiography. New York, Macmillan, 1971.

Cassirer, Henry R. Television Teaching Today. Paris, UNESCO, 1960.

Catalogue of Egyptian Documentary and Short Films. Cairo, General Egyptian Cinema Organization, 1969.

Catalogue Général des Films Français de Court Métrage. Paris, Unifrance Film, 1953.

Centrofilm. Turin, monthly, 1960–

Ceram, C. W. Archaeology of the Cinema. New York, Harcourt, Brace & World, undated.

Challenge for Change Newsletter. Montreal, National Film Board of Canada, 3–4 times a year, 1967–72.

Channels of Communication. New York, bimonthly, 1981–

Chaplin. Stockholm, quarterly, 1959–

Christensen, Theodor, and Karl Roos. Film. Copenhagen, Levin & Munksgaard, 1936.

Cinéaste. New York, quarterly, 1969–

Cinema Journal. Society for Cinema Studies. Iowa City, semiannual, 1961–

Coblentz, Gaston. See Drummond, Roscoe, and—

Codding, George A. Broadcasting Without Barriers. Paris, UNESCO, 1959.

Cogley, John. Report on Blacklisting, I: movies. Fund for the Republic, 1956.

Cogley, John. Report on Blacklisting, II: radio-television. Fund for the Republic, 1956.

Columbia Journalism Review. New York, Graduate School of Journalism, Columbia University, quarterly, 1962–

Conant, Michael. Antitrust in the Motion Picture Industry. Berkeley, University of California Press, 1960.

Contemporary Polish Cinematography. Warsaw, Polonia Publishing House, 1962.

Cook, Olive. Movement in Two Dimensions. London, Hutchinson, 1963.

Cooper, Merian C. Grass. New York, Putnam, 1925.

Counterattack: the newsletter of facts on communism. New York, American Business Consultants, monthly, 1947–55.

Cowie, Peter. Swedish Cinema. London, Tantivy, 1966.

Crankshaw, Edward. Khrushchev: a career. New York, Viking, 1966.

Creel, George. How We Advertised America. New York, Harper, 1920.

Crosby, John. With Love and Loathing. New York, McGraw-Hill, 1963.

Crowther, Bosley. The Lion's Share: the story of an entertainment empire. New York, Dutton, 1957.

Curtis, David. Experimental Cinema. New York, Universe Books, 1971.

Czechoslovak Short Films 1965–66. Prague, Czechoslovak Filmexport, 1966.

de Brigard, Emilie. Anthropological Cinema. New York, Museum of Modern Art, 1974.

de Heusch, Luc. The Cinema and Social Science: a survey of ethnographic and sociological film. Paris, UNESCO, 1962.

de la Roche, Catherine. See Dickinson, Thorold, and—

DEFA 1946–64: filmografie, studio für wochenschau und dokumentarfilme. Berlin, Staatliches Filmarchiv der DDR, 1969.

Deicke, Gunther. See Hellwig, Joachim, and—

Deslandes, Jacques, Histoire Comparée du Cinéma v. I (1966); Deslandes and Jacques Richard v. II (1968), Casterman,

Dewey, Langdon. Outline of Czechoslovakian Cinema. London: Informatics, 1971.

Dickinson, Thorold. A Discovery of Cinema. London, Oxford University Press, 1971.

Dickinson, Thorold, and Catherine de la Roche. Soviet Cinema. London, Falcon, 1948.

Dickson, W. K. L. The Biograph in Battle: its story in the South African war. London, Unwin, 1901.

Dizard, Wilson P. Television: a world view. Syracuse, Syracuse University Press, 1966.

Documentary Film News. New York, monthly, 1940–42.

Drobaschenko, Sergej (ed.). Dsiga Wertow: aufsätze, tagebücher, skizzen. Berlin, Filmwissenschaftliche Bibliothek, 1967.

Drummond, Roscoe, and Gaston Coblentz. Duel at the Brink: John Foster Dulles' command of American power. Garden City (N.Y.), Doubleday, 1960.

Durgnat, Raymond. Franju. London, Studio Vista, 1967.

Durgnat, Raymond. Luis Bunuel. Berkeley, University of California Press, 1968.

Edström, Mauritz. Sucksdorff: främlingen i hemmaskogen. Stockholm, Pan-Norstedts, 1968.

Educators Guide to Free Films. Randolph (Wis.), Educators Progress Service, annual, 1941—

The Eighth Art. Introduction by Robert Lewis Shayon. New York, Holt, Rinehart & Winston, 1962.

Eisenhower, Dwight D. The White House Years: mandate for change 1953–1956. Garden City (N.Y.), Doubleday, 1963.

El-Mazzaoui, Farid. Cinema in the U. A. R. Cairo, Ministry of Culture, 1970.

Elson, Robert T. Time, Inc.: the intimate history of a publishing enterprise, 1923–1941. New York, Atheneum, 1968.

Emery, Walter B. National and International Systems of Broadcasting: their history, operation, and control. East Lansing, Michigan State University Press, 1969.

The Factual Film. Report of the Arts Enquiry. London, Oxford University Press, 1947.

Faulk, John Henry. Fear on Trial. New York, Simon and Schuster, 1964.

Fielding, Raymond. The American Newsreel: 1911–1967. Norman, University of Oklahoma Press, 1972.

Film: the magazine of the Federation of Film Societies. Sheffield, quarterly, 1954–

Film Comment. New York, quarterly, 1962–

Film Culture. New York, irregularly, 1955–

Film Daily; later, Film and TV Daily. New York, 1918–69.

Film Daily Year Book of Motion Pictures. New York, 1919–69.

Film Heritage. Wright State University, Dayton (Ohio), quarterly, 1965–75.

Film and the Historian. London, British Universities Film Council, 1969.

Film Journal. New York, quarterly, 1972–

Film Library Quarterly. Greenwich (Conn.), 1967–

Film Quarterly. Successor to Quarterly of Film, Radio, and Television. Berkeley, University of California Press, 1958–

The Film Society Programmes 1925–1939. Prepared under the direction of the council of the London Film Society. New York, Arno, 1972.

Film Society Review. New York, American Federation of Film Societies, monthly, 1965–

Filmdokumentaristen der DDR. Berlin, Henschelverlag, 1969.

Filmfront. New York, National Film and Photo League, 1934–35. Merged with New Theatre.

Filmkritik. Munich, monthly, 1957–

Filmmakers Newsletter. New York, monthly, 1968–

Films for Historians. London, British Universities Film Council, 1972.

Films in Review. New York, National Board of Review of Motion Pictures, monthly, 1950–

Films for Television. Evanston (Ill.), Standard Rate and Data Service, 1955.

Flaherty, Frances Hubbard. The Odyssey of a Film Maker. Urbana, Beta Phi Mu, 1960.

Flaherty Oral History Collection. Interviews by Bruce Harding for International Film Seminars, 1973–74. Special Collections, Columbia University, New York. Unpublished.

Flaherty Papers. Letters, diaries, etc., of Robert and Frances Flaherty. Special Collections, Columbia University, New York. Unpublished.

Fraenkel, Heinrich. See Manvell, Roger, and–

Friendly, Fred W. Due to Circumstances Beyond Our Control . . . New York, Random House, 1967.

Galbraith, John Kenneth. Economics and the Public Purpose. Boston, Houghton Mifflin, 1973.

Geduld, Harry M. (ed.). Film Makers on Film Making. Bloomington, Indiana University Press, 1967.

Gessner, Robert. The Moving Image: a guide to cinematic literacy. New York, Dutton, 1968.

Gomes, P. E. Salles. Jean Vigo. Berkeley, University of California Press, 1971.

Greene, Felix. A Curtain of Ignorance: how the American public has been misinformed about China. Garden City (N.Y.), Doubleday, 1964.

Gregor, Ulrich, and Enno Patalas. Geschichte des Films. Gütersloh, Sigbert Mohn, 1962.

Grierson, John. Grierson on Documentary. Edited by Forsyth Hardy. Revised. London, Faber and Faber, 1966.

Griffith, Richard. The World of Robert Flaherty. New York, Duell, Sloan & Pearce, 1953.

Griffith, Richard, and Arthur Mayer. The Movies. Revised. New York, Simon and Schuster, 1970.

Griffith, Richard. See Rotha, Paul, with—

Guback, Thomas H. The International Film Industry. Bloomington, Indiana University Press, 1969.

Halliwell, Leslie. The Filmgoer's Companion. Revised. New York, Hill and Wang, 1970.

Hardy, Forsyth (ed.). Grierson on Documentary. Revised. London, Faber and Faber, 1966.

Haudiquet, Philippe. Paul Fejos: 1897–1963. Paris, Anthologie du Cinéma, 1968.

Hazard, Patrick D. (ed.). TV as Art: some essays in criticism. Champaign (Ill.), National Council of Teachers of English, 1966.

Hellwig, Joachim, and Günther Deicke. Ein Tagebuch für Anne Frank. Berlin, Verlag der Nation, 1959.

Hendricks, Gordon. The Edison Motion Picture Myth. Berkeley, University of California Press, 1961.

Henkel, H. Wij Filmen den Oorlog. Amsterdam, Roskam, 1943.

Hennebelle, Guy. African Cinema. New York, Pitman, 1973.

Hibbin, Nina. Eastern Europe: an illustrated guide. Screen series. London, Zwemmer, 1969.

Hillier, Jim. See Lovell, Alan, and—

Historical Journal of Film, Radio, and Television. Oxford (U.K.), IAMHIST, semiannual, 1981–

Hollywood Quarterly. Berkeley, University of California Press, 1945–51.

Hollywood Reporter. Hollywood, daily, 1930–

Hornby, Clifford. Shooting Without Stars. London, Hutchinson, 1940.

Houston, Penelope. The Contemporary Cinema. Harmondsworth (Eng.), Penguin, 1963.

Hughes, Robert (ed.). Film Book 1: the audience and the filmmaker. New York, Grove, 1959.

Hughes, Robert (ed.). Film Book 2: films of peace and war. New York, Grove, 1962.

Hull, David Stewart. Film in the Third Reich: a study of the German cinema 1933–1945. Berkeley, University of California Press, 1960.

Idestam-Almquist, Bengt. När Filmen Kom Till Sverige. Stockholm, Norstedt & Söners, 1959.

The Independent. New York, Foundation for Independent Film and Video, monthly, 1977–

Indian Documentary. Bombay, monthly, 1955–59.

Indian Film Culture. Calcutta, Federation of Film Societies of India, quarterly, 1962–

Indian Talkie, 1931–56. Silver Jubilee Souvenir. Bombay, Film Federation of India, 1956.

Innis, Harold A. The Bias of Communication. Toronto, University of Toronto Press, 1951.

Innis, Harold A. Empire and Communications. Oxford, Clarendon Press, 1950.

Intermedia. Journal of the International Institute of Communications. London, irregularly, 1973–

International Film Annual. London, annual, 1957–60.

International Film Guide. London, Tantivy, annual, 1964–

Ivens, Joris. The Camera and I. New York, International Publishers, 1969.

Ivens Papers. Letters and other documents of Joris Ivens. Nederlands Filmmuseum, Amsterdam. Unpublished.

Jacobs, Lewis. The Rise of the American Film: a critical history. New York, Harcourt, Brace, 1939.

Jacobs, Lewis (ed.). The Documentary Tradition. 2nd ed. New York, Norton, 1979.

Jacobs, Lewis (ed.). Introduction to the Art of the Movies: an anthology of ideas on the nature of movie art. New York, Noonday, 1960.

Jacobs, Lewis. See Manvell, Roger, and—

Jahnke, Eckart. See Klaue, Wolfgang; Manfred Lichtenstein; and—

Janicki, Stanisław. Film Polski od A do Z. Warszawa, Wydawnictwa Artystycze i Filmowe, 1972.

Jenkins, Clive. Power Behind the Screen: ownership, control and motivation in British commercial television. London, MacGibbon and Kee, 1961.

Journal of Broadcasting. Association for Professional Broadcasting Education, quarterly, 1956–

Journal of Popular Film. Bowling Green (Ohio), quarterly, 1972–78.

Journal of the Producers Guild of America. Successor to Journal of the Screen Producers Guild. Quarterly, 1967–

Journal of the Screen Producers Guild. Succeeded (1967) by Journal of the Producers Guild of America.

Journal of the Society of Film and Television Arts. London, 1971–

Kelly, Frank K. Who Owns the Air? Santa Barbara, Center for the Study of Democratic Institutions, 1960.

Kendrick, Alexander.   Prime Time: the life of Edward R. Murrow.   Boston, Little, Brown, 1969.

Khan, M.   An Introduction to the Egyptian Cinema.   London, Informatics, 1969.

Klapp, Orrin E.   Symbolic Leaders: public dramas and public men.   Chicago, Aldene, 1964.

Klaue, Wolfgang (ed.).   Alberto Cavalcanti.   Berlin, Staatliches Filmarchiv der DDR, 1962.

Klaue, Wolfgang, and Jay Leyda (eds.).   Robert Flaherty.   Berlin, Henschelverlag, 1964.

Klaue, Wolfgang, and Manfred Lichtenstein (eds.).   Filme Contra Faschismus.   Berlin, Staatliches Filmarchiv der DDR, 1965.

Klaue, Wolfgang, and Manfred Lichtenstein (eds.).   Französischer Dokumentarfilm.   Berlin, Staatliches Filmarchiv der DDR, 1966.

Klaue, Wolfgang, and Manfred Lichtenstein (eds.).   Sowjetischer Dokumentarfilm.   Berlin, Staatliches Filmarchiv der DDR, 1967.

Klaue, Wolfgang; Manfred Lichtenstein; and Eckart Jahnke (eds.).   Dokumentarfilm in Polen.   Berlin, Henschelverlag, 1968.

Klaue, Wolfgang; Manfred Lichtenstein; and Hans Wegner (eds.).   Joris Ivens.   Berlin, Staatliches Filmarchiv der DDR, 1963.

Knight, Arthur.   The Liveliest Art: a panoramic history of the movies.   New York, Macmillan, 1957.

Knight, Derrick, and Vincent Porter.   A Long Look at Short Films.   Oxford, Pergamon Press, 1967.

Knoll, Erwin.   See McGaffin, William, and—

Koury, Phil A.   See Smith, Albert E., in collaboration with—

Kracauer, Siegfried.   From Caligari to Hitler: a psychological history of the German film.   Princeton, Princeton University Press, 1947.

Kracauer, Siegfried.   Theory of Film.   New York, Oxford University Press, 1960.

Krishnaswamy, S.   See Barnouw, Erik, and—

Larson, Rodger, with Ellen Meade.   Young Filmmakers.   New York, Avon, 1969.

Leiser, Erwin.   Om Dokumentärfilm.   Stockholm, Pan-Norstedts, 1967.

Leprohon, Pierre.   Chasseurs d'Images.   Paris, Bonne, 1960.

Leprohon, Pierre.   Le Cinéma Italien.   Paris, Seghers, 1966.

Levenson, Claude B.   Jeune Cinéma Hongrois.   Lyon, Premier Plan, 1966.

Levin, G. Roy.   Documentary Explorations: fifteen interviews with filmmakers.   Garden City (N.Y.), Doubleday, 1971.

Leyda, Jay.   Dianying: electric shadows.   An account of films and the film audience in China.   Cambridge (Mass.), MIT Press, 1972.

Leyda, Jay.   Films Beget Films.   New York, Hill and Wang, 1964.

Leyda, Jay.   Kino: a history of the Russian and Soviet film.   London, Allen & Unwin, 1960.

Leyda, Jay.   See also Klaue, Wolfgang, and—

Lichtenstein, Manfred. See Klaue, Wolfgang, and—

The Listener. London, British Broadcasting Corporation, weekly, 1930–

Liu, Alan P. Communications and National Integration in Communist China. Berkeley, University of California Press, 1971.

Living Films: a catalog of documentary films and their makers. New York, Association of Documentary Film Producers, 1940 (mimeographed).

Lovell, Alan, and Jim Hillier. Studies in Documentary. New York, Viking, 1972.

Low, Rachael. The History of the British Film 1906–1914. London, Allen & Unwin, 1949.

Low, Rachael. The History of the British Film 1914–1918. London, Allen & Unwin, 1950.

Low, Rachael. The History of the British Film 1918–1929. London, Allen & Unwin, 1971.

Low, Rachael, and Roger Manvell. The History of the British Film 1896–1906. London, Allen & Unwin, 1948.

Lukacs, John. A New History of the Cold War. Garden City (N.Y.), Doubleday, 1966.

MacCann, Richard Dyer. Film and Society. New York, Scribner, 1964.

MacCann, Richard Dyer. Hollywood in Transition. Boston, Houghton Mifflin, 1962.

MacCann, Richard Dyer. The People's Films: a political history of U.S. government motion pictures. New York, Hastings, 1973.

MacDonnell, Kevin. Eadweard Muybridge: the man who invented the moving picture. Boston, Little, Brown, 1972.

Macgowan, Kenneth. Behind the Screen: the history and techniques of the motion picture. New York, Dell, 1965.

MacNeil, Robert. The People Machine. New York, Harper & Row, 1968.

Maelstaf, R. Henri Storck: mens en kunstenaar. Socialistische Federatie van Cinéclubs, 1971.

Mannes, Marya. More in Anger. Philadelphia, Lippincott, 1958.

Manvell, Roger (ed.). The Cinema 1950, 1951, etc. Harmondsworth (Eng.), Penguin, annual, 1950–

Manvell, Roger. Film. Harmondsworth (Eng.), Penguin (revised), 1950.

Manvell, Roger. The Film and the Public. Harmondsworth (Eng.), Penguin, 1955.

Manvell, Roger, and Heinrich Fraenkel. The German Cinema. London, Dent, 1971.

Manvell, Roger, and Lewis Jacobs (eds.). International Encyclopedia of Film. New York, Crown, 1972.

Manvell, Roger. See Low, Rachael, and—

Marey, E. J. Movement. New York, Appleton, 1895.

Martin, Marcel. See Schnitzer, Luda and Jean, and—

Mast, Gerald. A Short History of the Movies. New York, Pegasus, 1971.

Matthews, J. H. Surrealism and Film. Ann Arbor, University of Michigan Press, 1971.

Matuszewski, Boleslaw. Une Nouvelle Source de l'Histoire. Paris, 1898.

Matuszewski, Boleslaw. La Photographie Animée. Paris, 1898.

Mayer, Arthur. See Griffith, Richard, and—

Maysles, Albert and David, with Charlotte Zwerin. Salesman (transcript). New York, New American Library, 1969.

McGaffin, William, and Erwin Knoll. Anything But the Truth: the credibility gap—how the news is managed in Washington. New York, Putnam, 1968.

McLuhan, Marshall. Understanding Media: the extensions of man. New York, McGraw-Hill, 1965.

Meade, Ellen. See Larson, Rodger, with—

Mekas, Jonas. Movie Journal: the rise of a new American cinema, 1959–1971. New York, Collier, 1972.

Mesguich, Félix. Tours de Manivelle: souvenirs d'un chasseur d'images. Paris, Grasset, 1933.

Meyer, Han. Joris Ivens: de weg naar Vietnam. Utrecht, Bruna, 1970.

Miller, Arthur C. See Balshofer, Fred. J., and—

Miller, Merle. The Judges and the Judged. Garden City (N.Y.), Doubleday, 1952.

Monaco, James. Media Culture. New York, Delta, 1978.

Montagu, Ivor. With Eisenstein in Hollywood: a chapter of autobiography. New York, International Publishers, 1969.

Morin, Edgar. See Rouch, Jean, and—

Motion Picture Herald. New York, weekly, 1907–

Moussinac, Léon. Le Cinéma Soviétique. Paris, Gallimard, 1928.

Mullen, Pat. Man of Aran. New York, Dutton, 1935.

Murrow, Edward R. In Search of Light: the broadcasts of Edward R. Murrow 1938–1961. Edited by Edward Bliss, Jr. New York, Knopf, 1967.

Muybridge, Eadweard. Animal Locomotion. Philadelphia, Lippincott, 1888.

Myerson, Michael. Memories of Underdevelopment: the revolutionary films of Cuba. New York, Grossman, 1973.

National Film Archive Catalogue, Part I: silent news films 1895–1933. London, British Film Institute, 1965.

National Film Archive Catalogue, Part II: silent non-fiction films 1895–1934. London, British Film Institute, 1960.

Neergaard, Ebbe. Documentary in Denmark: one hundred films of fact in war, occupation, liberation, peace 1940–1948. Copenhagen, Statens Filmcentral, 1948.

Neergaard, Ebbe. The Story of Danish Film. Copenhagen, Det Danske Selskab, 1962.

Nemeskürty, István. Word and Image: history of the Hungarian cinema. Budapest, Corvina, 1968.

New Theatre; later, New Theatre and Film. New York, 1934–37.

Niver, Kemp R. Motion Pictures from the Library of Congress Paper Print Collection 1894–1912. Berkeley, University of California Press, 1967.

Nolan, William F. John Huston: king rebel. Los Angeles, Sherbourne Press, 1965.

Objectif. Montreal, irregularly, 1960–67.

Ophuls, Marcel. The Sorrow and the Pity. Filmscript translated by Mireille Johnston. New York, Outerbridge & Lazard, 1972.

Opotowsky, Stan. TV–the Big Picture. New York, Collier, 1962.

The Opportunity for Sponsored Films: how to make your program successful. New York, Modern Talking Picture Service, 1956.

Patalas, Enno. See Gregor, Ulrich, and–

Paulu, Burton. Radio and Television on the European Continent. Minneapolis, University of Minnesota Press, 1967.

Pennybacker, John H., and Waldo W. Braden (eds.). Broadcasting and the Public Interest. New York, Random House, 1969.

The Pentagon Papers: as published by The New York Times. New York, Bantam, 1971.

Petric, Vladimir. Soviet Revolutionary Films in America 1926–1935. Ph.D. dissertation, New York University, 1973. Unpublished.

PIEF Newsletter. Philadelphia, Program in Ethnographic Film, 1970–

Porcile, François. Défense du Court Métrage Français. Éditions du Cerf, 1965.

Porter, Vincent. See Knight, Derrick, and–

Potamkin, Harry Alan. The Eyes of the Movie. New York, International Pamphlets, 1934.

Prakke, Henk, and B. J. Bertina. Film in den Niederlanden. Assen, Van Gorcum, 1963.

Prédal, René. Jeune Cinéma Canadien. Lyon, Premier Plan, 1967.

Prism. Cairo, Ministry of Culture, irregularly, 1969–

Propaganda und Gegenpropaganda im Film 1933–1945. Vienna, Österreichischer Filmmuseum, 1972.

Public Television: a program for action. The report and recommendations of the Carnegie commission on educational television. New York, Bantam, 1967.

Quarterly of Film, Radio and Television. Berkeley, University of California Press, quarterly, 1951–57.

Quigley, Martin, Jr. Magic Shadows: the story of the origin of motion pictures. Washington, Georgetown University Press, 1948.

Racheva, Maria. Present-day Bulgarian Cinema. Sofia, State Printing House, undated (ca. 1968).

Ramsaye, Terry. A Million and One Nights: a history of the motion picture. New York, Simon and Schuster, 1926.

Rangoonwalla, Firoze. Indian Filmography: silent and Hindi films 1897–1969. Bombay, Udeshi, 1970.

Red Channels: the report of communist influence in radio and television. New York, American Business Consultants, 1950.

Reisz, Karel. The Technique of Film Editing. London, Focal, 1953.

Renan, Sheldon. An Introduction to the American Underground Film. New York, Dutton, 1967.

Richie, Donald. Japanese Cinema. Garden City (N.Y.), Doubleday, 1971.

Richie, Donald. See Anderson, Joseph L., and—

Richter, Hans. Filmgegner von Heute—Filmfreunde von Morgen. Berlin, Reckendorf, 1929.

Riefenstahl, Leni. Hinter den Kulissen des Reichsparteitagfilms. Munich, N.S.D.A.P., 1935.

Road, Sinclair. See Rotha, Paul, with—

Robinson, David. The History of World Cinema. New York, Stein and Day, 1973.

Roman Karmen: filmretrospective, New York. Sovexportfilm, 1973.

Roman Karmen: retrospektive zur XIV Internationalen Leipziger Dokumentar- und Kurzfilmwoche für Kino und Fernsehen. Berlin, Staatliches Filmarchiv der DDR, 1971.

Roos, Karl. See Christensen, Theodor, and—

Rosenthal, Alan. The New Documentary in Action: a casebook in film making. Berkeley, University of California Press, 1971.

Rotha, Paul. The Film Till Now: a survey of world cinema. With an additional section by Richard Griffith. London, Vision Press and Mayflower Publishing Company, 1960.

Rotha, Paul, with Sinclair Road and Richard Griffith. Documentary Film. Revised. New York, Hastings, 1952.

Rotha, Paul (ed.). Portrait of a Flying Yorkshireman: letters from Eric Knight in the United States to Paul Rotha in England. London, Chapman, 1952.

Rouch, Jean. The Cinema in Africa: present position and current trends. Paris, UNESCO, 1962 (mimeographed).

Rouch, Jean, and Edgar Morin. Chronique d'un Été. Paris, Interspectacles, 1962.

Rovere, Richard H. Senator Joe McCarthy. Cleveland, World, 1960.

Russell, Bertrand. War Crimes in Vietnam. New York, Monthly Review Press, 1967.

Sadoul, Georges. Dictionary of Film Makers. Translated, edited, and updated by Peter Morris. Berkeley, University of California Press, 1972.

Sadoul, Georges. Dictionary of Films. Translated, edited, and updated by Peter Morris. Berkeley, University of California Press, 1972.

Sadoul, Georges. Dziga Vertov. Preface de Jean Rouch. Paris, Éditions Champ Libre, 1971.

Sadoul, Georges. Histoire du Cinéma. Paris, Flammarion, 1962.

Sadoul, Georges. Louis Lumière. Paris, Seghers, 1964.

Sahlberg, Gardar. Levande Bilder. Stockholm, Bonniers, 1966.

Schickel, Richard. The Disney Version: the life, times, art and commerce
of Walt Disney. New York, Simon and Schuster, 1968.

Schiller, Herbert I. Mass Communications and American Empire. New
York, Kelley, 1969.

Schiller, Herbert I. The Mind Managers. Boston, Beacon, 1973.

Schlesinger, Arthur, Jr. The Bitter Heritage: Vietnam and American
democracy: 1941–1966. New York, Fawcett, 1967.

Schnitzer, Luda and Jean, and Marcel Martin (eds.). Cinema in Revolution: the heroic era of the Soviet film. New York, Hill and Wang,
1973.

Schramm, Wilbur. Mass Media and National Development. Palo Alto,
Stanford University Press, 1964.

Schramm, Wilbur (ed.). The Process and Effects of Mass Communications. Urbana, University of Illinois Press, 1954.

Scott, A. C. Literature and the Arts in Twentieth Century China. London, Allen & Unwin, 1965.

Screen: the journal of the Society for Education in Film and Television.
London, 1960–

Seldes, Gilbert. The New Mass Media: challenge to a free society.
Washington, Public Affairs Press, 1968.

Seldes, Gilbert. The Public Arts. New York, Simon and Schuster, 1956.

Seton, Marie. Portrait of a Director: Satyajit Ray. Bloomington, Indiana University Press, 1971.

Shayon, Robert Lewis. See The Eighth Art.

Shayon, Robert Lewis. The Crowd-catchers: an informal introduction to
television. New York, Saturday Review Press, 1973.

The Shell Film Unit 1933–1954. London, Shell, 1954.

Sherwood, Robert E. (ed.). The Best Moving Pictures of 1922–23.
Boston, Small, Maynard, 1923.

Shirer, William. The Rise and Fall of the Third Reich. New York,
Simon and Schuster, 1960.

Sight and Sound. London, British Film Institute, quarterly, 1932–

Sitney, P. Adams (ed.). Film Culture Reader. New York, Praeger,
1970.

Sixty Years of 16mm Film: 1923–1983. Evanston, Film Council of
America, 1954.

Skornia, Harry J. Television and the News: a critical appraisal. Palo
Alto, Pacific Books, 1968.

Skornia, Harry J. Television and Society: an inquest and agenda for improvement. New York, McGraw-Hill, 1965.

Skvorecky, Josef. All the Bright Young Men and Women: a personal history of the Czech cinema. Translated by Michael Schonberg. Toronto, Peter Martin Associates, 1971.

Small, William. To Kill a Messenger: television news and the real world. New York, Hastings, 1970.

Smith, Albert E., in collaboration with Phil A. Koury. Two Reels and a Crank. Garden City (N.Y.), Doubleday, 1952.

Snyder, Robert L. Pare Lorentz and the Documentary Film. Norman, University of Oklahoma Press, 1968.

Sopkin, Charles. Seven Glorious Days, Seven Fun-Filled Nights: one man's struggle to survive a week watching commercial television in America. New York, Simon and Schuster, 1968.

Sorensen, Thomas C. The Word War: the story of American propaganda. New York, Harper, 1968.

The Spanish Cinema. Madrid, Diplomatic Information Office, 1949.

Sponsor. New York, biweekly, then weekly, 1948–

Starr, Cecile (ed.). Film Society Primer. New York, American Federation of Film Societies, 1956.

Starr, Cecile (ed.). Ideas on Film: a handbook for the 16mm user. New York, Funk & Wagnalls, 1951.

Stott, William. Documentary Expression and Thirties America. New York, Oxford University Press, 1973.

Studies in Visual Communication. Philadelphia, Annenberg, quarterly, 1974–

Sussex, Elizabeth. Lindsay Anderson. London, Studio Vista, 1969.

Take One. Toronto, bimonthly, 1969–79.

Talbot, Daniel (ed.). Film: an anthology. Berkeley, University of California Press, 1966.

Taylor, John Russell. Cinema Eye, Cinema Ear: some key film makers of the sixties. New York, Hill and Wang, 1964.

Television Quarterly: journal of the National Academy of Television Arts and Sciences, 1962–69.

Thomas, David B. The First Colour Motion Pictures. London, Science Museum Monograph, 1969.

Variety. New York, weekly, 1905–

Wagenknecht, Edward. The Movies in the Age of Innocence. Norman, University of Oklahoma Press, 1962.

Wegner, Hans. See Klaue, Wolfgang, and–

Weinberg, Meyer. TV in America: the morality of hard cash. New York, Ballantine, 1962.

Weir, E. Austin. The Struggle for National Broadcasting in Canada. Toronto, McClelland and Stewart, 1965.

Wells, Alan. Picture-Tube Imperialism? the impact of U.S. television on Latin America. Maryknoll (N.Y.), Orbis, 1972.

Whale, John. The Half-Shut Eye: television and politics in Britain and America. London, Macmillan, 1969.

White, David Manning, and Richard Averson (eds.).   Sight, Sound, and Society: motion pictures and television in America.   Boston, Beacon, 1968.

Whyte, Alastair.   New Cinema in Eastern Europe.   London, Studio Vista, 1968.

Wilson, H. H.   Pressure Group: the campaign for commercial television in England.   New Brunswick (N.J.), Rutgers University Press, 1961.

World Directory of Stockshot and Film Production Libraries.   Oxford, Pergamon Press, 1969.

World Radio-TV Handbook.   Hellerup (Denmark), annual, 1947—

Woroszylski, Wiktor.   The Life of Mayakovsky.   Translation by Boleslaw Taborski.   New York, Orion, 1970.

Worth, Sol, and John Adair.   Through Navajo Eyes: an exploration in film communication and anthropology.   New York, Farrar, Strauss & Giroux, 1972.

Wyand, Paul.   Useless If Delayed: adventures in putting history on film. London, Harrap, 1959.

Wyckoff, Gene.   The Image Candidates: American politics in the age of television.   New York, Macmillan, 1968.

Yellin, David G.   Special: Fred Freed and the television documentary. New York, Macmillan, 1972.

Young, Vernon.   Cinema Borealis.   New York, Avon, 1971.

Zalzman, A.   Joris Ivens.   Paris, Seghers, 1963.

Zavattini, Cesare.   Sequences from a Cinematic Life.   New York, Prentice Hall, 1970.

Zwerin, Charlotte.   See Maysles, Albert and David, with—

INDEX